Study Hall: College Football, Its Stats and Its Stories

Bill Connelly

Foreword by Spencer Hall and Jason Kirk
Edited by Rob Weir

D1166865

Table of Contents

Foreword

By Spencer Hall and Jason Kirk

Spencer: I would like to state for the reader's benefit that Bill wrote this book while writing something like 40,000 words a week for his day job.

Jason: And feeling bad about writing only that many words. And also he ran two other websites that had nothing to do with those 40,000. And he raised a toddler.

Spencer: I assume that kind of productivity only comes with the willpower to wake up at 4:30 in the morning. I will never know this. I'm okay with that.

Jason: The waking-up-at-such-and-such-a-time thing is the most popular lie Bill Connelly tells. He actually doesn't ever sleep, and in fact taught Nick Saban everything he knows about not sleeping. Gross!

So one cool thing in this book that our friend, the reader, is about to glean is a sense of college football as a thing that a person is lucky to be exposed to. What would you say was the moment for you when the sport first became a thing worth loving?

Spencer: When Florida lost to Auburn in 1994. That was a game that featured Florida turning the ball over a thousand times, and still only losing on the final play of the game. That playcall was a smash combination, designed to split a cover 2 in half on one side. Bill Connelly can tell you all of this without looking it up like I had to, because he is not human. You?

Jason: I spent years split between caring more about (A) the NFL beyond the usually bad franchise I root for and (B) college football, with a long series of usually bad Georgia Tech teams forming my formative sports memories before that. But Vince Young over USC sealed it. Hadn't really thought about that until reading Bill's own top 10 list. Bill Connelly, always making you think!

Spencer: That's the worst part about this book. It reminds me of a lot of objectively wonderful things I feel subjective pain over. For instance, it reminded me about how very good the Nebraska of the 1990s was, and how badly they destroyed Florida in 1995. Thanks for taking another day of use off my liver, memories and Bill Connelly!

Jason: It is great and terrible having nowhere for your memories and assumptions to hide, and I think it's clear Bill feels the same way about tangling with his own numbers.

Spencer: That Bill can simultaneously work with numbers and write well in English is unfair, but if he has to do it I'd rather him do it about football, and not something I don't care about. There is a universe somewhere where Bill Connelly writes the most underappreciated agricultural surveys for the Missouri Ag board. This is the saddest universe I can imagine.

Jason: Well, he does write about tennis sometimes, which is at least more popular among certain people than agriculture, but we don't want to offend any Clemson fans here.

Spencer: You're assuming Clemson fans will read a book. Charity is in your heart.

Jason: True. This is a free-speech zone, seeing as it is made of written words. Vince Dooley would beat Danny Ford again if given the opportunity.

Spencer: So would Todd Berry, provided you spotted him his 2012 team. That might have been my favorite part, because I think Bill understands this better than any other college football writer: that the game is less about the top 25, and more about the backwaters and oddballs who survive throughout the whole ecosystem.

Bill will happily talk about Alabama, but he'd *really* like to talk about underdog tactics in the Sun Belt.

Jason: And he doesn't just do this because North Texas fans send him more glowing annual emails than Ohio State fans do, either. It's a sport that demands that level of broad affection, but most of us only have so much room in our minds (AND IN OUR HEARTS) to keep up with the absolute highest-level attention stuff. In numbers and in the way our man Bill (and certain others) approaches the game, there's an understanding of college football ... an engagement with it that I think surpasses what we can get out of any other American sport.

Spencer: In summary, raise your children in the middle of nowhere, Oklahoma, and have them watch terrible Missouri football for 20 years, and one day you too can create a Bill Connelly. He's proof great things come from terrible boredom.

Jason: Also, do not make him drive through Birmingham, Alabama, because he is the sort of person who will hate driving through Birmingham, Alabama[i].

Spencer: And there. We've found one way in which Bill is mortal and normal like the rest of us. Birmingham: It brings greatness to its knees, and then usually makes it say ROLL TIDE.

---

[i] Back story from Bill: I drove through Birmingham once and got caught in traffic for two hours. Birmingham's metro area houses more than one million people; its thru highways are tighter than those of Jefferson City, Missouri (population: 43,000). Driving through Birmingham is the worst, most soul-sucking experience imaginable.

1. It's Personal

Maybe your experience is similar[1].

It's probably an hour after I intended to show up, but I'm here. I park in a different lot than where the tailgate is located, but while that gets a bit frustrating at times, it does allow me to take in the scene as I hike to our chosen spot. On my walk, I can spy on tailgate food, take in bits and pieces of conversations and get an early feel for what attendance is going to be like ("At three hours to kickoff, this lot should be much more full than this…").

Within 30 seconds of my arrival, Seth hands me a beer, as he has for just about every tailgate I've ever attended. He always gets here on time At Homecoming it's all about the Bloody Mary with the infused vodka. After Halloween, I'll bring in growlers of the local pumpkin ale. Right now, it's just beer, even at 8:00 a.m. (if your team is unlucky enough to draw an 11:00 a.m. start time). The bottle is open, there are hours before kickoff, and it's time to settle in. I'm not thinking about numbers.

It's the same people, the same chairs, and the same tent with the same team colors each year. The grilling equipment gets upgraded from

---

[1] Parts of this chapter adapted from a piece that appeared at SB Nation on September 19, 2011.

1

time to time, and lord knows there are more children here than there used to be, but there is comfort in familiarity. I do not overtly fear change in my day-to-day life, but I like my tailgates the way they are. When the weather cooperates, there is nothing more relaxing. And it's still pretty good when the weather is temperamental.

****

In Lincoln, Nebraska, 85,000 people make an incomprehensible amount of noise watching on an enormous jumbotron as 100 young men walk through a hallway. In Columbia, South Carolina, old Southern men yell and wave towels to the pulsating beat of a nearly 15-year old song by Finnish trance DJ Darude. In Blacksburg, Virginia, engineering majors make an equal amount of noise following the opening notes to a classic rock song from Los Angeles-based Metallica.

In Madison, Wisconsin, after 45 minutes of play, the home crowd jumps along in disturbing unison to a decades-old song from faux-Irish rap group House of Pain. It is so fun you can occasionally catch members of the visiting team joining in on the sideline.

In Auburn, Alabama, a town of 53,000, up to 87,000 people show up to watch an eagle fly around a stadium. A retired eagle still hangs out on campus. (The team's nickname is the Tigers, by the way.) In Tallahassee, Florida, a student is given a scholarship to dress up as a Seminole chief, ride into Doak Campbell Stadium on a horse named Renegade, and plant a spear into the ground.

In Starkville, Mississippi, home fans clang cowbells incessantly, and they are the only fans in the country allowed to do so. This is a big deal. In Stillwater, Oklahoma, the Cowboy Marching Band plays "The Waving Song" after the home team scores. The fans don't clap along, of course; they wave.

In Clemson, South Carolina, the home team pats a rock and runs down a hill to thunderous applause. In College

2

Station, Texas, proud Aggies cheer along with male yell leaders dressed like milkmen, repeating chants that you don't understand and nodding quietly to the collie graveyard on the north end of the stadium[2].

In Shreveport, Louisiana, local Louisiana State fans show up at the Independence Bowl, a game in which their team isn't playing, just so they can get some tailgating practice. In Boise, Idaho, Utah State beats Toledo in the Famous Idaho Potato Bowl. The trophy they receive is basically a crystal bowl of potatoes. Winning this ridiculous trophy is one of the program's finest moments.

In stadiums throughout the country, men wearing different-colored shirts, with perhaps incredibly similar backgrounds, yell at and/or tussle with each other because of the actions of a bunch of 19-year olds wearing similar colors. And in stadiums throughout the country, men wearing the *same*-colored shirts yell at and/or tussle with each other because of the plays being called by a well-paid man in a box across the stadium from them.

Welcome to college football, where this all makes sense. From the tunnel walk at Nebraska, to "Sandstorm" at South Carolina, to "Enter Sandman" at Virginia Tech, to "Jump Around" at Wisconsin. From War Eagle at Auburn to Chief Osceola at Florida State. From CLANGA CLANGA CLANGA at Mississippi State to silent waving at Oklahoma State. From drunk LSU fans grilling meat for practice to jubilant Utah State fans cheering as their head coach holds a potato bowl over his head.

In the real world, you aren't allowed to dress up like a Native American and throw a spear into the ground. In college football, you can pay for an education doing this.

College football is the world's biggest insiders' club, a sport with too many inane, insanely enjoyable traditions to count. It is off the beaten path. It is messy and absurd. It is

---

[2] The collies are buried facing the south scoreboard so they'll always know how the home team is doing.

3

nonsensical. It is wonderful. It is always changing, and it never changes.

****

A guy named Michael down the line of cars has a deep fryer. He lives six hours away, but he comes in for every home game. He makes most road games, too, but the home games are special. "I have friends six times a year," he says. We talk about the game. I do not reference success rates, or leverage, or points per play. Maybe he asks me what "the numbers" say about this one, but he's really just asking who I think is going to win.

The air smells like grass and fried meat. The walk to the stadium from our lot is a nice one: mostly downhill (which means mostly uphill after the game, I guess), past the basketball arena (a nice Porta-Potty alternative), through the high-roller donor lot, past the buses blaring the same Jock Jams CD for nearly 20 years running, and down the drive toward the stadium where, if we time it just right (and we usually do), the marching band is serenading the crowd and making its way into the stadium like we are.

Kids and families stop to watch and listen as we weave through them. Some old alum is attending his 300th home game. Some 3-year-old, hypnotized by the band or the mascot, is attending his first. So, so many people attend college football games in this country; all of them have their own habits, goals and levels of alcohol and food intake. I probably do not have much in common personally, or politically, with most of the people around me, but right now we are wearing the same colors. In about 30 minutes, we'll be singing the same song. Hopefully at some point we'll be high-fiving.

****

If you count yourself among the millions of college football obsessives, chances are good that there was a moment when the bug bit you. In Alabama, or Oklahoma, or Nebraska, perhaps that moment was simply your birth. But maybe you were a Northwestern student during the Wildcats' Rose Bowl run in 1995. Maybe you attended Virginia when the Cavaliers made a miraculous (and brief) run to No. 1 in 1990. Maybe you were attending Missouri 17 years later when the same thing happened. Maybe you just got sucked into the game – the fight songs, the unexpected passion, the combination of chess and brutality, the vulnerability associated with life as an amateur – at any random school. Or maybe you were simply a six-year-old watching Doug Flutie complete a Hail Mary live on television one Saturday night in 1984.

College football is almost literally off the beaten path. There isn't much of a presence for this sport in New York City for example, and while there are games in or around Chicago and Los Angeles, those aren't what you would naturally call college football towns. Instead, the capitals of college football require a bit of a drive, even from smaller-market cities. Tuscaloosa, Alabama, is an hour from Birmingham. Lincoln, Nebraska, is an hour from Omaha. Norman, Oklahoma, is about half an hour from Oklahoma City. Eugene, Oregon, is almost two hours from Portland. Ann Arbor, Michigan, is about 45 minutes from Detroit. Baton Rouge is about an hour and a half from New Orleans. And, of course, South Bend, Indiana, is about an hour and a half from Chicago. You have to find college football; it's probably not going to find you. But oh, when you find it, it's all over for you.

"Sports define people in a given culture," notes Chris B. Brown of the wonderful website Smart Football. "If you grew up in the New England area, perhaps you grew up in a community with a pro football focus. But if you grew up in Alabama, it was all college. For me, I grew up playing the sport and college is probably the best blend of the things that make the game meaningful – doing it for team reasons, doing it in support of each other, working for a singular goal, not just for money or recognition, plus the noble, 'get knocked down and get back up' part – and the strategic side of it. With 100-plus teams, you get a lot more diversity, more effective problems.

5

"There is at least a little insanity involved in college football obsession, in the way it makes you think and feel," Brown continues. "Often, when you're rooting for a Purdue [his school] or a Missouri [mine], it's because it connects you with some community or cultural experience – four years of college, tailgating with friends, something you can continue to do each year. If you're a part of the Notre Dame or Alabama fan base, maybe you feel connected to something that's larger than you. Connecting to that gives you a better sense of who, and where, you are."

"I always laugh when people go to their first real college football game, maybe an SEC game" says *Sports Illustrated*'s Andy Staples, "and they see how different it is from the NFL. If you go to an Alabama-LSU game in Baton Rouge, there's really just nothing in the world that compares[3]."

CBS Sports' Bruce Feldman agrees. "It's always cool just to get down on the field late in a game, when things are ramping up. It always feels new. I love seeing when Oregon lets the students in; you're looking down from the press box, and it's pretty picturesque, and you have these students sprinting down the steps trying to get to their seats. Sometimes it's raining, and you think 'This is a bad idea.' And when Virginia Tech comes onto to the field, and you hear the sound of 'Enter Sandman' starting up? I get goose bumps every time[4]."

For Steven Godfrey, a writer for SB Nation, it took a little while to get bitten. "I grew up in an FBI family, and we

---

[3] More from Staples: "It's my favorite sport. I was born in Columbia, South Carolina. We moved around to Florida, another football-crazy state, and it just wasn't an option. Saturday was the holy day in our house. I went to my first game in 1983, and I was hooked." He would eventually walk on for Steve Spurrier and Florida in 1996 before deciding that writing about college football was far less painful.

[4] More from Feldman: "There are just so many moving parts in college football, and there's a different level of strategy that I think is fascinating. I covered college basketball for a while, and the level of detail in scouting and preparation and breakdown is 100 times more intense in college football than it is in college basketball."

moved a lot. We went to a Marshall game here, a VMI game there, but it didn't really click. I finished high school in Jackson, Mississippi, and we went to the Egg Bowl[5]. It was there that I began to see the disproportionate amount of passion to reason, the amount of time people spend obsessing over this. It was an immersion process.

"You have people with different coal politics in the West Virginia-Marshall rivalry. You've got Civil War ties to Kansas-Missouri. The stakes are just different in college football."

Godfrey later came back to Oxford to finish his degree at Ole Miss and decided to give beat writing a chance. His first job: covering Ole Miss for the 2003 season. One of the most dominant programs in the country in the late 1950s and early 1960s, Ole Miss had not been ranked higher than 15th in the AP Poll since 1970 and hadn't won a conference title since 1963. But behind quarterback Eli Manning, the Rebels made a charge toward glory in 2003 ... eventually. They first fell to Memphis and Texas Tech and began the season 2-2. But they beat No. 24 Florida and No. 21 Arkansas, surged to No. 15 in the polls, and found themselves undefeated in conference play when No. 3 LSU came to town on November 22. A win would give them the SEC West title and a chance at the SEC championship.

"Ole Miss-LSU was the perfect college football experience," says Godfrey. "I remember thinking, 'This is the most passion I've ever seen from a group of people about anything in my life.' If I ever get football fatigue, I always remember that. Their passion is my passion, I guess.

"Ole Miss was lining up to kick a field goal at the end of the game, and a CBS production guy comes running by me. They were taking their cameras off of the goal posts. I said,

---

[5] The annual Ole Miss-Mississippi State game is called the Egg Bowl because ... well, because it's college football, basically. The winner of the game earns possession of the Golden Egg, over which these two schools have been fighting since 1927.

'What are you doing? Why are you doing that?' He said, 'Look around. This place is about to fucking explode[6].'"

"My dad is from Louisiana, and my mom is from Georgia. College football provided context for every aspect of my life." C.J. Schexnayder is discussing how he never really had a chance in avoiding the college football bug. Schexnayder, an Alabama fan who has written for sites like Roll Bama Roll and [my own] Football Study Hall, loves the backstories almost as much as the game itself. "The historical and sociological aspect of college football is just fascinating," he says.

"So many plays have an 'Immaculate Reception'-like impact on so many fan bases and cultures," Schexnayder notes. He's right. The NFL has a storied history, with plenty of crazy, fate-changing plays like Franco Harris' deflected-catch-and-run from the 1972 AFC playoffs. But in sheer quantity, it cannot hold a candle to college football. Every program has an Immaculate Reception, a play or a game that changed its fortunes (for better or worse), a near-miss that still hurts 40 years later, a great play that is still celebrated 20 years later. Ask a Florida State or Miami fan about Wide Right I, Wide Right II, Wide Right III, or Wide Left. Ask a Georgia fan about Run, Lindsay, Run. Ask an Arkansas fan about Right 53 Veer Pass. Ask a Missouri fan about the Fifth Down or the Flea Kicker. Ask an Alabama or Auburn fan about Punt Bama Punt. Ask a Nebraska fan about Tommie Frazier's run or Johnnie Rodgers' punt return. Ask an Ole Miss fan about Billy Cannon. Ask a Texas fan about Michael Crabtree. Et cetera. You'll never actually learn about every incredible moment, every incredible game, every classic gut punch. There are just too many of them.

"As I've gotten older, and I've read more books and

---

[6] Kicker Jonathan Nichols, who made 25 of 29 field goals for the season as a whole, missed a 47-yarder late in the second quarter, then missed a 36-yarder wide right with four minutes remaining in a 17-14 loss. Ole Miss still hasn't won a conference title since 1963.

talked to more people," says Brian Fremeau of Football Outsiders, "the history of college football that I have come to understand more fully has produced such a rich culture, richer than what I would call the 'sterile' culture of professional sports. There are these great little stories from every season, and they have been happening for more than 100 years. People want to tell you about this amazing little nugget of a story from 60 years ago. People in a pro sport maybe talk about records or the team that held the Lombardi Trophy so many years ago. But they don't really share the stories that build up to a 'This is why we rally around this team' conclusion. The little stories are what make this such a passionate sport."

At the same time, there are bigger, broader stories, which is another draw to college football for football academics like Schexnayder. "Football allows us to talk about complex cultural issues in a safer, less threatening way. You can see what's happening socially in the country through college football."

Football was a backdrop for the desegregation battles of the 1960s, from the fight over James Meredith's enrollment at Ole Miss in 1962 to the integration of Alabama's football team (and Arkansas', and Texas') a few years later. College football is, like politics, local. And a look through time at your team's history will tell you so much about your school's, your town's, and your state's history as well.

I began writing about college football for Football Outsiders in September 2008. My job was to talk about the numbers I had begun to play with over the previous year or two, but I wanted to make sure I knew what I was talking about when it came to college football as a whole – its traditions, its history, its rivalries, its collective joy and bitterness. This didn't seem like a difficult task; I had obsessed over the sport since I was about three years old.

I grew up in Oklahoma, where college football is basically the pro sport of choice. Some relatives of mine were the type of obsessive OU fans that made me both revere them and despise them. I remembered the controversial tie between OU and Texas in 1984, and people talked about the Sooner Schooner's premature celebratory arrival onto the Orange Bowl field (and subsequent penalty) for years. I knew just about every player on Oklahoma's 1985 national title team. Jamelle Holieway was my first official favorite player.

I had the Heisman winners memorized going back a decade or two, and I could recite for you national title winners like they were Super Bowl champions. I knew who the All-Americans were, I knew where all the top NFL players attended school, and my love for college football only grew when I began attending major (sometimes) college games at Missouri in the late 1990s. And a decade later, I was getting paid a little bit to write about this sport and its numbers? This was going to be great.

I began to snatch up every college football book I could think of on eBay and Amazon.com. I read everything Dan Jenkins ever wrote for *Sports Illustrated*. I took in the known classics and the out-of-print, only-locals-will-probably-care autobiographies of successful coaches (John Vaught's *Rebel Coach* is my favorite). I recorded and watched just about every old college football game ESPN Classic would show and complained when they didn't show nearly enough variety.

After nearly three decades as a college football obsessive, I came to realize something during this immersion process: I didn't know shit about college football.

I knew about Oklahoma, Nebraska and the Big 8. I knew about Bud Wilkinson and Barry Sanders and Sal Aunese and the tunnel walk in Lincoln. I knew everything there was to know about my alma mater's football program, from Don Faurot creating the Split-T (and teaching it to future Oklahoma coach Bud Wilkinson during World War II), to Dan Devine nearly winning a national title in 1960 (damn Kansas beating Ol' Mizzou with an ineligible player), to the big upset wins (and ridiculous upset losses) of the 1970s, to the cratering of the 1980s and the early 1990s, to the Fifth Down, to the Flea Kicker (which I had the honor of seeing in person).

I didn't, however, know about how dominant those late 1950s and early 1960s Ole Miss teams were. I didn't know enough about the Ten Year War between Michigan's Bo Schembechler and Ohio State's Woody Hayes. I didn't know how dominant Pittsburgh and Minnesota used to be. And Fordham. And St. Mary's. I didn't realize how important the Third Saturday in October (the annual battle between Tennessee and Alabama) was. I didn't know Oregon State had a Heisman Trophy winner. I didn't know about Harvard "beating" Yale, 29-29. I didn't realize just how good Herschel Walker and Bo Jackson were, at least not until they reached the pros.

"Every college football team has a 500-page biography," says the *USA Today's* Paul Myerberg. "Oklahoma's is 1,000 pages. Notre Dame's is 2,000. Every game has a back story." When Michigan and Ohio State face off in Ann Arbor in 2013, they will not only be fighting for present-tense supremacy, but they'll also be *re*-fighting all of the battles that came before, in Michigan's home stadium and elsewhere. The same goes for conference battles throughout the country. The more you learn about college football, the more you find out you have to learn.

"College football fandom is a niche," says college football historian and sociologist (and former Notre Dame star) Michael Oriard. "You are a fan of your school, or your conference, more than you are a fan of college football." College football's history is incredibly rich but regionalized; because of travel and a limited sample size, your team barely played teams out of its region (aside from bowls) until the last 40-50 years. Shared facts do not extend far beyond Heisman winners and national champions, and even the mythical national champion from a given season is often up for debate. Five teams claim a share of the 1926 title (Alabama, Lafayette, Michigan, Navy, Stanford). Another five claim the 1927 title. In the 12 seasons from 1931-42, at least three teams claim a

11

title from 10 of them. If you added up claimed titles, you would guess that college football has been played since about 1650 A.D.

Now, it should be noted that this is changing a bit. Unlike 30 years ago, you can find more than a couple of nationally televised college football games airing on a given Saturday. And as it has for everything else, the Internet has made the world a lot smaller. Blogs and Twitter have helped even further in this regard. But this is a new development. The shared history of college football has just begun.

Of course, college football's history has only so much to do with actual results. For many, the reason for obsession over college football actually has little to do with the game on the field and everything to do with the events *surrounding* the game on the field. The word "pageantry" ("an elaborate display or ceremony") was meant for college football. You probably clap (or wave) to the same fight song that your parents (or alums your parents' age) clapped to a generation before. And while your program's stadium may have been stretched and expanded a few times through the years, the field probably hasn't moved. The grass (fake or real) that hosts a given game on a given Saturday was probably hosting the cleats of athletes decades earlier. Schools don't move their teams like pro franchises. Where you play is quite possibly where you have *always* played.

In this vein, college football is, to Football Outsiders' Matt Hinton, "a body regenerating itself." New players come and go every year. Coaches stay anywhere between a couple of weeks and a couple of decades. But for the most part, the school colors remain the same[7]. The tailgates don't change that often. Season ticket holders plop down in nearly the same seat from one year to another. You meet up with people on fall Saturdays that you don't get to see the other nine months of the year, and you will meet up with them again next year. The

---

[7] Oregon and its flexible (for lack of a better word) color scheme are the exception, not the rule.

game day experience keeps you coming back even when the names associated with the team change.

This is a communal experience, a constant in life. You plan one-third of your calendar year around it. Everything else in your life may change; fall Saturdays aren't going anywhere. And hell, when the fall ends, bowls, recruiting, and spring football are right around the corner.

****

There is a lovely old couple in the row behind us. They were as excited as Seth's parents the first time they got to see his new baby one fall. A couple of years later, they got to meet Child No. 2. They probably don't care about opponent adjustments or what "PPP" stands for, but they love my school as much as I do. The first home game of the season is like a family reunion, really. It's the same people sitting in the same places around us. Sometimes you can move up a few rows if others have canceled their season tickets, but when your school is doing well, that doesn't happen too often. Winning comes with a price[8]. That's okay, though: We've talked ourselves into the "From the 61st row, you can really see the plays develop!" line of thinking[9].

When you attend games for years (I'm getting ready for my 17th season as a ticket holder, which pales in comparison to others), seemingly subtle changes are noteworthy. A couple of years ago, a new director took over the marching band. They played different songs at different times of the game, and we reacted as if we were listening to Questlove DJ'ing in a club. "Ah, he chose this song now? Interesting transition.[10]"

We also got a new P.A. announcer a couple of years ago, the first change in that seat since I came here. We complained about him all fall, even though he probably wasn't actually that bad.

---

[8] Winning also comes with bandwagon jumpers, horrible traffic, more ridiculous expectations and embarrassing behavior by some of the people around us. Also: It's much, much better than losing.

[9] For what it's worth, you really *can* see the plays develop from up there.

[10] Later on: "Is this Lady Gaga? Wow, the last guy definitely wouldn't have chosen this. Very progressive."

****

Even if we are born into college football, we can probably still look back on specific moments, specific games, that truly reeled us in. Here are 10 formative games that helped to turn me into the fan I have become.

1. November 23, 1984: Boston College 47, Miami 45.

A six-year-old in 1984 had almost no choice but to love Doug Flutie. He was kind of wild, he was a magician, he had the belly shirt, and to top it all off, it seemed he was about the same size as me. If you were playing football in the front yard, or in your room, or with friends, you didn't have to look very far to find your muse in 1984. And this game, with the Flutie-to-Phelan Hail Mary, and the classic call from Brent Musberger, and the ebbs and flows of the game itself ... it had it all. Even before the final play, this was a classic. Boston College jumped to a 14-0 lead, Miami charged back, the game was tied 31-31 heading into the fourth quarter, Miami's Bernie Kosar passed for 447 yards, Flutie passed for 472, and Miami took a 45-41 lead with 28 seconds left. It was an outstanding game before that final pass. It was a classic after it.

I was led to believe Hail Marys like this worked all the time.

2. January 1, 1986: Oklahoma 25, Penn State 10.

I loved that 1985 Oklahoma team. Then seven, I was addicted to the brash, sometimes ridiculous personalities, and the talent level was simply ridiculous – linebackers Brian Bosworth, Dante Jones and Paul Migliazzo; nose tackle Tony Casillas; defensive back Rickey Dixon; and of course all of the wishbone talent you could possibly want: quarterback Jamelle Holieway, fullback Lydell Carr, halfbacks Spencer Tillman and Patrick Collins. The buzz entering the season was about how

14

Barry Switzer had adapted his offense to account for the star talent of quarterback Troy Aikman. But when Aikman broke his ankle against Miami in the fourth game of the year, adaptation went out the window. Switzer inserted Holieway, a true freshman, into the lineup, and Oklahoma wrecked shop.

I used to have a VHS copy of this game. My grandparents had two VCRs and did a lot of recording, which was pretty crazy (and felt a little illicit) in 1986. I watched this tape so much I remember the commercials. Does anybody remember a show called *Blacke's Magic*? It starred *Barney Miller's* Hal Linden and *M*A*S*H's* Harry Morgan. It was about a retired magician (Linden) who uses his tricks to solve crimes. It lasted just 12 episodes. I'm sure it was terrible. But NBC pushed it multiple times during the telecast. I remember that. I also remember the perfect play-action bomb from Holieway to magic tight end Keith Jackson, and I remember Carr eventually finding room to run up the middle. I was never an unabashed Oklahoma fan like a lot of my friends and family, but I did love this particular team.

3. January 2, 1987: Penn State 14, Miami 10.

The BCS era has left us unfulfilled in a lot of ways due to its inability to fit three deserving teams onto the same championship field. But it has spoiled us in one regard: It guarantees an end-of-year battle between the No. 1 and No. 2 teams. In 1986, these matchups were rare. That undefeated Miami and Penn State were facing off was an absurdly big deal then. Add to it the sort of "good (Penn State) versus evil (Miami)" tone most of the coverage of the game took (coverage that makes you a little queasy upon reflection, after the sexual abuse conviction of then-Penn State defensive coordinator Jerry Sandusky), and this was one of the most highly anticipated college football games in memory.

Not only did the "good versus evil" theme take hold, but the narrative was fulfilled during the game as well. Those cocky, no-good Hurricanes were shown up and beaten by the good, wholesome young men from Penn State; Sandusky's defense picked off Miami quarterback Vinnie Testaverde five times, and Penn State won, 14-10, despite being outgained 445-162. This was the first college football game I could remember truly receiving Super Bowl-level hype; and to say the least, the game (and its narrative) lived up to the hype. I think it was the only time my father, never a Joe Paterno fan, ever rooted for Penn State.

4. October 16, 1993: Missouri 42, Oklahoma State 9.

And now we take a left turn. The first three games on the list are relatively well known. This one, however, makes the list for two reasons. First, it was just the second major-college football game I had ever attended (the first: Missouri 41, Oklahoma State 7 in 1991). Second, it featured what still might be the greatest catch I have ever seen. This game taught me the "You never know when something memorable might happen" lesson more than any game has since.

I don't remember a single play from this game except this one: Sometime in the second half, with Missouri already winning comfortably (they were up 28-9 at halftime after scoring all of 20 points in their five previous first halves), freshman receiver Rashetnu Jenkins went deep. The way I remember it now, he was well covered by a poor OSU defender but made a diving, one-handed catch around said defender. I have never attempted to find film of this play or make any sort of corroborative effort that might ruin my memory of it. All I know is, I left this game assuming Jenkins was going to be an All-American by the time he graduated. I probably do not need to tell you that did not happen.

5. January 2, 1996: Nebraska 62, Florida 24.

16

By this point, I was a junior in high school. Raised a Missouri fan in a sea of Oklahoma fans, I grew up with a healthy dislike of all things Nebraska. But in this game, that just didn't matter. Whatever Big 8 pride I had came out in droves during the Fiesta Bowl, which saw stoic Tom Osborne defeat cocky Steve Spurrier and saw Tommie Frazier rip off one of the most famous plays in college football history; he ran into a wall of Florida defenders, then ran right *through* the wall for a 75-yard touchdown. He broke somewhere between five and 26 tackles on the play, and his score gave the Huskers a jarring 49-18 lead.

That 1995 Nebraska team was just one of the most dominant I've ever seen. In summer 2010 at Football Outsiders, I compiled a list of the Top 100 teams of the last century based on calculations similar to those that give me the S&P+ ratings we will discuss in a future chapter. Because of a relatively weak strength of schedule and their propensity for allowing garbage-time points here and there, the 1995 Cornhuskers ranked just 47th. That alone made me question whether I should publish the countdown at all. I'm glad I did – it was a fascinating, enriching comparison of what one era calls great to what another era does – but the rankings were the perfect example of numbers being used to *start* a dialogue, not end it[11].

6. November 8, 1997: Nebraska 45, Missouri 38.

---

[11] The Top 20 of this list, by the way? 20. 1943 Notre Dame (9-1). 19. 1986 Oklahoma (11-1). 18. 2004 USC (13-0). 17. 1962 LSU (9-1-1). 16. 1952 Georgia Tech (12-0). 15. 1979 Alabama (12-0). 14. 1987 Miami (12-0). 13. 2000 Oklahoma (13-0). 12. 1971 Nebraska (13-0). 11. 1946 Notre Dame (8-0-1). 10. 1946 Army (9-0-1). 9. 1972 Oklahoma (11-1). 8. 1962 Alabama (10-1). 7. 1957 Auburn (10-0). 6. 2001 Miami (12-0). 5. 1945 Army (9-0). 4. 1944 Army (9-0). 3. 1966 Notre Dame (9-0-1). 2. 1961 Alabama (11-0). 1. 1959 Ole Miss (10-1). That a one-loss team could qualify as the greatest team ever is the most perfect representation of both college football's oddity and a season's small sample size. What was the late Beano Cook's response to some of the odder results here (1959 Ole Miss, 1957 Auburn, 2000 Oklahoma) when I spoke to him about it? "Well, it's your list." I miss Beano.

Welcome to life as a Missouri fan, kid.

Mizzou fans of a certain age will perpetually struggle to let their collective guard down, mostly because of what happened when they did so in the 1990s. First, you had the Fifth Down in 1990, when the officials lost track of downs in the final minute of Missouri's upset attempt against eventual national champion Colorado[12]. Then, you had Mizzou's 1995 upset bid of eventual basketball national champion UCLA done in by a 4.8-second, length-of-the-court drive by Tyus Edney in the second round of the NCAA Tournament. But I experienced those from afar. The Colorado-Missouri game wasn't on television in Oklahoma, and while Tyus Edney crushed me, I was still not yet fully invested in Mizzou fandom. I was only about 95 percent or so.

This game, on the other hand? I was fully immersed. This was my fourth home game as a Mizzou student. I was in the 14th row of the student section. When Corby Jones found Eddie Brooks on a perfect play-action pass, one that you could see had worked while the pass was still in the air, for the go-ahead touchdown midway through the fourth quarter, it was my first true experience of college football joy and bedlam, hugging strangers and not being able to hear myself screaming because of all the chaos around me.

By the end of the game, with Missouri up 38-31 on the No. 1 team in the country, the 14th row was standing on about the seventh row of the bleachers. The crush was ready. It almost misfired when squatty linebacker Al Sterling nearly made a diving interception earlier in Nebraska's final drive[13], but it was so very ready.

---

[12] By the way, Colorado quarterback Charles Johnson was down before he reached across the goal line on fifth down. You can never tell me otherwise.

[13] I still swear he caught it before it hit the ground, and if the game is on ESPN Classic, I make sure to look away for this play so I don't have to be proven wrong.

I still clearly remember every millisecond of the final play of regulation. Quarterback Scott Frost threw over the middle to receiver Shevin Wiggins at the goal line; two Missouri defenders were there to bat the pass away, and it fluttered away from Wiggins. The student section surged toward the field, collectively thinking Mizzou had just won the game. Some Nebraska player behind the play dove to the ground for some reason, and the official's arms signaled touchdown. At this point I was basically in the front row, charging toward the field involuntarily (*getting* charged toward the field, I guess), one of the only people around me to see the official's arms in the air. A dorm mate, attacking from the northeast corner of the stadium, was the first person to reach the goal posts. Memorial Stadium went from unabashed joy to confusion and chaos and absurdity and a little bit of anger in seconds.

I assume you probably know what happened, but in case you don't: When Wiggins was knocked to the ground, with the ball falling away from him, he swung his legs up and kicked the ball back into the air. Freshman receiver Matt Davison – who would walk on to Nebraska's basketball team a couple of years later and get booed vigorously for 40 straight minutes by Missouri fans at the Big 12 tournament – dove for the ball and caught it. Wiggins later admitted he kicked the ball intentionally, which is illegal, but there was no way for officials to understand that at the time.

Once in overtime, the outcome was a foregone conclusion, of course. Nebraska scored, Missouri didn't, et cetera. We knew what was going to happen, and then it happened. We had to sit patiently until the inevitable took place, then we had to trudge back to the dorms to figure out what the hell we had just seen.

I still remember that night, too. Reality sank in. By 11:00 p.m., a group of friends and I had come together in a dorm room, and we almost literally just stared at the tiles on the floor for a couple of hours, then went our separate ways.

19

College football is great, but college football is often just cruel. The Flea Kicker: my own Immaculate Reception.

7. November 20, 1999: Kansas State 66, Missouri 0.

There are a lot of ways for college football to break you. There is the steady build-up of hope that is finished off by a bolt of devastation, not unlike the Flea Kicker. But then there is the steady, week-to-week crumbling we sometimes get to witness in slow motion.

Missouri finished with a losing record for 13 straight years, from 1984 to 1996. In 1997-98, however, under Larry Smith, the Tigers had surged back. They went 7-5 in 1997 despite the Flea Kicker, and they went 8-4 in 1998, leading every game at halftime before eventually losing to Ohio State, Nebraska, Texas A&M and Kansas State (and trying their damnedest to do the same in the Insight.com Bowl versus Marc Bulger and West Virginia).

Each of the four losses was terribly disappointing in its own way, but no matter: Missouri is good now! So they're losing quarterback Corby Jones, running back Devin West and a host of difference-makers on both sides of the ball; recruiting has picked up! Mizzou has started to win now, and they're never going to stink again! That's all in the past!

In 1999, at a naïve 21, I actually believed this. Despite the fact that I really didn't actually have any money, I bought tickets (via student charge, of course) to every Missouri game, including the five road games. I watched as the revenge attempt against Nebraska went awry immediately, with two snaps bombed over the punter's head in the first five minutes of the game on the way to a 40-10 loss[14].

I made the 11-hour drive to Boulder to watch Missouri fall behind against Colorado, catch up, fall behind again, catch up again, and lose in overtime, 46-39. I watched as quarterback

[14] The poor long snapper's name: Ben Davidson. That I can remember a long-snapper's name 14 years later tells you he did something creatively awful.

Kirk Farmer broke his leg after getting pushed out of bounds during Homecoming against Iowa State; I was on the hill on the north side of the stadium with my parents, so unlike most of the student section on the east side, I apparently missed witnessing him screaming, throwing up, and passing out. And I watched Missouri somewhat justifiably fall apart afterward and lose, 24-21. I drove to Lawrence the next week and watched the Tigers get thumped, 21-0, by a really bad Kansas team.

I drove to Norman two weeks later and watched Missouri lose, 37-0, to Oklahoma. I watched a desperate Larry Smith tear the redshirt off of Justin Gage late in the fourth quarter. This was the ninth game of the season. Gage would become one of Missouri's all-time great receivers, but in 1999 he was a raw, dual-threat quarterback. He was of no help. This all came after I almost got arrested the night before the game[15].

---

[15] I drove down to the Oklahoma game with seven friends in two cars and stayed at my parents' house in Oklahoma City. Late that night, after being denied service at a Whataburger, we went to a 24-hour Wal-Mart in Yukon, just on the outskirts of Oklahoma City, to get … something. I have no idea what we were getting there, and it couldn't be less important to the story. Passing the toys section, three of us stopped to grab bouncy balls from the giant display and bounced them on the ground for about three seconds when a man in a leather jacket and sweat pants told us, "You either need to buy those, or put them away and leave." We put them away and moved on to the next aisle, and he followed us. "I said *leave!*" We were getting kicked out of the store before we really had a chance to do anything worth getting kicked out about, and we thought the man doing the kicking was some repressed 3 a.m. Wal Mart security guard. Turns out he was a cop. The friend in the passenger seat of my truck made sarcastic noises about flipping him off on the way out of the parking lot. I noted that this was a bad idea, being small-town Oklahoma and all. Without my knowledge, he did it anyway. The cop moseyed over to his car, called for backup, and pulled us over on the on-ramp to the interstate. After we spent about 20 minutes with our hands in the air, on our knees, behind the truck, the friend with the finger received a ticket for disorderly conduct. I got a ticket for a busted tail light; I didn't know I had a busted tail light – I thought it was going to turn into a scene from a terrible movie ("What busted tail light?" *crash* "*That* busted tail light.") – but it turned out there was indeed a tiny hole in the upper left hand corner of the left light. Thirteen years later – and this is no lie, I promise – I met a woman at an MBA happy hour at Mizzou. Turned out, she was a graduate of Yukon High School. Upon finding that out, I immediately told her this story. Two years and two months later, we were married.

The next week, I watched Missouri quarterbacks complete 14 of 39 passes in a 51-14 home loss to Texas A&M.

And in the coup de grace, I watched Kansas State score 28 points in the first 10 minutes in Manhattan, cruise to a 42-0 halftime lead (it could have been 70-0 if they wanted), and try their damnedest not to score anymore after going up 52-0 midway through the third quarter.

And I watched Missouri say "No really, I insist," handing them a pick six, then allowing a blocked punt for a touchdown when KSU wasn't even really going for the block.

I walked back to my truck after the game and found a parking ticket on my windshield.

The entire 1999 season was a slow-motion car crash, and I was there for every second of it. Okay, that's a lie; I was not there for the final minutes of the Kansas State game. We all have our limits.

More than anything else, this season taught me the moral value of loyalty. Endure the losses, stay on the bandwagon, and you will feel twice the reward when something good happens[16].

8. October 11, 2003: Missouri 41, Nebraska 24.

Revenge is sweet. In 1999, we just *knew* Missouri was going to get revenge for the Flea Kicker, but instead we watched Ben Davidson become immortalized. We also watched Matt Davison score another damn touchdown. In 2001, we just *knew* Missouri was going to get revenge, but instead we watched Eric Crouch avoid a sack in his own end zone, then race about 104 yards for a touchdown. But in 2003, it happened. In a driving rainstorm, Missouri scored 27 fourth-

---

[16] That's a load of crap, by the way. What the 1999 season really taught me is that I have masochistic tendencies I didn't previously know about or understand. Many sports fans do. I could have just stayed at home and held my hand to a lighter for a few hours each Saturday, but instead I chose to abuse my parents' Conoco gas card, doing the metaphorical version of the same thing.

quarter points, turning a 10-point deficit into a laugher. With Nebraska leading, 24-21, Missouri lined up to attempt a field goal to tie the game. I couldn't watch, so I turned my back, only to hear my friend Seth scream, "Oh they *faked* it!" with a cracking voice. I turned around in time to see backup quarterback Sonny Riccio's lob falling into tight end Victor Sesay's arms in the end zone. I watched Missouri force a three-and-out, then score again, then pick off a pass and score again.

After the game, while rushing the field along with every other Mizzou fan in attendance, I grabbed Riccio while he was doing a postgame interview and screamed, "I love you SO MUCH." His response: "Thank you?[17]" I made snow angels (plastic pellet angels) on the 50-yard line with a friend. I bought the poster.

9. November 24, 2007: Missouri 36, Kansas 28.

This was the most important game in the history of both the University of Missouri's football program and that of its biggest rival. Both Missouri and Kansas were having dream seasons. In 2002, they had combined to go 7-17. In 1988, 4-17-1. But heading into a matchup at Arrowhead Stadium over Thanksgiving weekend 2007, they were a combined 21-1. With LSU's loss to Arkansas the day before, the winner of this game would almost certainly be No. 1 in the BCS standings, with only a date with Oklahoma in the Big 12 title game separating them from a spot in the BCS Championship game. It had been 47 years since Missouri had spent its lone week at No. 1 in the rankings. (They had beaten Oklahoma that year, moved to 9-0 and No. 1, then lost to Kansas, of all teams, and lost the national title.) Kansas had never reached the top spot. Kansas was known mostly for basketball, Missouri for ... self-pity, I

---

[17] Riccio transferred two months later. The commonly accepted reason was that he was going to be stuck behind quarterback Brad Smith on the depth chart for the rest of his career. But I knew the real reason.

guess? Regardless, this was the one game in the series that Missouri just absolutely, positively *had* to win.

And they won. After a tense first few minutes, quarterback Chase Daniel did what Chase Daniel did all year. He found tight end Martin Rucker for a touchdown on fourth-and-goal late in the first quarter. He scrambled around for about a day and a half and found receiver Danario Alexander for a touchdown early in the second quarter. He completed 40 of 49 passes and helped to stake Missouri to a 28-7 lead heading into the fourth quarter. Kansas made a late charge, but in the Jayhawks' last gasp, the entire Missouri defensive line piled on top of quarterback Todd Reesing for a safety with 12 seconds left, solidifying a 36-28 win and a No. 1 ranking.

I was not at Arrowhead, by the way. I had committed to meeting family in Oklahoma for Thanksgiving long before, and while everyone involved would have probably understood if I changed plans … I didn't want to. This was too personal a moment; I decided I didn't want to share it with anybody else. I watched in our dark basement with the laptop pulled up (to Rock M Nation, my Missouri blog, of course), fought the urge to curl into the fetal position, and called Seth when it was over.

Missouri lost the next week, of course. In the third quarter of a close game, Rucker let a ball go through his hands and into the hands of Oklahoma linebacker Curtis Lofton, setting into motion a brief domino effect from which the Tigers wouldn't recover. They lost, 38-17, then destroyed Arkansas in the Cotton Bowl and finished 12-2.

We don't all get to be Alabama fans. For the week after Arrowhead, I got to bask in the fact that Missouri won, that they were in the "Final Four," so to speak. I got to help my former roommate Andrew Lawrence, a *Sports Illustrated* writer, piece together feature story ideas on the off chance that *SI* would be making a "Congrats, your team just won the national title!" commemorative edition a few weeks later. Most of us will follow college football for all of our lives without getting to experience the feeling of actually winning a title. This was my moment to bask in the almost.

10. December 17, 2011: UL-Lafayette 32, San Diego State 30.

We finish this list with some randomness. The 2011 season was my first as a full-time college football writer for SB Nation. It was a job, complete with 60-hour work weeks and occasionally smattered with tasks I didn't really care about or enjoy (like a weekly Heisman column, for instance). But it was a job *writing about college football*. All fall, I felt paranoid that this was some elaborate prank, and that I would have to go back to my old job, one I liked at times but didn't *love*.

The 2011 season was full of "I cannot believe I get paid to write about this" moments. The New Orleans Bowl was potentially my favorite. While most were mourning the fact that we got a national title game – an Alabama-LSU rematch – that few wanted to see, some of us watched a game that reinforced all of college football's strangeness and sheer joy. San Diego State and UL-Lafayette faced off in the Superdome. For Louisiana, it was the program's greatest moment. Drifting through the Southland conference, three years in the Big West (despite being west of very little), two stays as an independent, and more than a decade as a Sun Belt also-ran, the Ragin' Cajuns had never been to a bowl game and never threatened to get noticed by the college football world. But in head coach Mark Hudspeth's first year in Lafayette, his Cajuns came out of nowhere to go 8-4 and earn their first ever bowl invitation.

Hudspeth and his team treated this minor bowl as their Super Bowl. He had them doing the Oklahoma Drill – a risky, full-contact, one-on-one tackling drill, basically – on the sidelines before the game. He dipped into every page of the playbook. The Cajuns took a 19-3 lead early in the third quarter, completely ran out of steam (there's a reason why you don't usually do the Oklahoma Drill before you have to play a

25

real, 60-minute game), and eventually fell behind, 30-29, with 35 seconds remaining. But as time expired, kicker Brett Baer made a knuckling, wobbling, terribly unlikely 50-yard field goal, snaking it just above the crossbar and just inside the right goal post. And the team celebrated like it had won the national title. A couple of fanshots from the stands made it onto YouTube. From the first game of the year to the national title game, everything matters to somebody. What was a minor, inconsequential bowl to some was the greatest sporting moment of some Louisiana fans' lives. It was an absolute joy to watch.

So that's my list. It directly reflects where I grew up and where I went to school. I wanted to see the same lists from other college football fanatics, however; the best way to illustrate how regional college football's history is, is to look at the games that had an impact on people from different regions. So I approached a few of my favorite blogger friends – a man who goes by "Senator Blutarsky" at his blog, Get the Picture, and the duo that runs the Solid Verbal Podcast (Ty Hildenbrandt and Dan Rubenstein) – for their takes as well. Here are their lists and explanations. You'll notice almost no overlap whatsoever from list to list.

Senator Blutarsky, Georgia fan

1. November 19, 1966: Notre Dame 10, Michigan State 10

"This was the first college football game that seeped into my (then 10-year-old) conscious mind. Lots of pre-game hype, followed by lots of post-game second guessing, thus proving that the Internet and ESPN are evolutionary, not revolutionary, developments."

2. November 25, 1971: Nebraska 35, Oklahoma 31

"A game-of-the-century game that lived up to the hype and then some. It cemented one of college football's great rivalries for me, which is one reason why the collateral damage from college football's current realignment obsession saddens me so."

3. October 28, 1978: Georgia 17, Kentucky 16

"Three years of watching Virginia's football program go down the toilet had soured me on the sport as a whole. [Georgia radio announcer] Larry Munson rekindled my love in one night with a radio call that Lewis Grizzard aptly described as 'better than being there.' Munson never did call the winning kick good. It didn't matter."

4. November 8, 1980: Georgia 26, Florida 21

"The one game here that needs no explanation[18]."

5. January 1, 1981: Georgia 17, Notre Dame 10

"When it's your team winning its only national championship of your lifetime, yeah, it's gonna make the list."

6. November 1, 1997: Georgia 37, Florida 17

---

[18] Quick background, just in case: With Georgia's national title season hanging in the balance, the No. 2 Bulldogs rallied to beat No. 20 Florida late in the game when quarterback Buck Belue found Lindsay Scott for a 93-yard touchdown pass on third-and-long to pull off an improbable 26-21 win. Larry Munson called it like this: "Florida in a stand-up five. They may or may not blitz. Buck back, third down on the eight. In trouble ... he got a block behind him. Gotta throw on the run ... complete to the 25. To the 30. Lindsay Scott 35, 40! Lindsay Scott 45, 50! 45, 40! Run, Lindsay! 25, 20, 15, 10, 5! Lindsay Scott! Lindsay Scott! Lindsay Scott!" Georgia would win the national title two months later. Run, Lindsay, Run: Senator Blutarsky's Immaculate Reception.

"While it didn't herald the next step in the program many hoped it would, this game was still the only win Georgia claimed over Steve Spurrier during his time in Gainesville. Robert Edwards' clinching touchdown marked the closest I've ever come to fainting at a game due to sheer joy."

7. November 16, 2002: Georgia 24, Auburn 21

"The game that marked the return of Georgia to SEC relevance after nearly two decades. It was kind of a big deal, in other words."

8. January 4, 2006: Texas 45, Southern Cal 42

"The high water mark for the BCS (and Texas head coach Mack Brown, too, come to think about it), a game matching the undisputed top two teams in college football that went down to the wire."

9. November 23, 2007: Arkansas 50, LSU 48

"This was the insane capper to an insane season, still my favorite college football season of all. Arkansas' Darren McFadden running a mutant version of the Wing-T ... what's not to love? Added bonus: [Arkansas head coach] Houston Nutt's post-game babbling."

10. December 1, 2012: Alabama 32, Georgia 28

"If part of being a fan is suffering through pain, then this game surely qualifies. I still haven't worked up the resolve to watch the replay, although I can't bring myself to erase it from my DVR, either."

Ty Hildenbrandt, Notre Dame fan

1. January 2, 1989: Notre Dame 34, West Virginia 21

"My earliest euphoric experience due to a college football game. West Virginia never had a chance as Lou Holtz cemented his legacy as a great coach by winning his first national championship in the then-Sunkist Fiesta Bowl."

2. November 25, 1989: Miami 27, Notre Dame 10

"My mom thought it'd be a novel idea to arrange a trip to Miami to see this game for my eighth birthday. Consequently, it's my earliest (and only) memory of having beer bottles thrown at me for wearing a Notre Dame T-shirt. Miami's improbable third-and-44 conversion was just insult to injury."

3. January 1, 1991: Colorado 10, Notre Dame 9

"My first exposure to untimely officiating, as Rocket Ismail was robbed – robbed, I say![19] – of a game-winning punt return in the 1991 Orange Bowl."

4. November 14, 1992: Notre Dame 17, Penn State 16

"As a Pennsylvanian, no game defined my fandom for the Irish more than the famous 'Snow Bowl,' in which Rick Mirer hit Reggie Brooks for a game-winning two-point conversion. This dramatic victory over 'hometown' Penn State – a school from which I would eventually graduate – cemented my

---

[19] Yeah, I concur. The clipping call that negated what would have been the game winner in the final minute was, at best, an illegal block that happened far behind Ismail's return and, at worst, non-existent. Colorado's run to the 1991 national title (well, co-title) was blessed, to say the least, by this penalty and the Fifth Down incident discussed earlier.

rooting interests and forever labeled me as the oddball among friends and fellow alumni."

5. November 20, 1993: Boston College 41, Notre Dame 39

"A week after Notre Dame's watershed victory over Florida State, the cold-blooded foot of Boston College's David Gordon taught me the cruel reality of let-down losses and, really, life in general.[20]"

6. September 4, 2004: BYU 20, Notre Dame 17

"My most vivid memory of a look-ahead loss. I watched this game, with unfettered excitement and inebriation, from The Rathskellar in State College, Pennsylvania, and proceeded to spike my cell phone into a million pieces in the middle of the bar. Notre Dame came back the next week and knocked off Michigan."

7. October 15, 2005: USC 34, Notre Dame 31

"The ultimate stomach punch game. I watched in a catatonic state from the stands of Notre Dame Stadium as the 'Bush Push[21]' kept USC unbeaten. As history would show, this game may have been the ceiling for [Irish head coach] Charlie Weis."

8. November 7, 2009: Navy 23, Notre Dame 21

---

[20] Gordon's field goal gave Boston College an improbable win and knocked No. 1 Notre Dame from atop the polls. In one of the best examples of the "It's better to lose earlier than later" meme that dominated our poll-driven sport for a long time, Notre Dame's loss boosted Florida State back to No. 1 in the AP poll. The one-loss Seminoles would finish the season No. 1, just ahead of the one-loss Fighting Irish who had beaten them in early November.

[21] USC scored the game-winning touchdown with just seconds remaining when quarterback Matt Leinart sneaked over the goal line with help from what was probably an illegal push from running back Reggie Bush.

"With Notre Dame's second straight home loss to Navy, it became a near certainty that the Irish would fire Charlie Weis and, again, be looking for a new coach to shepherd their program back to greatness. Also, it was really embarrassing to be a fan, especially after losses to Pitt, UConn and Stanford soon followed."

9. September 3, 2011: South Florida 23, Notre Dame 20

"The game during which every Notre Dame fan wondered if head coach Brian Kelly would have a heart attack, get struck by lightning, or both. After months of anticipation, a sloppy, home loss to South Florida with weather delays and backbreaking turnovers kicked off a season of quarterback controversies and disappointment."

10. October 27, 2012: Notre Dame 30, Oklahoma 13

Possibly Notre Dame's biggest win in 20 years – on the road in Norman, Oklahoma – with a freshman quarterback in the midst of an undefeated season. It was significant for the program on so many levels, and a symbolic breath of fresh air for self-loathing Irish fans around the country."

Dan Rubenstein, Oregon Fan

"Having parents who didn't go to schools with big football tradition, I wasn't born into team loyalty, so I generally grew up watching big national games and a random smattering of west coast games with my dad. This is my story."

1. January 2, 1996: Nebraska 62, Florida 24

"I was late for a parks league basketball game because my eyes were too wide open from watching both Tommie Frazier break *all of the tackles* and the Blackshirts[22] completely swallow up the fun 'n gun."

2. December 5, 1998: Miami 49, UCLA 45

"At least in today's statistical terms, Cade McNown was pretty ordinary, but man, did he look great to my 15-year old eyes, which made the possibility of the local team going to the national championship kind of fun until Edgerrin James was all like, 'Nope[23].'"

3. January 1, 1999: Wisconsin 38, UCLA 31

"I always had really good Chinese chicken salad (big ups, Abe's Deli) at an annual New Year's Day party, so the bummer (but secretly fun) experience of watching Ron Dayne run all over UCLA was made a little easier by both wonton noodles and announcer Craig James brilliantly calling the Badgers the 'worst team to ever play in the Rose Bowl' before they dominated the Bruins."

4. September 22, 2001: Oregon 24, USC 22

"It was my first Duck game at Autzen Stadium my freshman year, which meant it was the first time I walked the footbridge from campus to the stadium and the first time I experienced the wall of Autzen sound when Joey Harrington led a comeback win against the Trojans late in the fourth to seal a

---

[22] That's the nickname given to the Nebraska defense. It stems from the Bob Devaney era, when defenders wore black pullover jerseys in practice.

[23] UCLA was undefeated and ranked third in the BCS standings until a trip to Miami in early December. No. 2 Kansas State had lost to Texas A&M in the Big 12 title game earlier that day, and all UCLA had to do was beat Miami to get a shot at Tennessee in the national title game. Instead, James rushed 39 times for 299 yards and three touchdowns, and Miami scored three fourth-quarter touchdowns to win, 49-45. UCLA gained 670 yards but lost.

win, ultimately leading me down my personal and professional college football path."

5. November 19, 2005: USC 50, Fresno State 42

"With shrugging apologies to Vince Young et al, Reggie Bush's college football thesis was the single most dynamic performance I've seen in a single game[24]."

6. January 4, 2006: Texas 41, USC 38

"I didn't really like either team going in, but I couldn't ever turn away from watching Reggie Bush, so I went west coast and had the privilege of rooting for a team that looked great, predictable, dumb, and helpless in a matter of minutes."

7. November 18, 2006: Ohio State 42, Michigan 39

"I watched this in a great, packed Palo Alto, California, bar called The Old Pro, which was split down the middle with Wolverines and Buckeyes, and I couldn't have been happier to watch Troy Smith and high level (No. 1 vs. No. 2) Big Ten football without a rooting interest other than for cool things to keep happening."

8. January 1, 2007: Boise State 43, Oklahoma 42

"I watched this game alone because one of my then-roommates was jet lagged and passed out and the other was still traveling. So nobody heard my screaming when Boise State broke out the hook-and-ladder and Statue of Liberty play[25]."

---

[24] Bush rushed 23 times for 294 yards and two scores, caught three passes for 68 yards, and threw in 151 return yards to boot.

[25] A Statue of Liberty play is when the quarterback fakes a pass while handing the ball to the running back behind his back.

9. September 8, 2007: Oregon 39, Michigan 7

"I was traveling for work and had to watch it a day late on the DVR, but the introduction to America of [new offensive coordinator] Chip Kelly and the great version of quarterback Dennis Dixon, which included both a Statue of Liberty play *and* fake Statue of Liberty, was the first of countless giggle sessions, both as an Oregon fan and a college football fan."

10. October 20, 2007: Oregon 55, Washington 34

"Beyond Chip Kelly realizing that Washington's defense wasn't going to stop *anything* on the ground (and running the same three plays all game), the sound of the Husky crowd cheering running back Jonathan Stewart getting blown up on a zone read while Dennis Dixon was 18 yards down the field running with the ball always makes me smile."

These four lists produced 40 games, and only two were listed twice: Tommie Frazier's iconic decimation of Florida, and the USC-Texas game that felt more like a Super Bowl than a lot of Super Bowls. The four of us have all obsessed over college football for the vast majority of our respective lives, and we produced 38 different games as sources of our obsessions.

****

College football is, literally and figuratively, an antique; the flaws, no matter how serious, somehow just accentuate the charm. Shady academic dealings? Free tattoos? Envelopes of cash in recruits' pockets? Head injuries? Sham degrees? Okay, sure, but ... fight songs! Bratwursts! Friends! Homecoming! Jumbotrons! Hugs from strangers after touchdowns! The local R.O.T.C. unit firing off a cannon!

I was a college football fan long before I was a numbers guy. I've always been far too analytical about this sport (and most other things), and the numbers have simply informed my analytical ability. I thrive in the gray area to which most people are allergic when it comes to sports debates (or any debates, really), and numbers give you more "Yeah, but... material than just about anything else. Ranking teams is only the start of it.

Because of numbers, I know just how important a fast start to a game truly is. Or how those long, satisfying, 15-play, seven-minute touchdown drives do not happen often enough to rely on them. Or how much of a difference second-and-8 can make over second-and-6 in the long run. Or how random fumble recoveries (and games that turn because of them) can be. Or how one team's offensive personality differs from others'. These are innate truths to me now; I don't need to keep a running track of a team's success rate in my head, and I don't need to calculate a team's average yards per play on first down while I'm watching. Numbers have simply given me a better intuitive feel for this game I love. They have also given me a stronger voice[26].

I obviously talk about numbers a lot, but they aren't what made me a college football fan, and my obsession with them has not been some sort of attempt to beat the game or pound others over the head with them. As I say many times in my pieces, if you don't like numbers, skip to the words. Hopefully some of them are worth reading. Numbers help me set better expectations, both for my team and for others, but when the game's on, the game's on.

****

"I'm getting 18-year old young men and helping them grow as people. When they leave here in four or five years, they have a degree, and they have a clear picture of what they want to be in the future. They are learning to prioritize their life. I want them to be great people, great fathers, great husbands, great businessmen. Football is a vehicle for this. It builds character and reveals character. It's a tough, tough game

---

[26] They also give me a way to talk about the sport every single day of the year.

35

Every day I'm making a little bit of a difference in people's lives."

Colorado head coach Mike MacIntyre is explaining why he has dedicated his life to coaching the game of football, and why college football has drawn him in so much. An NFL assistant for five years, he returned to the college ranks as Duke's defensive coordinator in 2008, earned a promotion to head coach of San Jose State in 2010, turned a flailing program around in just three years, and was hired to do the same at Colorado following the 2012 season.

"I enjoy the college process," he says. "When I was coaching in the NFL, I got my Ph.D. in coaching – Bill Parcells [his mentor with the Dallas Cowboys], Eric Mangini [his boss for one year with the New York Jets] were great. But I missed the everyday interaction with these kids. You are mentoring kids."

Head coaches are paid quite well at the higher levels of college football. But when you get into coaching to begin with, you don't know that you're going to make it that far up the ladder. Nick Saban, a national title-winning head coach at LSU (once) and Alabama (three times), spent five years as a low-level assistant at Kent State. Texas head coach Mack Brown spent seven years as a low-level assistant, at four different schools, in the 1970s. Pete Carroll, most recently the head coach at USC and for the NFL's Seattle Seahawks, spent five years as a graduate assistant: four at the University of the Pacific and one at Arkansas.

There were no guarantees of future success and four-million-dollars-per-year contracts when these coaches got started in the business. They followed their chosen path because of the game itself.

"I didn't know it was something I was going to do when I went to college," says California head coach Sonny Dykes. "I was actually playing college baseball. I started to think about my life without football, and honestly, I got into it because I couldn't imagine my life without it. It's a strange way to make a living, but it's something I enjoy doing. If I won the lottery tomorrow, I would keep doing it."

And while it is easy to become cynical about the money involved in college football, and the way it has impacted the game as a whole[27], that cynicism does not pervade the coaching ranks, especially at the mid-major level.

Ball State head coach Pete Lembo: "I have no desire to coach in the NFL. College football is the whole package, the whole organization. I love everything that goes into making Saturday happen: the recruiting process, program management the organization of practice week. I really enjoy bringing the right people into the organization – athletes, coaches, support staff – and helping those people develop and maximize their potential, academically, socially, personally, and athletically. I love seeing assistant coaches thrive and grow. It's applying business management principles to running a football program I enjoy a lot of the macro, too: the dealing with constituents, interactions on campus, all of the different areas you deal with.

UL-Monroe head coach Todd Berry: "It's really the opportunity to work with this age group. They're into the game, and you know it, and they're fascinated with learning the game at this age. We don't have to deal with the ego and the divas. The NFL thing's just not for me. Younger than this age is fun, too, but they're not quite as into the game as I am. This group's a lot of fun to work with. It's easy to get a really strong team mentality at this point."

Ohio head coach Frank Solich: "I love working with young men. To me, the job of a college football coach is threefold. You have to help a player maximize his goals academically, athletically, and personally. You can have an influence on college kids. I want them to have a lot of opportunities open to them when they leave here. I enjoy that part of it. Now, I know as well as anybody that you need to win football games, or someone else will be in your job. That's

---

[27] Trust me, that conversation is coming.

the nature of the business. But I see my job as much more than just that."

Wake Forest head coach Jim Grobe, who bounced around as an assistant at quite a few mid-major schools early in his career: "I wanted to play. I wish I was still playing – I'm still waiting on the NFL guys to call me! I would rather play than coach. I just wasn't good enough to play at the next level, and when I figured that out, I decided the only way I could stay in football and stay a kid was to coach. I would have been perfectly happy being a high school coach for my entire career. A colleague ended up at Emory & Henry, so I went along with him. Then another colleague ended up at Marshall, then a Marshall coach ended up getting defensive coordinator job at Air Force. It's not your plan where you're going to be or what level you'll coach at. I just knew I wanted to stay in football."

New Mexico head coach Bob Davie, who spent a decade as an ESPN color commentator after a five-year stint as the head man at Notre Dame: "I had a lot of time to reflect on this and think about it. I had been in college coaching for 25 years, and I spent 10 at ESPN. The biggest thing about it is, 365 days a year, you have a chance to compete, and you have a chance to make a difference. There are so many different facets – the fall, and the games, and then recruiting. Think about the time involved in just those two things. And then you've got player and staff development in the spring. It's such an energized environment year-round.

"I loved television, and I loved going to games. But the reality is, when the game was over, you didn't have anything to do with the outcome. You didn't have the development, the preparation, the thought process. It was kind of hollow. It's kind of a shock when you get out of coaching, and you realize that there's a whole other world going on. There's such a tunnel vision going on in coaching, and in a lot of ways that's a positive and a negative.

"Every year, the demons would take over, and I'd want to get back into it."

The origin of those "demons" could go far back, to high school or even earlier. For former Air Force head coach Fisher DeBerry, football gave him structure that didn't otherwise exist. "I was a product of a single-parent home. My mother had to work all the time. If it hadn't been for my coaches, I don't know where I would have landed.

"All I wanted to do was be around athletics," DeBerry says. He played baseball and football at Wofford College in South Carolina and saw playing time on both sides of the football field as a receiver, linebacker, and defensive back. He coached in South Carolina high schools throughout the 1960s, ended up an assistant at Wofford for two years, moved to Appalachian State as part of Jim Brakefield's staff in the 1970s, landed on Ken Hatfield's coaching staff at Air Force in 1980, took over as offensive coordinator in 1981, and landed the head coaching gig when Hatfield moved to Arkansas in 1984. From his freshman year at Wofford to his final year as Air Force's head coach, he was "around athletics" for more than 50 years.

****

We hang around, join arms, and sing the alma mater after the game. We think we're trying to set an example for others, but really we just do it because it feels good and we don't want to leave the stadium yet. We eventually make the weary walk back uphill for liquids, brownies and some general lingering. We are hoarse, tired and dehydrated. Some have to make a two-hour drive east or west to get home.

Maybe you grew up in a large metropolitan area, where pro football is king. Maybe you attended a school that was smaller or more prestigious (and less football-inclined). Or maybe you simply grew up in an area of the country that doesn't give a damn about college football. You may like pro football more than college — plenty do — but you aren't me. When you grow up in an area obsessed with this sport, and when you take in the collegiate game day experience enough, it becomes a large portion of your identity, more than perhaps any other sport in this country. You

39

cannot fathom another way to spend autumn Saturdays. You get nervous when friends announce they're getting married in September. Cracking open a beer at 8:00 a.m. is, on Saturdays, completely defensible. Driving 12 hours round trip for a big conference game? Not only logical, but necessary. NFL fans who say things like "Well, I don't really follow college football..." make you question both their integrity and their morals. You perhaps cannot justify some of college sports' shadier dealings, but you believe there is enough good to outweigh the bad, and it is difficult to imagine what might change that.

By Monday, I'll have pored through the box score of every game, looking for the important stories, stats and narratives. But today, I am a college football fan in the heart of Saturday's America, tired and buzzed and trying to get home. Depending on how many people left early, or how horrendous the new event staff plan for directing traffic may be, I find my destination between 15 and 75 minutes after I got in my car (with no traffic, it would take me about eight). On the drive home, I have been plotting what I will be writing and saying about the game, replaying virtually every play in my head, listening to the local post game show hosted by Former Player A and Former Coach B, charging my cell phone and trying to pull in some scores. I shower, I grab a bite to eat, and I open the laptop. It's time to start getting ready for next week's game.

****

"It's typically at this moment when I get very sad and nostalgic about another season gone. Miss you guys. Let's do it again soon."
– Paul Myerberg on Twitter after the 2013 BCS title game

Being a college football fan is like wearing a special members-only suit jacket (like the ones that bowl committee members were known for wearing and probably still do). When you find another one out in the real world, you just smile at them and nod.

In this way, the Internet has allowed for this club to grow. You can find like-minded individuals in seconds. And in recent years, that club has taken to Twitter, the Internet's version of a sports bar, to bond and commiserate. It is how I got to know Paul Myerberg, for instance. Author of a well-known, and excellent, college football blog called Pre-Snap Read before he was snatched up by *USA Today*, he and I bonded over nerdery: We had both written lengthy previews about all 120 (then 124, now 125) FBS teams through the years in the football offseason, we had compared notes, and we had chatted at length – with others, of course: Spencer Hall and Jason Kirk from SB Nation, Andy Staples and Stewart Mandel from *Sports Illustrated*, Holly Anderson from Grantland, Bruce Feldman and the blogger team from CBS Sports, Adam Kramer, Michael Felder, and company from Bleacher Report – over time. We have met in person just once. But when he posted the above quote, it hit me hard. I knew just how he felt.

"I got caught up working harder on college football this year than I ever had," he says. "I didn't realize until the year was over, but ... I think I'm sadder this year than I ever have been before." The more involved you get with college football, the more you grow to love it, it seems.

College football is, quite simply, about bonding. It's about players and coaches, players and players, coaches and coaches, players and fans, fans and writers, writers and writers. It is about shaking hands with somebody you haven't seen for nine months each September. It's about the weird traditions. It's about the way Twitter erupts when something amazing happens anywhere in the country. It's about hugging your old stars on the way out the door[28]. It's about hoping your new stars are right around the corner. It's about making snow angels at the 50-yard line. It's about some town of 50,000 becoming the center of the universe for a few hours on a

---

[28] Myerberg: "Your heart explodes when you see [Outland Award winning Texas A&M offensive lineman] Luke Joeckel writing a letter to the A&M fan base, thanking them before leaving for the pros. Reading that made me very sad." I got to experience the same thing watching Missouri receiver Jeremy Maclin choking back tears while announcing he was going pro following the 2008 season. Head coach Gary Pinkel basically had to talk him into leaving because he was desperate for a reason to stay but had nothing more to prove.

Saturday. Sure, it's about the bad things, too. And we're getting ready to talk about those. But the loyalty this sport engenders starts from a pure place. It's also a silly, irrational, ridiculous place. But it's pure. And sometimes it's beautiful.

2. An Ungovernable Mess

"The moment schools realized they could charge admission for their games, college football was in trouble."

— Michael Oriard

In April 2013, Harvard marketing professor Doug J. Chung published a study titled "The Dynamic Advertising Effect of Collegiate Athletics." The goal was to "estimate the impact of athletic success on applicant quality and quantity." In other words, he wrote a paper about the Flutie Effect.

You've probably heard the story by now, of course. With Doug Flutie lined up at quarterback, Boston College won football games at what was then a rather unprecedented level. In the final three years of his career at BC (1982-84), the Eagles went 27-8-1; as a senior, he won the Heisman Trophy, and BC went 10-2 (most memorably beating Miami via the Hail Mary from the last chapter), won the Cotton Bowl, and finished fifth in the AP poll. Two years later, applications to Boston College had risen by 30 percent. Chung's study shows that this wasn't simply a Boston College thing. He notes other examples like Georgetown during the Patrick Ewing basketball years (applications rose by 45 percent) and Northwestern during its unexpected Rose Bowl run of 1995 (21 percent).

I got to witness the same effect in 2008. Following Missouri's 2007 run to 12 wins and a No. 4 finish in the polls, Mizzou welcomed its largest freshman class ever. Call it the Chase Daniel Effect. From a morale standpoint, there was simply nothing like walking around campus the week after the Tigers beat Kansas to reach No. 1 in the country. The vibe was different, happier. College football has, for better or worse, become a status symbol. The team's success is indirectly your success[29].

Chung likened athletic success to advertising, "as a stock of goodwill that decays over time." It raises awareness about the school, and it creates buzz. Alumni become more engaged (and generous), as well. And he found that, indeed, such success has a rather stark impact on both the quantity and quality of applicants received by a given school.

> "When a school goes from being 'mediocre' to being 'great' on the football field, applications increase by 17.7 percent, with the vast proportion of the increase coming from low-ability students. However, there is also an increase in the applications from students at the highest ability level. In order to attain similar effects, a school must either decrease tuition by 3.8 percent or increase the quality of education by recruiting higher-quality faculty who are paid 5.1 percent more in the academic labor market."

So to increase enrollment, you can either drop tuition, pay your professors more, or figure out how to play good

---

[29] Consequently, the team's failure sometimes feels like your failure. Fans take losing personally (and act out accordingly), and while that is certainly irrational and often ridiculous, that doesn't make it unnatural.

football. Which of those three do you figure would have the most support among the general alumni base?

That college football can actually do some good for your school is just about the worst thing possible, really, because all we need is a reason to go crazy. All we need to hear is that there might be some health benefits to chocolate, and we eat the whole bag of Oreos. As Chung himself said, "I am hesitant to say schools choose to invest in athletics just because of the spillover effect into academics." But the horse has long since left the barn.

****

It is generally true that your best traits are also your worst. Someone who is renowned for being relentlessly driven to succeed in his or her chosen career path might also be a little too intense or tactless away from the office. Someone who is seen as a great friend who never says no and never ignores a phone call might also end up struggling with priorities when it comes to relationships or parenting[30].

For football, these rules also apply. The "violence" portion of the chess-and-violence formula that so many Americans find so appealing can lead to serious health issues down the line. And for college football in particular, the popularity of the game itself has led to more money than the model was ever designed to distribute. It has led to more exposure, more televised games, better amenities, a happier fan experience, and plenty of issues regarding where all of this extra money is going, especially since it can't go directly to the players.

---

[30] Me? I've always considered my best-and-worst quality to be the speed with which my brain seems to move. When I'm on the right track, I get there really quickly. When I'm on the wrong track, I go careening in the wrong direction, and it takes me a long time to figure out where I made a wrong turn. You can't have the good without the bad.

45

College football's uniqueness and oddities, its strange traditions and small towns and closed doors, make it amazing to follow. You are constantly learning things about this sport, and you are never in danger of knowing everything. This sport is constantly surprising. It is also an ungovernable mess. And with each passing decade, its pool of money has grown, seemingly exponentially. Really, though, *only* the money has changed. The other problems have been mostly omnipresent.

Francis Wallace's *Dementia Pigskin* is a narcissistic, self-congratulatory read, an indirect autobiography for a screenwriter, columnist, and Notre Dame fan. It is also incredibly accurate in the way it describes the game of college football we have come to know. Some highlights:

> "Coaching, for instance, is a perilous pursuit from which the average artisan derives only a modest living, with a headache for every dollar and a heartache for lagniappe."

> "The players, prohibited by college law from deriving any financial benefit from the sport in which they engage, receive from the colleges, in most cases, an even exchange of an education. ... From a strictly financial angle, the lads are grossly underpaid."

> "The most distinguished members of the Football Nuts of America are the faculty men who make up the National Collegiate Athletic Association, which strongly resembles the political U.N. – loud voice and baby teeth."

> "Up to now, the faculty men have taken themselves off the horns of their gridiron dilemma by adding a new regulation to take care of any development which threatens their paradox of making money out of an amateur sport."

46

"The amateur system, in practical operation, shapes up like a Rube Goldberg invention. Everybody knows there hasn't been an honest amateur in big-time football for quite sometime now."

"As presently conducted, college football is a business where, to make the round peg fit into the square hole, it is understood that everybody can cheat a little but nobody should cheat enough to embarrass everybody else."

"The only real developments in football during the last two decades have been increased emphasis upon speed and passing. ... There used to be a theory that passing could not become a primary formation, that it must always be supplementary to a sound running offense. The pros exploded that, and the college game is following this pro trend."

"All through the night, and all through the week, the season, the discussions, arguments, analyses, the praisings and second-guessings, the idolatry and disgust. Football is the big thing in the small town during the season; a healthy thing; a constructive thing; a typically American thing, nationalistic and narrow as hell."

And my personal favorite:

"Football is something like sex. You might overemphasize it but you're never going to make it unpopular."

If not for the Rube Goldberg reference and use of the word "lads[31]" (and the description of coaching salaries as "modest," though the average coach does not make what Nick Saban makes), you would have no idea this book was written in 1951.

In December 2012, *Sports Illustrated*'s Andy Staples wrote the definitive column in this vein. It was titled "The college football apocalypse is nigh! Or is it?" and pointed out that the things we consider threats to the sport, have always been threats to this sport. Serious injuries? *The New York Times* said "Public sentiment is yearly growing stronger against the brutality of the game," in 1905. Threats to the sanctity of the NCAA? NCAA president J. Neils Thompson said, "If we don't start doing something, we're not going to have an NCAA farther down the road," in 1977, when big schools were threatening to break apart and form a new association. Too much television influence? NCAA president John Toner said, "A small number of television networks now can manipulate the college football market the way they wish," in 1984.

College football has been the driving force behind everything good (it quite often pays the budget for your school's rowing or tennis team, and again, it can positively impact the makeup of your student body) and bad (see: every major scandal regarding football players, coaches, or administrators taking advantage of their status and/or the need to win football games, for the last century) since athletic departments were created.

With more money and influence, of course, come more complaints about the negative side of the sport. This is understandable. One could write a volume of books about this, but let's run through the major grievances.

---

[31] Okay, fine, I also had to look up the word "lagniappe." It means, among other things, "something given or obtained gratuitously or by way of good measure." The more you know…

"Football is too powerful."

Between 1941 and 1949, Missouri played Ohio State eight times, all on the road. According to Bob Broeg's *Ol' Mizzou: A Story of Missouri Football* (1974), the Tigers did this because head coach and athletic director Don Faurot would use the payout from the yearly trip (and loss) to fund the athletic department's budget for the rest of the year. According to a former Mizzou administrator, quoted by Broeg, "That series, more than any other, permitted Don to wipe out athletic-department indebtedness."

Football has been the driving force of the athletic budget for quite a long time, in other words. This was the case in the 1940s, and it is certainly the case now. Due mostly to television rights, college football is making more money than ever. Live sporting events are pretty much the most valuable advertising commodity television has in the days of DVR; college football Saturdays do not quite have the drawing power of NFL Sundays, but while the sport as a whole was undervalued for decades, this is no longer the case.

Just over the past decade or so, we have seen per-year television revenue figures jump to unfathomable levels. With its exclusive NBC television deal, Notre Dame was once in possession of just about the most lucrative television contract on the market. But when the ACC renegotiated its rights deals in 2012, Notre Dame's per-year revenue figure was lower than Boston College's. In 2012-13, ACC teams were expected to make in the neighborhood of $17 million a year from television. Big 12 teams were to make just under $20 million on average, Pac-12 schools about $21 million. Big Ten schools were to make close to $25 million, thanks in part to the Big Ten Network. And when the SEC Network makes its debut in August 2014, the conference is expected to exceed even the Big Ten's numbers.

And this says nothing, of course, of the money train that will be the four-team College Football Playoff, which begins in the 2014 postseason.

"It's off the charts financially," says UTSA head coach Larry Coker, a 2001 national champion at Miami. "I was at Ohio State for a few years, and Woody Hayes felt money corrupted the coaches and changed everything. He didn't want anything to do with it."

"The money has become absurd," says author and former Notre Dame star Michael Oriard. "It has pushed to extreme lengths the positioning battle between athletics and academics."

It should come as no surprise, then, that college football and its TV contracts have become the primary force behind the rash of conference realignment moves between 2009 and 2013. That Jim Boeheim's Syracuse Orange basketball team will no longer battle it out for Big East conference supremacy with John Thompson III and the Georgetown Hoyas (just like he did with John Thompson, Jr., and Georgetown 30 years ago) was of little concern when Syracuse made the move to the ACC. And when the proud basketball tradition of the Big East conference was usurped by the additions of programs like Houston and Tulane, it became more clear than ever which sport was calling the shots.

"I hate realignment," says *Sports Illustrated*'s Stewart Mandel. "With each domino that fell, it got less and less appealing and more, 'Why is this happening?' It's becoming less about like-minded schools and rivalries and familiarity, and more about bundling as much television programming as possible to sell to cable networks.

"How far do they go before they meet resistance from the fans?" Mandel continues. "Maryland moving to the Big Ten was the first example of a move in which a good portion of the fan base was openly hostile to the move."

When the Big Ten announced that it was adding Maryland and Rutgers in 2012, the conference added two more strong academic institutions; but the moves suggested that not even football matters – only football revenue does. Maryland brought part of the Washington, D.C., market into the reach of the Big Ten Network, and while Rutgers does not exactly own New York City, the idea has long been floated that adding Rutgers would add a strong amount of market share to NYC cable packages. More than ever, schools have become commodities for television. It has been both unseemly and detrimental to rivalry in the short-term. In 2012, thanks to Missouri's move to the SEC, Mizzou and Kansas didn't play against each other for the first time since 1918 (when neither program fielded a team). Pittsburgh and new Big 12 member West Virginia didn't play for the first time since 1942. Nebraska's long conference affiliation with the Big 8 schools ended in 2011. Things have changed.

Meanwhile, revenue has risen so much, so quickly, that it is impossible not to see at least a little bit of a bubble effect. "This is like we're watching the bubble before it bursts," says Mandel. "There is so much money getting thrown around, but it cannot last forever, can it? Conference commissioners operate under the assumption that the sport will always be as popular as it is now, if not more so; but what happens if you reduce your product to something not as recognizable as fans are accustomed to? At what point do the casual fans get turned off?"

It isn't just writers and fans who are a bit dismayed by all of the positioning and repositioning. "I'm a traditionalist," says Colorado head coach Mike MacIntyre. "Somebody asked my what my ideal season and conference alignment would be. I said you play your first game after Labor Day, you play your rival on Thanksgiving, you play 11 straight games, and every conference has eight teams. I'm just hoping realignment doesn't hurt college football, where you're taking away the rivalries, the pageantry. I don't want fans thinking it's just another game in a given week."

"Everybody's trying to make their conference better, stronger, more sellable to television networks," says UL-Monroe coach Todd Berry. "From a university standpoint, you don't want to be left out in the game of musical chairs. You're trying to posture yourself in that regard. That forces universities to move around a lot – TCU[32] – and that makes them more apt to be searching."

In April 2013, the remaining members of the ACC signed on to a 15-year, "grant of media rights" deal[33] that may have ended the short-term burst of conference realignment, at least at the major-conference level. We don't yet know what kind of effect the series of moves – Nebraska, Maryland, and Rutgers to the Big Ten, Colorado and Utah to the Pac-12, Syracuse, Pittsburgh, and Louisville to the ACC, Texas A&M and Missouri to the SEC, TCU and West Virginia to the Big 12, and countless moves at the mid-major level that have basically reduced the Big East (now the American Athletic Conference) to New Conference USA and Conference USA to New Sun Belt – will have on rivalries, fan interest, or the game itself; but if anything else, most can welcome a break from the soap opera, if only so we can catch our collective breath.

"...and the players don't see a dime of this!"

When it comes to whether or not football players (or college athletes as a whole) should be further compensated for

---

[32] TCU has had a fascinating journey over the past two decades. A member of the Southwest Conference until its dissolution in 1995, the Horned Frogs were passed over for Big 12 membership in favor of Baylor. TCU joined the WAC for five years (1996-00), moved to Conference USA for four (2001-04), resided in the Mountain West for seven seasons (2005-11), and briefly agreed to become part of the Big East before getting 'called up,' so to speak, to the Big 12, where it began play in 2012.

[33] This means that the schools agree to sign over revenue from broadcast rights to the conference. If a school leaves the conference during the duration of the deal, it forfeits that revenue. It is, in effect, an exit fee so steep that few could afford it. Every major conference except the SEC has agreed to such a deal. And nobody's leaving the SEC.

their efforts, it has become nearly impossible to have an honest conversation. People in favor of paying players will, more often than not, tell you how the athletes are working "for free," and if they get riled up, they'll break out terms like "plantation" or "modern-day slavery." People opposed will lean on the word "amateurism" until it breaks in half. They'll tell you that most athletic programs are operating "in the red" and that paying players would have awful, unintended consequences to all of college athletics.

The dramatics of this exchange, for the most part, prevent a serious conversation from taking place. It has become like a political debate in all the wrong ways. And that's a shame.

First of all, college football players are not working for free. In political negotiation, we often hear about anchors, where somebody arguing one side will start in the far extreme so that, when they compromise, they end up where they logically would have started all along. This is a pretty good example of that. Students receive tuition, room and board, food, academic support, and, to say the least, access to a pretty good gym. They are free to leave for another school[34] or quit the sport altogether. This is not a plantation. These players are not modern-day slaves. We can argue about whether they are compensated *enough*, but they are indeed compensated at a level to which most of their school classmates are not. This makes some degree of sense, of course, considering the demands on their time and, again, the impact a successful football team can have on the university as a whole.

Second, the very concept of student-athletes and amateurism is based on the idea that, as Andy Staples puts it, "in the 1930s and 1940s, somebody decided it was a bad idea if these athletes get paid." So many of us still lean on

---

[34] That said, in most cases they must sit out of action for a year if they transfer to another school, and in one of the rules I hate the most, a school losing a given player to transfer can specify which schools they are or are not allowed to attend.

"amateurism" as if nothing about the sport, or the term, has changed in the last 75 years. "It is very similar to the war on drugs," Staples says. "We're spending all of these resources fighting this. In a couple of states now, marijuana is legal. In 20 years, that'll be almost every state. People's ideas just change over time. So when the next generation is in charge of higher education, people aren't going to think it's a bad thing. We need some old fogies to retire and some youngsters to take their place. You can't imagine there was a time when half the population wasn't allowed to vote."

Now, Staples' assertion quickly veers toward the realm of "arguable," to put it conservatively, but the point remains: The world has changed, and the sport makes a lot more money than it used to. Since we aren't paying students any more than we ever have, that money has instead gone toward coaches' salaries, weight rooms and other amenities that, at best, only indirectly benefit the athletes in question.

Michael Oriard's *Bowled Over* (2009) describes the history of the 'student-athlete' comprehensively. "Criticism of too much commercialism and too little academic emphasis in college football is nearly as old as the game, and so too is public indifference to these perennial 'problems.'"

In response to the concern that athletes were professionals in disguise, the NCAA instituted an athletic grant-in-aid scholarship (with an emphasis on 'scholar') in 1956. "The NCAA understood this fiction to be just that," Oriard writes. "Executive director Walter Byers promoted the term 'student-athlete' expressly to deny the inherent professionalism of students paid to play sports. For Byers, at issue was not some lofty ideal of amateurism but the more pragmatic and dangerous prospect of paid athletes' entitlement to workers' rights."

After a series of tweaks in the 1960s, the NCAA adopted a serious change in 1973, one that benefited football programs a lot more than student-athletes. Here's how Oriard describes the change in *Bowled Over*:

"The establishment of the athletic grant-in-aid in 1956 set the stage for the debates at NCAA conventions in the 1960s that culminated, in 1973, in the one-year scholarship, renewable at the coach's discretion. I will argue that this little-noted and mostly forgotten reinvention of the athletic scholarship marks a crucial turning point for big-time college football. ... The one-year scholarship, backed by the mindset that it represents, exposed so-called student-athletes to the mounting pressures of an increasingly commercialized sport while denying them a share in its new bounty."

As a former state government employee, I have long held empathy for governing bodies like the NCAA, which, even if run perfectly, would still be handcuffed and hamstrung in attempting to enforce an infinite, arcane set of rules (one that grows daily to account for the changing world) and govern a less-than-equal populace equally. But moves like this one – giving coaches the right to rescind a scholarship agreement after one year for no reason better than "This guy stinks" – makes defending the NCAA more difficult[35]. And to be sure, it has made plenty of similarly questionable decisions through the years.

As Oriard points out, we have had debates about commercialism and amateurism for as long as we've had college football. But with every new television contract and with every obscene weight room expansion, the issue grows larger, and the demand for further compensation for players grows louder[36].

---

[35] In recent years, the NCAA has made a multi-year scholarship available to schools on an optional basis. So you *can* guarantee a player multiple years if you want to, but you don't have to.

[36] Former Arizona State linebacker Mike Nixon: "When I was at ASU, we remodeled the locker rooms twice in four years. Save whatever you're spending on that, put it in a piggy bank, and when these players graduate, give them a share of it!"

Oriard, himself, has come around on the idea. "There is no easy solution to player compensation, but the fact is that these players do make money for so many others. A head coach might make $4 million in a given year, assistants might make $700,000, school presidents make $1-2 million so it won't look bad that they're making so much less than the head coach. Players have to get more than they're getting."

Certain conferences appear willing to move on the idea. In 2011, the Big Ten proposed an increase to college football players' scholarships to include what they called "full cost of attendance." There is concern that student-athletes don't necessarily break even when it comes to the aid they currently receive, and basically a little bit of extra money – the typically accepted figure is an extra stipend worth between about $2,000 to $3,000 per year – would make sure students come out ahead. When the idea stalled, in part because of the damage it might do to smaller schools at the FBS level, SEC commissioner Mike Slive brought it back up. In April 2013, Slive told an audience at an Associated Press sports editors meeting in Birmingham, "It's a disappointment that it's not taken care of yet. We truly believe that we ought to do more for our student-athletes than just the room, board, books and tuition. We're hopeful that we can continue to make that work. ... I think it's fair to say it's an idea that's not going to go away."

Of course, not every FBS school has an extra $2,000-$3,000 to give to scholarship athletes. And technically, since we're dealing with a not-for-profit situation here, *no* school has it without giving up something else.

"All the money has already been spent," says John Infante, writer of the wonderful Bylaw Blog on NCAA compliance and NCAA Expert for Athnet, a company that, according to its website, works "to bring college recruits and their families the advice and resources they need to get recruited and find athletic scholarships."

"So Ohio State has $150 million in revenue, but they're spending $150 million," Infante notes. "If they're going to pay players more, what are they going to stop doing? They're not going to pay [head coach] Urban Meyer less, because if they pay Urban Meyer less, they might eventually make less money. They're not going to cut the football team's expenses. They're not going to have fewer football players. These senior staff members are probably not going to decide to cut their own salaries. They're going to cut sports. And athletes in those sports, who are totally happy with what they have and are getting this amazing opportunity that, honestly, doesn't exist anywhere else in the world, aren't going to have it anymore."

The same issue blocks logical progress on the "pay-for-play" front as well[37].

"I think we should put a little something extra in these athletes' pockets because of the time they spend," says California head coach Sonny Dykes, "but then you end up with gender equity issues, more sports getting money ... and eventually schools cutting sports."

"The middle class kids are the ones that might have it the toughest," says Ball State head coach Pete Lembo. "If you're wealthy, and you get a scholarship, you're fine. If you're a kid from a tougher socioeconomic background, you're likely to get a Pell Grant, which can be over $2,000 per semester. If you manage that money well, that should give you plenty to assist with your education. But the middle class kid who's perhaps from a situation where it's tough for his family to send him some spending money, that's the kid who I think needs the help. He's not getting a Pell Grant, so he's got to manage his money closely." Lembo won't sign on to a pay-for-play concept for obvious reasons – anybody outside of a major conference would probably be crazy for doing so – but the cost-of-attendance idea has grown on him.

---

[37] "Pay-for-play" is the term typically used to describe the idea of paying athletes not as part of a stipend, but basically as employees. Doing this would quite possibly also open schools up to insurance and worker's compensation issues that very few schools could afford over the long haul without making cuts.

"I'd be really interested to see a push that says, 'We only want to talk about new money,'" Infante continues. "You have these nice, well-funded athletic departments, aside from a few exceptions[38], but let's talk about new money that comes in. We don't want anything with the money that you're using to have a swim team, a volleyball team, a soccer team, and a baseball team. The new money that comes in in these new television contracts, let's talk about that and what portion of that is going to go toward players. And that overcomes at least one big objection, which is that you'd have to stop doing something to pay players."

In January 2013, the Texas A&M athletic department published a press release talking about the impact of the Aggies' highly successful 2012 football season, in particular the unexpected run of quarterback Johnny Manziel to the Heisman Trophy. "Research conducted by Joyce Julius & Associates shows that the redshirt freshman winning the prestigious trophy produced more than 1.8 million media impressions, which translates into $37 million in media exposure for Texas A&M," it said.

This release elicited two common responses: "Wow," and "…and Manziel is seeing none of that money!" Now, anybody who follows Manziel on Twitter knows that he is doing alright for himself[39] and has a pretty good life at the moment. He could suffer a terrible injury in coming seasons, and his situation could change dramatically, of course. But the fact remains that some players are worth much, much more to

---

[38] While we often overstate programs' financial difficulties, there are programs that have genuinely struggled with money in recent years. Those include California, which announced in September 2010 that it would have to cut five sports, including baseball, to meet budgetary concerns. After a fund-raising push, it was able to walk back some of those cuts. Meanwhile, money was allegedly one of the major reasons Maryland agreed to join the Big Ten. As in, the Terrapins needed a lot more of it, and the Big Ten has it.

[39] Let's just say Manziel chatted with a lot of famous people and attended what appeared to be a lot of fun get-togethers.

their schools than others are, and for many, that means they should be more well-compensated than others.

Staples says he has the perfect solution to the payment issue. "I'll tell you the best way to deal with this: Schools are allowed to give scholarships, food, room, and board. That's it. Nothing more than you give now. You've got to give the same number of scholarships, and nothing more. Anybody else who wants to pay them, pays them. Anybody." Companies looking to secure endorsement deals? Yes. Agents looking to secure their services following school? Yes.

"We're already paying football players – with scholarships," Staples continues. "And 99 percent of them aren't worth more than that. You're just not worth more than four years at Stanford. But if American Express wants to give Andrew Luck an endorsement contract, who does that hurt? Nobody!"

Now, this absolutely destroys the notion of amateurism. And because of that, it would meet extreme resistance, probably too much to actually pass. But if you want the cleanest solution to this issue, this might be the one. "Everybody wants to change this idea, but what do you change?" Staples asks.

"If schools do it, then these players really are employees You have to pay payroll taxes, pay worker's compensation if they get hurt. And if schools give football players extra benefits, Title IX[40] dictates that others get those same benefits. But in my system, everyone the market deems worthy gets paid If a female athlete is deemed worthy, if [rapper] Lil' Wayne is wearing [former Notre Dame women's basketball player] Skylar Diggins' jersey on stage, Skylar Diggins is probably getting an endorsement deal after that."

---

[40] Title IX is also known as the Equal Opportunity in Education Act. As it pertains to athletics, this means that spending and assistance on male and female athletics must be "substantially proportional" to each other. At this point what it basically means is that if you add male sports, you must add female sports; and if you cut female sports, you must cut male sports.

Of course, as Infante points out, "The NCAA's job is to prevent exploitation. But at the same time there are claims that they are themselves exploiting the kids. And I think if they simply just said, 'Well, you're on your own now. If you get exploited and screwed by an agent who said they were giving you $25,000 a year, but it actually turned out to be a loan, and then you didn't get drafted, and now you owe the guy $75,000 … or the agent threatens to cut you off, and now you have to declare for the draft instead of finishing your degree or coming back for a national title run…' that's a bad look for the NCAA. It's not something they're going to allow." So perhaps, in a perfect world, the endorsement part of Staples' plan can stay, but the agents still have to stay away.

It is perhaps likely that the cost-of-attendance grant will eventually fall into place. The extra money has given this discussion some traction, and it seems like suitable middle ground between "give them nothing" and "Johnny Manziel should be paid millions of dollars." But an even larger shift in how money is distributed could be dictated by a court case that is, at print time, still in process. Since the outcome is not yet known, we won't spend a lot of time on it here, but in the *In re NCAA Student-Athlete Name & Likeness Licensing Litigation* case, otherwise known as *O'Bannon v. NCAA*, former UCLA basketball player Ed O'Bannon has led an attempted class-action strike against the NCAA for using current and former student-athletes' likenesses in video games without compensating the athletes in any way. If the plaintiffs win, the NCAA would be forced to pay recent student-athletes (and others who were part of "classic" teams sometimes featured in these games) an undetermined amount of money. Perhaps the NCAA beats this case back like it has others in the past. Perhaps the plaintiffs win, and the NCAA is forced to pay $1 or some ridiculously small fee – something that would basically serve notice that the NCAA will need to make changes in the future but would not financially cripple the organization because of what has happened in the past. And perhaps the plaintiffs win, and the NCAA is forced to pay an exorbitant sum.

In issues like this, an inability to make suitable changes in the short-term can backfire when a court or market force ends up making decisions for you. Over the coming year or two, we will find out if the NCAA makes changes on its own or has changes forced upon it.

"The big schools should just break apart from the NCAA.

Over the course of a lengthy Q&A with *The Columbia Daily Tribune* in December 2012, Missouri athletic director Mike Alden used the term "like institutions" four times. As in, "I still think there are schools continuing to try to line themselves up with *like institutions*."

The term could take on a lot of different meanings. Air Force head coach Troy Calhoun used a similar phrase when discussing aligning his school with institutions with common backgrounds, academic standards, et cetera. But it was pretty clear what Alden meant when he used it. Here is perhaps the most vivid use of the phrase:

> "When I used to be at Texas State, we were always looking at: How can we be like 'them'? Well, the reality of that is, the chances of us ever being like 'them,' there was probably never, ever a chance of that. So it really gives all the other institutions that continue to try to elevate themselves at whatever cost an opportunity to step back and focus their attention more on *like institutions*."

Even as a Missouri fan whose school hit the realignment lottery in moving to the SEC, the hair on my arms stood up when I read this quote. Alden is an excellent athletic director, and he has been very good for Missouri from a big-picture standpoint. But this was the clearest, most business-

61

speak acknowledgement of the sentiment that the big boys are really not interested in sharing their toys with the little schools anymore.

Throughout the conference realignment saga, people have long assumed that we were simply working our way toward "super-conferences," a term we typically use to describe four 16-team conferences that either break apart and form a new subdivision for college football or break apart from the NCAA altogether. Interviewees for this book were almost unanimous in this view, ranging from former Air Force coach Fisher DeBerry ("I assume we'll eventually end up with a super-conference structure with four leagues, and that 64 teams will break apart in probably the next five to six years") to Football Outsiders' Matt Hinton ("I think the move toward super-conferences is nearly inevitable, though very long. I think you'll end up with a structure more like a pro league, with 40-50 teams or whatever, instead of 100+"). Because of the stability culled from the grant-of-rights deals, it is conceivable that the five major conferences – the ACC, SEC, Big 12, Big Ten, and Pac-12 – are all strong enough to exist for quite a while, at least until these grant-of-rights deals begin to expire. But whether we are dealing with four super-conferences or simply the structure of five major conferences with which we are used to dealing[41], that top tier is stratifying itself away from the rest of college football. With every new media deal, that gulf grows.

"There's a feeling that the big guys want a different set of rules than the small ones," notes Coker, "and 'Hey, we can do things that the others can't do.'"

Financially, these "big guys" already have broken apart, and there's no catching them unless, like TCU, you get invited

---

[41] Technically, there have been six "major" conferences, i.e. those whose champions automatically qualify for a BCS bowl, over the last couple of decades. But the American Athletic Conference, formerly the Big East, has been picked apart by other conferences to an extent and, again, is closer in resemblance to the old Conference USA than to a major conference at the moment.

to join the club. But in terms of the structure of what we call the Football Bowl Subdivision[42], the big guys and small ones are still all playing for (unequal) shares of the same pie. Many are encouraging the baking of a new pie, so to speak.

"The current system we have is an unsustainable Frankenstein's monster," says Smart Football's Chris B. Brown "even vis-à-vis the smaller schools. They went out and created this BCS and had to append some sort of goofy formula[43] to avoid antitrust implications. If they could actually avoid the antitrust implications by simply hiving themselves off," it would potentially make sense to do so.

The guilty liberal in me hates this. One of my own favorite aspects of college football is watching a Boise State rise out of nothing. The playing field is tilted drastically in favor of the haves, but the have-nots have a chance to reach an elite level if they make enough of the right moves in a row. Dirk Koetter (26-10 from 1998-2000) was a good hire for Boise State, Dan Hawkins (53-11 from 2001-05 after Koetter left for Arizona State) was a better one, and Chris Petersen (84-8 since 2006 after Hawkins left for Colorado) was the best one yet. Boise State has invested in its program, made moves that were beyond smart, and has finished in the nation's Top 10 four times, and in the Top 5 twice, in the last seven seasons The Broncos have won two BCS bowls in that time: the 2007 Fiesta Bowl (over Oklahoma) and the 2010 Fiesta Bowl (over

---

[42] For reasons I still do not understand, the two subdivisions of Division I went from being called 1-A and 1-AA to the Football Bowl Subdivision (FBS) and Football Championship Subdivision (FCS). The FBS name will become at least partially outdated when its playoff championship begins in 2014, but hey, bowls will still exist, so perhaps it's accurate enough.

[43] Due to political involvement and the aforementioned antitrust issues, the BCS had to come up with a way for teams from conferences without an automatic BCS bowl bid to get in. The series of steps changed over the years, and last year Northern Illinois automatically qualified for a BCS bowl (the Orange Bowl) by finishing both in the Top 15 of the BCS standings and ahead of at least one automatically-qualifying BCS conference champion.

TCU, a fellow mid-major at the time) [44]. If the major conferences were to break apart, then unless we institute a system of promotion and relegation[45], that all but closes the door for future Boise States.

"The Boise States have no leverage," Brown continues, "other than antitrust and other legal ramifications. And ultimately the tectonic plates will shift in the direction of the leverage." Even though Boise State has built itself into one of the nation's sturdier programs, it still might not carry the historical heft, the fan base, or the television market share to really play a serious role in the business side of the sport. And its geographical limitations might assure that it never does. Amid all of the hubbub of conference realignment, Boise State's only option for moving up in the hierarchy was a move to the Big East; when the Big East began to look more like a horizontal move instead of a vertical one, BSU decided to stick with the Mountain West.

If the major conferences were to truly break apart from the rest of FBS, the *next* Boise State, whatever school that might be, might not even have a path to follow to the top. That is both unfair and logical. It is a heartwarming story to follow, but it doesn't make the sport a lot of money, and as we've clearly seen through the decades, that matters more than we might wish it did.

So what might college football look like if the haves were to form a 60-70 team subdivision atop the rest of the

---

[44] You could make the case that Miami is another example of a have-not becoming a have. In hiring Howard Schnellenberger in 1979, then following up with Jimmy Johnson in 1984 when Schnellenberger left for the USFL, the Hurricanes found the perfect pair of coaches to connect with the local recruits and community and show off a serious level of coaching prowess. They had finished ranked in the AP polls just five times before Schnellenberger but won four national titles in nine seasons in the 1980s and 1990s. Of course, Boise State had never finished ranked and was barely in its FBS infancy when it began its run of great play. There is no direct comparison to Boise State.

[45] Seriously, promotion and relegation is the greatest thing ever and would fit as well with college football as it does with European soccer. It will never, ever happen, but it should.

sport? "There could be a situation where they have sort of a junior varsity," Brown suggests, "and they want to expand the reach of football, the imprimatur of college football, for the Wednesday nights and late-night Saturdays, and maybe to the extent of bowl games. And you could end up with a situation that, optically, looks like what we have now." Perhaps the remaining FBS teams would form a new subdivision with some of the stronger FCS programs, fight for their own national title, and duke it out for TV deals similar to what conferences like the MAC have now. Perhaps teams in that new, higher-up subdivision would still be allowed to schedule teams in this subdivision without penalty[46], and perhaps we'd still see some big conference vs. little conference bowl games here and there.

But as Brown points out, "the only reason Northern Illinois was involved in a BCS bowl, or Boise State, or even TCU, was because they had to be involved. So unless these other schools can find a way to create the leverage, they're not going to have much of a say. And the fact that they all [temporarily] jumped to the [former] Big East is not a good sign that they have a lot of leverage here."

Brown uses the "L" word one more time. "It's leverage versus quality. The quality of play would be hurt by the exclusion of Boise State and TCU [from bigger bowls or the national title race] as much as it was hurt by the *in*clusion of Hawaii [which went undefeated in 2007, qualified for the Sugar Bowl, and was destroyed by Georgia, 41-10] and Northern Illinois [which went 12-1, won the MAC, qualified for the Orange Bowl, and was thumped by Florida State, 31-10[47]]. If

---

[46] The guilty liberal in me all but demands this, as the lower-FBS teams make a decent percentage of their annual revenue from the payments they receive for being a BCS team's cannon fodder (and occasionally pulling a fun upset).

[47] In fairness, NIU-FSU was a seven-point game in the third quarter. This was by no means an embarrassment on the scale of Hawaii-Georgia. NIU was physically outmatched, but a) just about everybody was physically outmatched versus FSU in 2012, and b) NIU was small even for a MAC team. More often than not, the Huskies made up for it with speed.

you meet certain standards, and those standards are enforced, and want even a tiny seat at the big boys' table, you can have it. But when aggregated, do these schools support the upper echelon of college football enough to make it worthwhile to give them a bone?

"A lot of this depends on a subjective view from fans of what their preferences would be and what would make them watch more college football. And the sentiment can turn really quickly. Boise State was awesome, but watching another blowout of Hawaii makes you turn the TV off. There will be more than enough money made through a playoff that you could support mid-majors if you want, instead of building a new rowing facility at Michigan. But the playoff would need to produce a TCU or Boise State and avoid a Northern Illinois or Hawaii to make the mid-majors' case."

"That's the debate, isn't it?" notes Grantland's Holly Anderson, succinctly. "It's quality of opportunity vs. quality of outcome.[48]"

"In the short term – say, four or five years – the playoff will help those lower FBS conferences," Pete Lembo says. "But when you think about the money that the higher-end conferences are going to get from that, it's potentially going to create an even bigger wedge."

And that's only if there remains an FBS as we know it.

There have long been rumors of the top schools breaking apart from the "corrupt," "incompetent" NCAA altogether. But while the NCAA has indeed been each of those adjectives at times, again, its job is impossible. A new governing body would find a lot of the same struggle. That's

---

[48] More from Anderson: "Any efforts to level the playing field are never, ever going to work. UAB is never going to be Alabama. If every player at both schools were to get an extra $2,300 a semester, Alabama will just pile on top of that. Anything done here will just continue to price out Tulane. And by the way, why is it that underdogs in the NCAA [basketball] tournament are so embraced, and in football they're so reviled? Everybody loved VCU going to the Final Four [in 2011]. And can you imagine if a school of that size – like UL-Monroe – makes the playoff ahead of a second SEC team?"

life when you have, by design, "no central brain in college football," as Hinton describes it. "It's the best and worst thing about college football. It gives everything flavor but also creates chaos."

"There will always be an overseer," says Infante. "If it isn't the NCAA, it'll be some other governing body. Everybody who criticizes the NCAA thinks they're doing something reasonable, and the NCAA is very radical or extremist. The thing I want to remind people is that, if you think athletes should be paid, and these aren't even really students, remember that there are already people on the other side saying that it's already too promotional, that it's already not connected enough to academics, that there shouldn't be athletic scholarships, that we should play fewer games. And there are people who are now saying that this sport is too dangerous to even play at all. The NCAA is always attempting to hold a compromised position. Any governing body will."

There are also plenty of people within the NCAA who wouldn't mind being disassociated with the top level of college football. "Because football doesn't contribute anything to the NCAA[49], I think it's just this giant drain on the organization," says Infante. "And whether or not it would be better for the sport to be governed differently, I think it would certainly be better for college athletics as a whole if it was, one way or the other."

"If the big schools have the money and want to spend it that doesn't bother me," says Wake Forest head coach Jim Grobe. "It's our responsibility to do what we can in that environment. The biggest conflict is that you still have to have some rules to govern fair play and keep some semblance of the student-athlete experience intact. It can get crazy. There's a danger there. I don't believe you want it to be a no-holds-barred environment, but there is some credibility to letting

---

[49] The NCAA handles enforcement but does not handle its national title race – hence the existence of the BCS – and does not directly benefit financially from its postseason.

people that have the ability to have bigger stadiums, weight rooms, et cetera. If they want to have that, let's not hold them back. But let's remember that we're asking them to be students first.[50]"

Fisher DeBerry makes a similar point: "These TV demands – playing mid-week, playing a team cross-country – lead to more missed classes. The game still belongs to the players, and that should always be the foremost thing."

That, of course, leads us to another debate[51]: *Does* the game belong to the players, to the *student*-athletes?

"If we are going to tout education as the way these athletes are being compensated, we need to make sure the education they are getting is a real one," says Oriard. It is common for a given school to have one or two go-to majors for a majority of student-athletes, of course. Some are more blatantly obvious than others – "General Studies," for example; that's the way it has been for a long time. But if you are getting a degree that isn't really going to assist you in finding a career path if or (more likely) when football doesn't work out, then you're not really getting much of a degree.

"At ASU, there was a thing called the 'BIS,' the Bachelor's in Independent Studies," says Mike Nixon, former Arizona State linebacker and captain. "You pick two things – say, sociology and communications – and you walk away with a BIS degree. What is that education worth? It's different if somebody's going into chemistry, then going to med school. But it's tough to do that with the hours that are required from football."

---

[50] More from Grobe: "I do feel like there's a struggle right now between haves and have-nots. I'm not sure Wake Forest and some of the 'for real' academic schools are in the same boat as some of the slam-dunk 'haves.' We get great revenue, but as far as stadium size, attendance, big alumni base … we don't have it. We graduate about 1,000 kids every year. There are some schools that have larger schools than we have living alums."

[51] College football has a lot of debates. As the offseason progresses, we just go from one, to another, to another.

There are plenty of examples of student-athletes excelling in both aspects of that title; Myron Rolle, the former Florida State safety and Rhodes Scholar, is an obvious one. But for every Rolle-esque success story, you've got countless students who end up with a different experience.

"The ones that drive me nuts are the schools that talk the smart kids out of majoring in something they want to major in," says Staples. "It just goes against what you're there for."

"I'm a big advocate of athletics as a major," Infante says "To me, a kid getting a degree in athletics performance or athletics education – getting a bachelor's degree in coaching, basically – that is a valuable degree. We need more coaches, especially in football. With the changes that are coming, from the NFL to youth football, we probably don't need uneducated volunteers teaching our kids this game. You'll need coaches who are trained in proper techniques and first aid, recognizing concussion symptoms, managing concussion syndrome. That could be a massive market for the people who play football now to stay involved with the sport they love, even if it's not as a professional player, and make a bunch of money doing it."

Infante continues: "In a perfect world, the one I get to create, I've always thought that college sports as an amateur thing that is more about getting an education – instead of just serving as a minor league – that makes sense. The problem is that we don't have another viable option for players, especially in football. If you don't have an alternative, a real professional environment, in terms of principle, you have a problem. The NCAA's always going to have to maintain some sort of academic standards.[52]"

---

[52] More from Infante: For most sports, the model works out fine. "Think about the amount of money baseball players will turn down to go to college. Recent high school graduates picked in the first round are saying, 'My college scholarship, which until recently could only be guaranteed for one year ... and if I blow my arm out, I could be kicked to the curb immediately ... I'd rather do that and have the opportunity to make more money down the road than in

I share this opinion. In my own perfect world, only players who want to play college football, to be student-athletes in the intended sense, are forced to play college football; if all you are looking for is a professional football career, there should be a developmental league into which you can enter. The problem is, in the NFL's eyes, there already *is* a quality developmental league where players can enhance their skills and craft their brands before they get to the big stage; its name is college football. And there is absolutely no motivation to create a new league that might fail when this one is running just fine.

Of course, while we have all of these running debates on an annual basis, every single one of these topics only matters with the assumption that people will still be playing football 30 years from now. Or, at least, the football we recognize.

****

"It was during two-a-days before my senior year. We were running inside drills, just the front seven. We had to run a lead-block fullback sweep. I blocked it right, I guess. [Fullback] Trey Millard came up to ask me about it afterward. 'Why'd you do it that way?' It turned out that I thought we were running a different play and just accidentally got it right. I was completely mixed up. And I started to get really confused. 'Was I just in? Was I playing?' Trey said, 'Dude, there's something wrong with you,' and he took my arm and led me to the doctor."

Trent Ratterree is recounting his experience with what was either a concussion or a series of them in August 2011.

---

some cases lock in a two- to three-million dollar signing bonus.' It's hard to sign off on that as a parent instead of saying, 'We'll put a couple hundred thousand of that in a trust fund, and you'll have it whenever you feel like using it.' I think it says a lot about the value to athletes: When the NCAA competes in the free market, and the NCAA restricts how good a deal it can offer athletes, it still does well."

Ratterree is, in many ways, the type of player college football is meant for[53]. He was the best player on his high school team, he was a stud basketball player, and he seemed to have the frame for big-time college football (6'3" or so, looking skinny as hell at 220). His speed and athleticism were fine, but they didn't jump off the charts. He struggled to get film out to the schools that wanted some, he didn't field any major offers (schools like Colorado State and Iowa State took a decent, late look at him but passed), so he decided to pursue his dream of becoming an Oklahoma Sooner.

Ratterree walked onto the team at tight end, redshirted in 2007, and saw increasing playing time over the course of his first three seasons. He caught 11 passes in 2009 and won fans with a phenomenal hustle play against rival Oklahoma State; in the late stages of a 27-0 Oklahoma win, with the shutout still on the line, OSU's Justin Gent (a three-star recruit according to Rivals.com, with offers from major-conference schools like Arizona State, Kansas State, North Carolina and Texas Tech) recovered a fumble and raced toward Oklahoma's end zone. After 55 yards, however, Ratterree not only tracked him down but stripped the ball loose and recovered it. The shutout remained intact.

Ratterree caught another 10 passes in 2010, scoring his first career touchdown in a 30-point romp over Florida State. Heading into 2011, he was rewarded for four years of hard work when head coach Bob Stoops awarded him a scholarship for his senior season. But things went awry a bit in August.

"They asked me what was wrong, and I said my head hurt really bad. I was woozy, and I couldn't really think straight. They were razzing me: 'What's new?' I told them every time I get hit there's a huge blast of light. I know my eyes are closed, but I can still see massive amounts of light. So they said, 'Yeah, you're done,' and they snatched my helmet out of my hand as quick as they could.

---

[53] In the interest of full disclosure, he's also the little brother of my childhood best friend.

"The air bubbles in my helmet had busted, probably two days before, and I didn't know it. And I'd been practicing for two days with no air in my helmet. They took me to the tent, and I pretty much had to be led where I was going, otherwise I would drift off aimlessly. I didn't ever know where I was going. They sat me down, and I was crying, then laughing, then crying, then laughing.

"I was out for two weeks because, to get back in, you basically can't feel sick at all, you can't feel dizzy at all, you can't have any light sensitivity, you can't have any symptoms for a set amount of time. And then you have to take a concussion test, which at OU is a computer program that gives you patterns and a memory quiz. That helps them decide that the swelling is gone, and your brain is relatively back to normal.

"There were three or four days there when they told me I shouldn't be driving my car and that I should go back home. I couldn't do anything. I literally just slept all day, and when I got up it felt like the world was turning around on me. I was dizzy, but it was … different. It was like the world was actually moving. It was really weird, and it's all in your head.

"There's a part that totally screws athletes. There's a point where you're doing better, you're getting close to where you can possibly think about coming back in a few days, and it seems like there's nothing wrong. And you're confused and wondering if the doctors dug symptoms out of you or something. 'Did I really have a concussion, or am I just being a baby?' 'Well, of course I had a concussion. I was crying in the tent at practice.' I think everyone experiences that part. At the end, you wonder if you ever had a problem.

"It mixes up your brain chemistry to where I think it causes you to have a lot of irrational thoughts. There were two other players who had a concussion when I did, and they were confused like I was. I would decide I was being a baby, and I would get up and try to run, but it would feel like my head was going to explode, like I was having an aneurysm or something. 'No, I actually had a concussion.' You can't do anything but sit

72

around forever, and it tricks you. There was one point where I called my mom, and I was all pissed off because I thought the coaches hated me. I thought they were just after me for some reason.

"Concussions are the scariest thing, I think because there's a certain part of you that doesn't really come back from it."

Now, for all we know, Ratterree suffered a series of small concussions over the period of time in which he was playing with a broken helmet. This might not have simply been a single concussion. One of the scariest aspect of the head injuries issue is that every concussion is different, and there is not an easy, "If A, then B," way to diagnose or treat it.

But that was still just one incident. He did not suffer from multiple known concussions over the course of his playing career, and he thinks that there's a part of him that didn't really "come back from it." There's a reason why, in the words of Brown, "compared to bowls, amateurism, and the other issues on the table, head injuries are going to lead to much bigger, more substantive changes."

With every instance of a former NFL great developing Chronic Traumatic Encephalopathy (CTE) – and in the cases of former safety Dave Duerson and former linebacker Junior Seau, committing suicide by shooting themselves in the chest so that their brains could be preserved for research – or a high schooler dealing with repercussions from multiple concussions it becomes more and more well-accepted that while football has long been known as a dangerous sport (it's part of the innate draw), it might be a little too dangerous. It might have more negative long-term effects than we thought. Slowly but surely, rules have been tweaked to deal with some of these issues, but many assume that bigger, more substantive changes are on the way.

"More kids than ever are interested in the sport of football," says Bryan Fischer of the Pac-12 Network. "But from a parent's perspective, it's never been scarier."

Staples (again, a former walk-on lineman at Florida) agrees: "My kid, I know he's going to be big – he's my kid! And my wife's tall. So he's going to be a big guy, and they're going to tell him to put his hand on the ground [as a lineman]. I'm not sure I want that. I'm not sure I want him to take all of those sub-concussive hits.[54]"

Again, there could (should, even) be many books written about this issue. But to stay as succinct as possible, there are basically seven things we need to know when it comes to the current debate about head injuries and the future of football. The situation seems to change almost daily, but here's where the conversation stands in the summer of 2013.

1. Concussions are tricky.

"The science is just not very old, and the research process is just so young," says Nixon. "Maybe we eventually find the right answer, but it's so hard at this point. I've had multiple concussions. In baseball, as a catcher, I took a bat to the back of the head, and it knocked me out cold. They put me on the 10-day disabled list, and after a week, I felt good enough to get back in and start trying to hit baseballs coming at me 95 miles per hour. But look at Sidney Crosby [a hockey star for the Pittsburgh Penguins]. He couldn't be on the ice for eight months. If you try to come up with a universal plan for dealing with them, it's going to be difficult."

Lembo concurs. "No two concussions are the same. If you can fully recover from the first one, your chances of getting a second, third, fourth one go down substantially." But the problem comes in getting concussions diagnosed properly at all. And the *other* problem comes in the simple fact that the

---

[54] More from Staples: "What people don't understand is, when you wear that equipment – and I haven't put on pads in 15 years, so it's probably even more so now – you feel invincible. You feel like you cannot be hurt. Now the equipment's even lighter, and people are even faster and stronger."

sub-concussive hits that pile up over time actually do as much or more damage than the concussions you know about.

"They say that every time you see stars, that might be a small concussion," Nixon continues. "Well, you pretty much see stars on every other big hit, just coming downhill and hitting a fullback. The scary thing about it is that it's not the really big, over-the-middle hit that messes you up. It's those repeated hits that do more damage. I went head-to-head with 300-pound offensive linemen 45 times a day in practice. I would have my bell ringing more in practice than in a game. In that sense, limiting contact in practice might really help."

"Back when I was playing, they used smelling salts," says Grobe. "As soon as you were conscious, you were back in the game. People think you just take a kid who's had a concussion, and as soon as he counts to two, you put him back in there. That's just not the case anymore. We have a list of questions that we ask each specific player in August, tough things they have to think about to answer. And until they can answer those questions, they can't go back onto the field. You have to fully recover because a couple in close succession can be really bad."

"We've learned a lot since my playing days," Grobe continues, "especially with the AFCA [American Football Coaches Association]. We've tried to be out front with better ways to tackle. But the problem you run into is that there's no way to guarantee that. No matter how much you teach good fundamentals, you can't guarantee it. The game is so big and fast and physical, there are going to be times when you can't avoid helmet contact."

2. Boxing was once one of the most popular sports in the country.

What was arguably the most popular sport in the first half of the 20th century barely makes a ripple on the national consciousness anymore. The game of football is actually responsible for two of the nation's three most popular sports – the NFL and college football – but there's nothing saying this always has to be the case. However the sport goes about addressing the issue of head injuries, if enough people feel the changes aren't sufficient and stop watching, and if enough parents steer their children toward playing other sports, then football's grasp on America as a whole could change.

Once upon a time, we admired boxers in much the same way as we admire football players today: for their tenacity, for their technical prowess, and for their ability to take a hit and keep trying to move forward. But some combination of corruption and queasiness has changed public admiration for the sport as a whole. Regarding the former, it does bear mentioning that with scandals involving official scorers, trainers, promoters, and basically every title within the sport, boxing has accomplished a level of corruption through the years that makes college football's issues seem quaint and naïve. And for every person who was turned off by seeing a punch-drunk, Parkinson's-addled Muhammad Ali (or any other star afflicted the same way) unable to speak, perhaps there were a few who just got annoyed with the corrupt aspects of the sport. That mixed martial arts (MMA) has risen at the same time that boxing has fallen certainly suggests that violence alone isn't the source of boxing's downfall.

Still, boxing is a perfect example of how a sport can go from indescribably popular to an afterthought. Major League Baseball is another, less tenuous example. If boxing wasn't someone's favorite sport in the first half of the 1900s, baseball was. Now it's barely holding on to second place, at best.

As Holly Anderson puts it, "Are our kids going to be watching what we're watching?" It only takes a couple of generations for sentiment to have shifted dramatically. Football lovers probably aren't ever going to stop loving football, but their grandchildren might not care about it very much.

Brown thinks college football will be "squeezed" in the coming years. "Media will put an awful lot of focus on pro football, and then the rubber will meet the road when kids and their parents are deciding to play football at the grade school or high school level. Essentially, you're deciding whether to have your kid play football, and you're told about getting CTE from playing high school football. That could ultimately suck the life out of the sport a bit."

For the most part, coaches have seen plenty of changes in practice and awareness in recent years.

Dykes: "The good thing is that people recognize there's a problem and are trying to deal with it. It had become a nasty little secret, but I'm glad people are acknowledging there's an issue and are focusing on the long-term health of the kids playing the game, from the youth level on up. The technology of the helmets will continue to get better. Teaching fundamentals, there will be more of an emphasis put on that. Punishing people who commit personal fouls. Coaches have to be smarter about how we practice now, too: How much are we hitting? How much full contact? And all the macho drills we do before practice (Oklahoma drills, etc.), they are potentially hurting kids. We've tried to stay ahead of the curve in terms of the way we practice, without a tremendous amount of contact. We're trying to be prudent in the way we take care of kids."

Lembo: "In my opinion, the game is much safer today than it was when I played 20 years ago. There's more baseline testing, and there's more of an emphasis on better protective equipment, better technique in tackling. Some of the rule changes are making a positive impact on awareness. Just the knowledge that's being transferred from the experts to the trainers, coaches, and student athletes about playing smart and being aware of conditions that are symptomatic of concussions it's light-years ahead of where it was. Like so many things, the media can play a role in magnifying or distorting things. What I can say from being in college athletics for 20 years now is that the awareness is much improved at every level."

Coker: "Awareness and feedback from medical professionals are key. I'm from the old school of 'You shake it off and play.' What you're seeing now is, when the NFL gets concerned about it, then everybody gets concerned about it. At the college level now, we test our kids. If they have symptoms of head injuries, then they're held out, and they have a battery of tests before they can return."

Grobe: "We've changed the game a lot. As coaches now, we're always looking out for the safety of the player. When I played, it was a much different mentality. You led with your head, your helmet was a weapon, and you wanted to hurt people with your helmet. 'Put your hat on 'em.' One of the coolest things for a player was to have your helmet all scratched up and beat to death. It was old-school, tough-guy stuff. I thought that was how I should be. But once you have your own children, you realize you want to coach the way you'd want them coached or treated. The mentality of the general public is that we don't have the kids' best interest at heart. I think it's the exact opposite."

Calhoun: "I think we've made enormous strides in terms of standardizing protocol. In terms of detection, we're being very conservative when it comes to some of the symptoms – the eye's responsiveness, for example – and the technology at hand. That we have medical personnel that are not aligned with the participants is a nice step. But this is a legitimate concern that has to be confronted, and by and large, you'll see that coaches have genuine concern for their players. They want to be proactive."

Still, while changes have been made, they are perhaps only keeping up with the physical changes in the game itself. "Hands down, the biggest difference [between his playing days and now] is the sheer force at impact," says Calhoun. "Larger bodies moving more swiftly – the physics involved is much different than it was 20-30 years ago. So the bang is going to be much louder and have more of an impact."

Plus, the game is and will always be surrounded by a football culture. "There's an attitude in football: You wipe the blood off your chin, pull yourself up by your bootstraps, and get back into the game," says Ratterree. "But with concussions, you can't just shake your head and go back in. That'll make it worse! It's a culture thing. When I was at OU, a starting lineman had a concussion, and he didn't know, nobody knew. He was telling coaches he didn't feel good, but he thought he was just tired or something, and the coaches were calling him a pussy. He started throwing up and fell down. He couldn't stand up anymore, and they were like, 'What the hell is going on here?' It had gone unnoticed for a couple of days." And it's not like that's an Oklahoma thing. Far from it. Football coaching is, in part, about instilling a level of toughness in your players; but the ways in which you go about doing that will also cause you to miss some very important physical issues.

3. It's not the NFL we have to worry about.

At the higher levels, you can, to some degree, justify the danger by saying that the players know what they're getting into. NFL players are paid handsomely to risk their physical well-being, and college players are at least rewarded with a scholarship. If this sport were to crumble, it would likely be because of what's happening at the lower levels.

In January 2013, as reported by ESPN's *Outside the Lines*, researchers at UCLA were able to identify the protein that causes CTE in the brains of living patients. The tau protein was found in five former football players, aged 45, 50, 59, 64, and 73. This was justifiably seen as a significant victory in the football community. If you can identify CTE before it begins to do its most serious damage, you can go about beginning to figure out how to treat it or, even better, prevent it.

Infante, however, saw it in a slightly different way. "I heard that report and thought, 'Wait until someone turns this machine on to a bunch of high school football players and sees what type of damage they might already have.' If you do that, and you indeed find some pretty significant damage that young, then you've already lost the war. The race is now on to make changes instead of waiting until the next round of research that says how widespread CTE is or how early it starts and the public just says, 'We've got to stop this. It's too dangerous to even test your new rules.'"

"If we're finding out that 12-year olds are getting brain damage, then there's a moral responsibility to do something about it," notes Staples.

"If you're under a certain age, I think if you get one concussion, you should be done for the year," says Ratterree. "With the way your brain develops, do you really want to slosh those chemicals around? The NFL – they're professionals. That's like being an underwater welder: You're going to make a ton of money, and you know in advance that it's dangerous. But honestly, if you get a concussion in elementary school or even junior high, you should probably be done until high school. I think once people start learning more about this, it's only going to get scarier. Knowledge isn't going to make people more comfortable with it."

It is incredible how big pee-wee football has become in the last couple of decades, by the way. Just back in the early- to mid-1990s, when I was going through school, the first time full-contact football was offered was in seventh grade. Some schools offered it in sixth grade. And this was in the heart of football country, Western Oklahoma. Just two decades later, children in my former hometown can begin playing pee-wee football at age five and playing full-contact by age seven. It is conceivable that the biggest changes in the management of the game will come at the lower ages, and I cannot say I would even be remotely resistant to the implementation of an age limit in the sport, at least when you're dealing with full contact. Flag football is perfectly fine for 10-year olds.

4. Nobody knows what (further) changes are coming.

"I don't know if the type of changes they've made to date – leaving the game if your helmet comes off, strict helmet-to-helmet penalties – are the type of changes that are needed to keep the sport viable," says Infante. Coaches will tell you that these changes have made a serious impact, and maybe they have, but most consider this level of change as something that is buying time before bigger changes come down the road, and the market is going to dictate the amount of change that is needed.

"We're very early in the changes," Brown says. "Everybody's trying to be proactive and dampen negative media exposure. Big change comes when external forces come into play: winning lawsuits versus team owners, coaches, or players, for example. The type of equipment you wear will change. There will be resistance, and it's going to take probably 20 years to all unfold. Once the issue starts threatening the economic viability of the sport, once an NFL team realizes 'this isn't making us money anymore,' once television contracts begin to fall apart, then things change quickly."

"Change will be very slow; it already has been," says Fischer. "And at first, it will be things like not only making better helmets, but making them cheap enough to get them to everybody, on down through high school and the lower levels.

But when it comes to bigger changes, things that go beyond equipment and strictly enforced helmet-to-helmet contact penalties? "Nobody has a clue," admits Dykes.

"The problem is that we really don't want much to change," Hinton adds. "Americans love this sport for a reason, and we don't know how you still have the sport without people butting heads. Re-teaching technique and penalizing helmet-to-helmet has been a good, sensible start, but bigger changes will be met with serious resistance."

A lot of interviewees for this book mentioned the idea of mandatory periods for sitting out following a concussion. For example, if you are diagnosed with a concussion, you must sit out a month, and if you are diagnosed with a second in that season, then you are out for the year. But that doesn't address the sub-concussive hits, and it doesn't deal with the fact that, again, every concussion is different. "And of course, if you keep a player out for the whole year, they're going to think you're attacking their livelihood," Ratterree says.

"You're going to have people just lying" if you institute mandatory periods away from practice or games, Nixon says. "I got pretty much knocked out by [star tight end] Rob Gronkowski against Arizona my senior year. I just kind of shook it off and walked straight to the sidelines. I couldn't really talk, but I knew it was a seven-point game, and I went back in on the next series. I looked at someone's helmet, and there were blue streaks coming off of the helmet from all the stadium lights. I literally one-eyed it for the last series of the game. My mom had to drive me home because I was still basically seeing laser beams everywhere. My school never knew about that. We ended up going to the Holiday Bowl, and I didn't want to sit out of maybe three weeks of practice or the game. If you tell me that if I get a concussion, then I'm out? Maybe for the whole year? I'm going to lie. It might be the right move for your health, but you want to play. And even at the high school level, you'll honestly have to worry about parents more than the kids. 'Oh no, no, no. He just got his bell rung.' And if dad's telling you you're okay, you're probably going to go back out and play."

So what other changes could be made? "I think you're going to see things like outlawing the three-point stance," says Staples [55] . "And why does rugby have so many fewer

<hr>

[55] Dykes' response? "We don't even line up in a three-point stance! So I guess we're ahead of the curve in that regard." That does give you a hint of where the game could be headed, however. If changes are made along the lines, where the most helmet contact takes place, then you could end up with more finesse and

concussions? Because you don't have a helmet, and you're not going to stick your face in there and break your nose! It's pretty simple. Stuff like that is going to get talked about, and people laugh now, but in 10 yards there are going to be serious discussions."

"We have a great game," Calhoun says, "but there's unquestionably a need for bigger changes. Hits to the head that occur, especially with build-up speed – crack-back blocks, things on kickoffs – we've made changes in those areas, but more are on the way."

Kickoffs actually offer us a look into how the public might react to future changes. In the summer of 2011, Greg Schiano, then the Rutgers head coach (he has since taken over as head coach of the NFL's Tampa Bay Buccaneers), told a radio station in Atlanta that, if it were up to him, we would get rid of kickoffs altogether. He noted that a researcher had told him that "17 to 18 percent of the catastrophic injuries in football happen on kickoffs, yet kickoffs are only about 2.5 percent of the plays in the game." He proposed replacing kickoffs with a fourth-and-15 for the scoring team; you can either punt or, instead of attempting an onside kick, you could simply elect to go for it on fourth down from where a kickoff used to take place.

In a lot of ways, this was a brilliant idea. Not only would you be getting rid of what is evidently one of the most dangerous plays in football, but you would also be replacing an onside kick, which is almost entirely based on a lucky bounce, with an actual play. It would be a step closer to determining a game with skill instead of luck (and in football, as we will discuss, there's a lot of luck involved).

The idea got plenty of national attention but went almost nowhere. It is potentially going to take changes of that magnitude (or larger) to sufficiently address the head injury problem – or convince the media and public it's being

---

short passing taking the place of get-a-hat-on-a-hat, slug-it-out run games. The game has been moving in that direction for a while already.

addressed, at least – and while we're all talking about the need for large changes, nobody has proven willing to take specific changes seriously just yet.

5. Head injuries are not proprietary to football.

This also bears mentioning, of course. Kids are going to play sports – they just are – and they will be in some danger for head injuries and concussions if they move to soccer, hockey, rugby, martial arts, tackle football in the front yard, or any other sport that serves some people's need to strike their peers. That need will always exist, and dangerous sports will always benefit from it. Football is not absolved from any responsibility – it has risen to prominence in part because of its violence – but if football were to dissolve tomorrow, the problem would not completely go away, and recognizing, treating, and preventing head injuries will continue to be a pressing issue heading into the future.

6. It will take a couple of decades to figure out if the changes were effective.

This is one of the other major issues at play. The biggest problem with CTE comes from accumulated contact over time. No matter what changes are adapted, big or small, we aren't going to know how effective they are for a while because CTE's symptoms and repercussions tend to unfold over a period of decades. This creates two opposing forces, really: the need to wait and see if the current changes are sufficient and the need to make drastic changes, knowing that we have to make them count.

7. Football rules have changed before.

"Nobody seems to remember that the sport almost went away 110 years ago," says Staples. John J. Miller's *The Big*

Scrum (2011) tells the story of how Teddy Roosevelt saved the sport of football from extinction in the early 1900s amid a series of deaths (18 in 1905 alone) and serious injuries. Citing America's sporting culture and the potential importance of the game to the country as a whole[56], Roosevelt helped to form a committee among college football's most influential figures and spur changes to the game instead of outlawing it altogether.

Here are some of the changes that came about: Instead of five yards for a first down, you would need 10, which meant that you were less likely to simply try to grind out two yards per play with one guy running up the middle behind a rugby-esque mass of bodies. Gang tackling was outlawed. A neutral zone was introduced at the line of scrimmage. No more than five players were permitted to line up in the backfield. And, of course, the forward pass was legalized. Plus, a body called the Intercollegiate Athletic Association of the United States was created to oversee the implementation of rules. It would soon become the NCAA.

In all, these new rules made the game nearly unrecognizable and, predictably, met with a lot of resistance. But the game survived, and as people grew more accustomed to the rules (which were tweaked many times through the years[57]), it thrived to a higher and higher level.

"Football does have a history of malleable rules," notes Brown. "That's the case even today. The Canadian Football League uses a wider, longer field. The Arena League uses half the field" and different motion rules. "Small high schools play eight-man football. Football has a history of reinventing itself, often in response to outcry." The odds that it will do so again are strong. And we'll keep watching. Bigger changes will

---

[56] He was certainly prescient in that regard, though I imagine he would still be downright shocked by the popularity of the sport 100 years after his time.

[57] For instance, a pass originally had to travel at least five yards beyond the line of scrimmage to be legal (something West Virginia head coach and Air Raid offensive maestro Dana Holgorsen would not enjoy very much) and couldn't cross the end zone in the air.

almost certainly come; again, it's up to the sport itself to be proactive or have changes forced upon it.

****

In *The Big Scrum*, Miller quotes a letter from Roosevelt to Harvard president Charles W. Eliot, then a major proponent for prohibiting the game of football from being played:

> "I do not agree with you that the game should be stopped," he wrote back. Then he scolded Eliot for his role in the controversy: "I further think that one reason why [football's abuses] are not remedied is that so many of our people whose voices would be potent in reforming the game, try to abolish it instead."

More than a century later, I found myself thinking basically the same thing as I watched the Slate/Intelligence Squared "Should College Football Be Banned?" debate. On May 8, 2012, four panelists – *The Tipping Point* author Malcolm Gladwell, *Friday Night Lights* author Buzz Bissinger, former NFL player and broadcaster Tim Green, and, for some reason, sports columnist Jason Whitlock – gathered at the Skirball Center for the Performing Arts at New York University to discuss the topic at hand. Gladwell and Bissinger were arguing for its prohibition; Green and Whitlock were arguing against it.

In the run-up to the event, I assumed that, since this topic had been beaten like a dead horse for most of the last 125 years, that the "banning" hook was just that: a hook. Once people were sucked into watching, I figured the debate would actually go to *fixing* the sport's issues. This seemed to me your typical anchor: Suck people in with an extreme headline, then say "Okay, no, but we do need to fix this head injuries issue." The inclusion of Gladwell, basically a professional thinker who had written some fascinating pieces about the makeup of football players and the savage beatings that offensive linemen take, gave me hope.

Lord knows the inclusion of Bissinger did not fill me with enthusiasm. Bissinger had published a terribly flimsy and, honestly, half-assed *Wall Street Journal* column that morning; in it, he cited Maryland's financial troubles as proof that the entire system was beyond repair and basically suggested that college is for book learning and nothing more, that a university doesn't in any way benefit from the sport[58], and that one's college experience comes completely from his or her studies. He brought up the most serious issue – head injuries – as almost a throwaway. And I found it pretty damning that he appeared to have no problem with *high school* football, about which he had once written a fantastic book and made, presumably, millions of dollars. Still, I thought the conversation might have some benefit.

I was terribly incorrect. Head injuries were barely brought up. Most of the discussion focused on "business" and "corruption" and football having "no place in institutions of higher learning." Almost every argument made during the panel could have been made about college basketball but wasn't. Even Gladwell found himself making arguments that were growing stale 75 years ago.

This sport has issues in desperate need of fixing. That much we know. Everything negative anybody says about the sport is probably true to some degree, and I want the sport to which I have dedicated my career to be as morally strong and beneficial to as many student-athletes (and fans) as possible. One day the real conversations will begin. But they didn't in May 2012, and really, they haven't since.

---

[58] He clearly wasn't a Boston College fan in the mid 1980s.

3. The Case for Computers

On November 22, 2008, nearing the end of one of college football's more fun seasons, here is how three Big 12 teams ranked in the Harris Poll[59]:

2. Texas Tech (10-0, 32 first-place votes, 2,737 overall points)
4. Texas (10-1, 2,476 points)
5. Oklahoma (9-1, 2,375 points)

In the BCS standings, Tech was second, Texas third and Oklahoma fifth. Tech's last-second win over the Longhorns had taken the Red Raiders to within two games of the Big 12 South title and within three games of a spot in the national title game. It was not to be, of course. That Saturday night, Oklahoma massacred Tech, 65-21, on national television and predictably made a nice jump. Here's how the poll took shape the next week:

---

[59] Adapted from a piece that appeared at SB Nation on September 30, 2011.

3. Oklahoma (10-1, 2,598 points)
4. Texas (10-1, 2,577 points)

In destroying the team that actually beat Texas, Oklahoma made up 122 points on the Horns in the Harris poll Texas held onto a narrow lead in the BCS standings, however: They were second, Oklahoma third.

That next week, Oklahoma went to Stillwater to face No. 11 Oklahoma State, a team Texas had beaten just 28-24 in Austin. In an incredibly fun game, the Sooners took out the Cowboys, 61-41. Meanwhile, the Horns hosted 4-7 Texas A&M, a team that had lost to Oklahoma at home by 38 points a few weeks earlier. They dilly-dallied a bit, leading only 7-0 midway through the second quarter, but they caught fire late and won, 49-9. Both the Sooners and Longhorns looked good, but Oklahoma clearly had the better week with their big win in Stillwater.

Here are the Harris Poll rankings that came out a couple of days later:

3. Texas (11-1, one first-place vote, 2,575 points)
4. Oklahoma (11-1, 2,569 points)

Texas gained 27 points and a first-place vote. Why did this happen? Because a) word came out that the computer rankings involved in the BCS standings were probably going to start favoring Oklahoma if they beat Oklahoma State, and b) Texas head coach Mack Brown (a politician in another lifetime[60]) went on every television network that would have him to advocate for his squad. And to at least a small degree, it worked. And I was horrified.

Granted, it didn't matter in the end. Because of the computer rankings component of the formula, Oklahoma did indeed finish ahead of Texas in the BCS standings; and because of the otherwise unbreakable three-way tie between

---

[60] Okay, he's basically a politician in this one, too.

Oklahoma, Texas, and Texas Tech, the BCS standings were used to send Oklahoma to the Big 12 title game, where the Sooners lit up Missouri and advanced to the BCS title game, a narrow loss to Florida. Texas, meanwhile, held off Ohio State in a 24-21 Fiesta Bowl win, and Texas Tech limped away with a 47-34 loss to Ole Miss in the Cotton Bowl.

I thought about the developments of late 2008 when I began playing with CBS' wonderfully entertaining, interactive AP voting bias tool in 2011. You can lose hours of your day both looking at how voters from certain regions perceive certain teams, and you can lose even more hours trying to figure out the narrative behind it. Why was Texas A&M overrated on the east coast? Why was Clemson underrated in their backyard and Top 10 in the Pacific Northwest? Why did New York love Texas so damn much? Why did the West Coast overrate Oregon before the Ducks' loss to LSU, and why did they underrate them later on? It is a fun way to both reinforce your own assumptions – an East Coast bias, a hometown bias, etc. – and create new ones.

It is also a way to prove the fallibility of the folks who have the biggest impact on who gets to play for (or, in the pre-BCS days, win) the national title.

In theory, the marriage of human polls and computer ratings makes an infinite amount of sense. There are some really good computer ratings systems out there – I even have one of my own that I like quite a bit – and I trust them to make evaluations more than I do my own, or anybody else's, lying eyes. Computer rankings typically look at a team's performance over an entire season, and they don't naturally overreact to late losses over early ones[61]. They aren't swayed by external criteria like "Coach A shook my hand and sure is a nice guy" or "Coach B is a total jerk, and his team didn't look very good that one week I watched them." They do a much better job of painting the big picture than we do.

---

[61] They don't unless they are programmed to do so, anyway.

However, there is a certain level of context that often gets lost with computer rankings – injuries, head-to-head results, and so forth. And for that reason, I like that human voters play a role, too. I'm a numbers snob, but I'm not a complete numbers snob.

But the way the BCS rankings have unfolded in recent years, humans have had too much on-the-fly control. When they see a ranking they disagree with, they change their own vote to rectify it. When computers produce a result they don't like at the end of the season, they change the formulas or reduce the weight of the computer rankings. And that ruins the entire marriage[62].

To be sure, I was not appalled about Texas' strange, Thanksgiving 2008 poll improvement because I didn't think the Longhorns had a case. Clearly they did; among other things, they had, after all, beaten Oklahoma on a neutral field in October. I was dismayed because voters were changing their votes because of factors other than what happened on the field that week. Either they heard computers were doing something they disagreed with, or they were swayed by Mack Brown's glad-handing, but in either case, they abused the system. Their job is to rank the 25 best, or most accomplished, teams in the country. Their job is not to right the wrongs of other pieces of the BCS equation.

The formulas used for the computer portion of the BCS rankings have been marginalized to remove margin of victory, which just so happens to be one of the most telling, evaluative pieces of data you can glean from the data most BCS formulas use: points scored and points allowed. Yes, a margin of victory component can add to the likelihood of a team attempting to run up the score on an overwhelmed opponent. But doing so

---

[62] The same thing happens when a voter makes an unconventional vote, of course – he or she gets mocked and ridiculed for not thinking like the rest of the pack, and his or her legitimacy as a voter is questioned. If conventional wisdom is going to be so rigorously enforced, we might as well just appoint a rankings committee of six or eight voters.

risks injury (since you are probably keeping your starters in longer) and backlash from pollsters. Proceed at your own risk.

Computers' impact on the overall BCS standings has shrunk as well. And when the computers do make an impact in one way or another, humans just figure out a way to neutralize them regardless. Computer rankings have been treated as an impediment instead of a contributor.

Human pollsters are weird, biased, and entertaining, in the most human way possible. And in college football, they hold too much sway[63]. We are all biased, and while that is okay, we need to be protected from ourselves sometimes.

[63] This will change, of course, with the implementation of the College Football Playoff for the 2014 season. A playoff committee will determine the four participants in said playoff, which is both scary and justifiable. On one hand, the committee will likely be populated with people who bring plenty of their own biases and blind spots to the table. On the other hand, we do entrust committees like this to determine playoff participants in other sports. And in a positive development, polls can now move back to their original purpose: rewarding success and encouraging conversation and debate. As the AP's Ralph Russo puts it, the type of politicization that occurred in 2008 is "the reason why the AP got out of the BCS business in the first place." (The AP's departure from the BCS formula opened the door for the even shakier Harris Poll to fill the void.) The football polls will become more like the college basketball polls – a way to keep track of who's doing well throughout the season – and nothing more. That's a very good thing. As Russo puts it, "Even if you knew Northern Illinois wasn't as good as Oklahoma State [in 2012], their record (12-1) deserved a reward." In an oligarchy like college football, a pat on the back like that is both quaint and to be encouraged. It just shouldn't have much of a role in determining the national champion.

4. You, Me, and Stats

It's the first day of March 2013, and I'm crammed into a ballroom chair deep in the recesses of the Boston Convention & Exhibition Center's third floor. I'm surrounded by a mix of sports personalities, sports executives and administrators, and young, incredibly hungry students and recent college graduates, mostly male (of course), looking to connect with said executives and administrators. The assistant dean of MIT's Sloan School of Management, Dr. S.P. Kothari, welcomes the 2,700 attendees, delivers a few scripted jokes, and cedes the floor to Houston Rockets general manager (and Sloan alumnus) Daryl Morey, conference co-founder (and Harvard alumnus) Jessica Gelman, and others. The next two days are booked with about 17 hours of panels and presentations. The seventh annual Sloan Sports Analytics Conference is underway[64].

---

[64] There's also a live video feed online for those who cannot attend. At this point, one could argue that this is one of the bigger, more-hyped business conferences in the country, in any industry. It trends on Twitter to the point where spammers flood the "#ssac" hashtag, rendering it unreadable.

It's been about 60 years since a man named Charles Reep began charting soccer matches in his own time, writing provocative pieces of data analysis for *Match Analysis* magazine and drawing conclusions that would become the basis for much of English soccer for the coming decades[65].

It's been 42 years since former *Sporting News* contributor L. Robert "Bob" Davids "sent a letter to about 40 people whom he knew to be interested in baseball history and statistical research – or, as he called them, 'statistorians'"[66] – and went about creating the Society for American Baseball Research (SABR). The terms "sabermetrics" and "sabermetricians" have become so commonplace that we apply them to anybody and anything associated with sports statistics. But since the "b" in "saber—" stands for "baseball," the usage is technically incorrect. Nobody seems to mind too much.

It's been 36 years since a Kansas security guard named Bill James published his first *Baseball Abstract* on a home mimeograph machine after years of playing with baseball play-by-play data in his off-time (at home and at work). It's been 32 years since *Sports Illustrated*'s Daniel Okrent published a magazine profile of James, which led to increased fame, adoration and outright scorn for the salty 31-year-old.

It's been 24 years since John Thorn, Bob Carroll and Pete Palmer published *The Hidden Game of Football*, one of the first major looks at advanced football statistics. It introduced concepts like net points, reemphasized the importance of special teams, and inspired a generation of sports nerds like Aaron Schatz, who would start a site called Football Outsiders about 14 years later.

---

[65] A lot of these conclusions were terribly misguided. For example, he was an early champion of the long-ball style, concluding long passes were the way to go since most goals were scored within three or fewer passes. Short-passing, ball-controlling Spain looks at all of its recent tournament trophies and smiles.
[66] From the Founders page of SABR's official website.

It's been 14 years since a stat nerd and baseball obsessive named Voros McCracken published his thoughts about "defense independent pitching" on a Usenet baseball newsgroup, and it's been 12 years since he published "Pitchers and Defense: How Much Control Do Hurlers Have?" for stat haven Baseball Prospectus[67]. If ever a single concept has changed the way we think about a sport, it is DIPS (Defensive Independent Pitching Stats). Bill James said in 2001 that he "felt stupid for not having realized … 30 years ago" that a pitcher only has total(ish) control over home runs, strikeouts and walks. Its spinoff, BABIP (Batting Average for Balls In Play), has introduced to us the idea that luck and/or defensive ability are to blame (or credit) for a lot of a pitcher's ERA and a batter's batting average. BABIP shifts pretty dramatically from year from year, but defense-independent stats do not, at least not as much.

It's been 10 years since Michael Lewis' *Moneyball* was unleashed on the world. The book, which chronicled the path of the 2002 Oakland A's and their general manager Billy Beane sold more than a million copies and inspired a Brad Pitt movie and a *Simpsons* episode. With his methods of using advanced stats to find and exploit market inefficiencies in baseball, Beane became a celebrity among nerds, proof that obsession with spreadsheets and baseball-on-paper can actually lead somewhere. Lewis opened himself up to severe backlash from scouts whose jobs might become threatened by nerds with calculators. And front offices throughout baseball and just about every other team sport began to wonder if they needed to start posting up for position amid the stat revolution.

It's been eight years since ESPN hired John Hollinger (born three months before McCracken), basketball writer and creator of the Player Efficiency Rating (PER), to produce content for its members-only Insider service. PER has slowly become the go-to "everything at a glance" basketball statistic.

---

[67] It's been 10 years, by the way, since the Boston Red Sox hired both James and McCracken as consultants (and eight years since McCracken left the team).

In late 2012, Hollinger was hired as Vice President of Basketball Operations by the NBA's Memphis Grizzlies.

It's been six years since the first Sloan Conference welcomed approximately 175 attendees and speakers. The keynote speakers were J.P. Ricciardi, then the general manager of the Toronto Blue Jays (and a one-time underling of Oakland's Billy Beane), and Jamie McCourt, then the chairman and vice president of the Los Angeles Dodgers[68]. The conference has since moved from MIT's campus to the monstrous Convention & Exhibition Center.

It's been a year and a half since the movie version of *Moneyball* was released, making the idea of using numbers to think outside the box all more palatable and easy to understand.

It's been a few months since Butler head basketball coach Brad Stevens hired stat analyst and former *Basketball Prospectus* contributor Drew Cannon, who just graduated from college, as a graduate assistant. A few weeks after the Sloan Conference, *Sports Illustrated*'s Pete Thamel will pen a piece about Cannon. Of the non-prevalence of stat guys on college basketball sidelines, Stevens tells Thamel, "I think whenever you publish this article, it's going to change."

The sports statistics industry, which crept along in the shadows for decades, has made major strides in a short amount of time. Whatever the catalyst – *Moneyball*, the coming of age of a new type of analyst/sports professional, or something else – people are paying attention to what the nerds are telling them now. All but one NBA team is in attendance at the Sloan Conference in 2013 (the Los Angeles Lakers are the lone holdouts), and there is healthy representation from the NFL and other professional leagues. Nobody quite knows what they are looking for just yet, but they're all there, just in case.

---

[68] Ricciardi was fired by Toronto in 2009, and McCourt renounced her claims on the team in 2011 as part of a nasty divorce with husband and Dodgers owner Frank McCourt.

So why numbers? What value do statistics and advanced statistics bring to your understanding of a given game that your eyes alone would not? It probably depends on what you're looking for, really.

In baseball, we can rather accurately measure a fielder's range, quickly catch on when a pitcher's cutter isn't cutting quite as much thanks to Pitch F/X data, or produce a list of hitters or pitchers whose numbers might be about to improve or regress with batted-ball data.

In basketball, we can analyze which players accelerate in which areas of the court, which shots are more likely to produce an offensive rebound, or how good defenders impact an enormous range of the court.

In soccer, we can track a player's path and mileage, his passing success rate, or his tendencies in different areas of the pitch.

In tennis, we can use Hawkeye data to measure the tendencies of the top players, or we can create a system of rankings far more accurate than the relatively arbitrary, luck-dependent tour rankings.

Hell, even in motorsports, we can use analytics to help drivers and teams make better in-race adjustments and prepare better between races.

And while we may be behind the curve a bit in football – we got a later start, and the pointy ball makes everything a little bit more random – we can still get an immediate feel for coaching tendencies, a quarterback's accuracy to different areas of the field, line analysis, and any number of other topics a typical box score doesn't cover.

"I don't have a particular affection for numbers themselves," says veteran baseball writer and former Bill James protégé Rob Neyer. "I didn't particularly enjoy math when I was in school – it was just something I had to get through. But there are a lot of questions I have about sports that are a lot easier to answer, in fact may *only* be answered, with the use of numbers. That's why I use them; if I didn't use them, I wouldn't be able to answer the questions I have."

"Stats are a way to cut through the nonsense," says Bill Barnwell of Grantland. "There is a level of objectivity using numbers that you just can't really find when relying on the fallacies of human memory and narrative creation." Numbers can be manipulated in service of narratives, of course, but when placed in capable hands, stats are wonderfully descriptive.

Just as a policeman can use numbers to perfectly recreate how a car accident unfolded in court, a talented and willing writer can use analytics to fill in gaps, confirm (or contradict) what the eyeballs saw, and give color, depth, and creativity to analysis. The eyeballs matter; of course they do. You have to have a great understanding of the game at hand to fully grasp what the numbers might be telling you.

Sometimes the numbers tell you something you didn't expect. "Understanding the statistics really teaches you how uncertain and random the game can be," says C.J. Schexnayder, college football historian and contributor to Football Study Hall. It offers endless shades of gray, which is sometimes not a welcome thing in a sports world filled with black-and-white assertions.

Stats can teach us what is truly important about a given sport, tell us where to focus our eyes, and give us a path for better understanding, and enjoying, a sport we most likely already loved. At the 2013 Sloan conference, Jonah Keri of Grantland will paraphrase Bill James: Stats help us tremendously in not aiming for the lowest common denominator, in flattering, engaging and challenging the reader. Some stats are easy to understand, and some aren't. Some are accompanied by you-can-do-it-too formulas, and some aren't. But at their best, they challenge and reward us, destroying some biases and confirming others.

Numbers are also communal to an extent. Neyer has a very descriptive term for this: "citizen science." "I see this term every so often when I read about bird watching. It's where Joe Blow goes out and counts birds and sends data in. It's incredibly useful for conservation efforts. One of the reasons why stats are so relevant now is that they're so accessible – from your home, you can actually do interesting work."

It took large-scale breakthroughs to get to the point where someone would pay attention to, and treat with respect, what the proverbial blogger-in-his-parents'-basement[69] might have to say about a given sport. "That certainly wasn't the case 40 years ago," says Neyer. "You had guys in the 1960s like Eldon and Harlan Mills[70] — these guys were doing stuff, and they were amateurs, so it's been happening for a long time. But it obviously exploded when Bill [James] came along. He inspired lots of people.

"If someone loves the sport, the easiest way to do something meaningful is to look at numbers. You're not going to show up at a game and pop into the broadcast booth and take over, but anybody who's interested and intelligent and can take some time can do some interesting work using numbers. The numbers, the blogs, are now a way in for people. That just didn't exist before."

"I often say I got into this to improve commentary, not to improve how well teams are run," says Aaron Schatz. "I think front offices in the NFL are smarter about things than fans give them credit for being. The trick for me in terms of regular fan acceptance is to get the color commentators and, particularly, the studio analysts used to it. We want the basic concepts to show up on broadcasts – success rates, yards per

---

[69] I use this term with great affection. At one point, I was indeed a blogger who lived in his parents' (well, in-laws') basement.

[70] Eldon and Harlan Mills co-authored a book entitled *Player Win Averages: A Complete Guide to Winning Baseball Players* (1970) and were pioneers in the field of looking beyond batting average and ERA in baseball.

down, fumbles luck, understanding the importance of opponent adjustments."

****

A good number of people aren't attending Sloan to learn how to describe a game, however. They are either looking for a job in sports or trying to find someone to hire.

In 2013, we are at a pivot point. The tools at our disposal are useful, impressive, potentially influential, and, again, incredibly descriptive. But we don't really know how these tools can change the process of decision-making or talent identification, at least not beyond what we already know. With every year at Sloan, there are new revelations, new approaches.

ESPN's presence at the Sloan conference is inescapable; the Worldwide Leader in Sports has put a lot of money, resources and man-power into its focus on analytics. This is, like so many things behind which ESPN throws its weight, both good and bad. On one hand, the Sloan Conference simply wouldn't be nearly as big, nearly as important, without ESPN. Plus, there are some really, really smart people working on important things because ESPN has dedicated itself to this venture.

On the other hand, when ESPN wants you to like something, or at least accede to it, the network makes it inescapable, omnipresent[71]. If the new concept or measure represents something truly innovative, something that makes the fan experience better, this isn't a bad thing. However, the

---

[71] "HAVE YOU HEARD OF THIS NEW MEASURE CALLED 'TOTAL QBR?' IT'S PRETTY AWESOME. YOU SHOULD DEFINITELY TRY TOTAL QBR. IT IS A GREAT WAY TO MEASURE A QUARTERBACK'S PROFICIENCY. IT'S MUCH BETTER THAN THE OLD PASSER RATING MEASURE. I'M TELLING YOU, TOTAL QBR CHANGES EVERYTHING. IT IS BRILLIANT. QBR, QBR, QBR. IT'S AMAZING. LET ME TELL YOU SOMETHING: TOTAL QBR IS HUGE. HUGE. QBR."

heavy-handedness can make you resent something you might otherwise appreciate, and it can perhaps make the numbers-resistant crowd doubly resistant.

There is a notable absence at Sloan, however.

****

Each year, Harris Interactive takes a look at the most popular sports in the United States. The NFL is an obvious, dominant No. 1, but baseball and college football have been duking it out for the No. 2 spot in recent years. College football holds the edge with the 18-to-24-year-old demographic, while baseball is the choice for the 50-to-64 crowd. If these two sports were political parties, we would say that college football is trending in the right direction thanks to its popularity with younger voters.

But there is virtually no college football presence at Sloan. There is a research paper proposing a "new football efficiency metric," but it is simply yards per point, which erstwhile college football magazine publisher Phil Steele has been using for a couple of decades.

In a few different, often unrelated, panels, someone will mention how random football is and how difficult it is to get a grasp for compared to other sports. "The ball's not even round," says professional gambler Bob Voulgaris in a Sloan panel. Voulgaris sticks mostly to NBA games because of both his enjoyment of the sport and the way he perceives the sport's general reliability.

In *The Success Equation* (2012), author Michael J. Mauboussin went into a little more detail but basically reached the same conclusion. His analysis determined that while the contribution of luck to an NBA basketball game determines about 12 percent of the result[72], it was closer to 38 percent for an NFL football game.

Randomness aside, football is generally a more complex game as well. You've got 11 players on each side of the ball, and some will only touch the ball if something went drastically wrong, so evaluating individuals, with different roles and jobs on a given play, is somewhere between difficult and a total lost cause. Whereas in baseball you've got some true, well-defined outcomes – player pitches ball, player hits ball, player fields ball – football is quite a bit more complicated.

"You've got 22 guys running around at the same time, and it's incredibly difficult to figure out how those things fit together with numbers," says Rob Neyer. "The down, the distance, the should-we-go-for-it stuff is easy, but how do you figure out how the left guard is doing? It's really hard. In basketball, you face the same sorts of issues, only there are half as many players. Baseball is easiest because you have this series of distinct actions that are relatively easy to put into a sequence."

Indeed, some of the things that make football such an appealing sport to so many Americans can cloud the perceived usefulness, or direction, of advanced football stats. "There is a set number of outs in baseball," points out *The Hidden Game*'s John Thorn. "The absence of a clock, the unpredictability of the outcome until the very last – these are virtues for baseball. But they are not for football, and that might be better for the modern fan.

"In football, stats can help you win in the offseason as much as anything. And they can help you understand the ramifications of certain strategies – going for two points here, going for it on fourth-and-2 there.[73]"

---

[72] Other sports: a Premier League soccer match was 31 percent luck, a Major League Baseball game was 34 percent luck, and an NHL hockey game was 53 percent luck.

[73] More from Thorn: "'When Runner X gets at least 100 yards, his team is 17-1.' 'When So-and-So throws for at least 300 yards, his team is 2-14.' It's mistaking the cart for the horse. And you've got garbage time stats being compiled in

Aaron Schatz sees three major hindrances when it comes to acceptance of advanced football stats.

1. The "best is the enemy of the better" concept. "The criticism is that there's no way that football stats will ever be as accurate or as easy-to-interpret as baseball stats," Schatz says. "But that doesn't mean they're not useful."

As an example, Schatz talks about charting data. Since about 2005, Football Outsiders has been charting each NFL game to derive extra information about formations, blitzes, distance of passes, broken tackles, etc. While it is wonderfully useful, "it's always going to be imperfect because we don't know what the play-calls were, what the assignments were. You have to accept it; you can't pretend it's not the case, and you can't pretend that, because that's the case, the measures we collect are useless."

2. The stats-versus-scouting dichotomy. Maybe there truly was a battle between baseball stats and scouts back when *Moneyball* was being written, he says, "but there isn't such a thing in football, especially not now. You always have to look at the context of a player's role.

"In baseball, you could take Josh Hamilton and throw him into the Angels' lineup instead of the Rangers', and as long as you adjust for park effects, you basically know what you're going to get. In football, it's not like that. You have to interpret a player's value both in terms of his stats and the relevant schemes."

3. The "Broken Tile" problem. "Think of your favorite mosaic[74]. What if there's a busted tile? That's where your eyes will go. Your eyes will always see the biggest miss, not the biggest hit. Combine that with the general misunderstanding of probability – Nate Silver seems to be

---

football and basketball that aren't in baseball. The 'when' is even more important in football than it is in baseball."

[74] Personally, I like the ones at the New York City subway stations.

always fighting that[75] – and it seems that football stats are worthless.

"You can't spend your whole life staring at the broken tile. If the team we projected to have a three percent chance of becoming a Super Bowl contender, becomes a Super Bowl contender, that doesn't automatically mean the system's broken."

"Football is a lot more complicated, a lot more rich, from offense being broken down into passing and rushing, to special teams," says Ed Feng of The Power Rank. "And you throw on top of that the fact that the college football season is so short, and that, for the majority of the season you're dealing with a scarcity of data. And even at the end of the season, the error bar is so big."

Ah, the sample size issue. In basketball, pro teams play 82 games, and college teams play at least 30. In baseball, you play 162 games in the pros and potentially 60-70 in college. In football, though, it's 16 and 12, respectively. Maybe you get up to 20 and 14 including the postseason. We make drastic conclusions based on 12 results – we don't have a choice, really – even though things are obviously a lot more complex than that.

To more clearly demonstrate the issue of sample sizes, imagine if college basketball teams played just 12 games, as in college football. If you sampled 12 games from a 30-game, real-life college basketball schedule, you could define a team's season in drastically different ways. Take 2013 NCAA basketball champion Louisville, for example. The Cardinals

---

[75] Sliver is perhaps the most well-known data nerd in the country right now. After serving as one of baseball's stronger stat voices in the 2000s, Silver decided to give political data a try. His site, Five Thirty Eight, was eventually scooped by the *New York Times*, and his work in the fall of 2012, leading up to the November presidential election, proved that a good portion of the country – and an even greater portion of political analysts – still don't understand probabilities very well. He went to great lengths to show how Barack Obama's odds of winning election were quite high and drew inane criticism from those who would simply point to the tight national opinion polls and say "That can't be true!" It was, of course.

went 35-5, finished 14-4 in the brutal Big East, won the Big East Tournament, rolled through the tournament's Midwest regional, and took out Wichita State and Michigan in the Final Four to win the title. They ranked first in Ken Pomeroy's efficiency ratings – fifth on offense and first on defense. They were great. The team had athleticism, length, and incredible toughness. For head coach Rick Pitino's style, this team was the culmination of his search for, as Bob Dylan would call it, that "thin, wild mercury sound."

But a 12-game sample could have told you two completely different stories.

Table 1: Louisville basketball (2012-13), 12-game samples		
	Sample A	Sample B
Non-Conference Schedule	Kentucky (W, 80-77) Manhattan (W, 79-51) at Charleston (W, 80-38) vs. Missouri (W, 84-61)	W. Kentucky (W, 78-55) N. Iowa (W, 51-46) at Memphis (W, 87-78) vs. Duke (L, 71-76)
Big East Schedule	at Syracuse (W, 58-53) at UConn (W, 73-58) at Rutgers (W, 68-48) at Seton Hall (W, 73-58) Marquette (W, 70-51) St. John's (W, 72-58) Notre Dame (W, 73-57) S. Florida (W, 64-38)	at Villanova (L, 64-73) at Georgetown (L, 51-53) at DePaul (W, 79-58) at S. Florida (W, 59-41) Syracuse (L, 68-70) Pittsburgh (W, 64-61) Providence (W, 80-62) Cincinnati (W, 67-51)
Final Record	12-0 (8-0 in conference)	8-4 (5-3 in conference)

Louisville began the season projected ninth in Pomeroy's rankings, reached second on December 29, and never fell out of the Top 4 the rest of the way, reaching No. 1 for good after a dominant Elite Eight win over No. 7 Duke. The Cardinals were very consistent and very, very good.

But two 12-game, football-styled samples told two completely different stories about the same team. In Sample B, with a tricky non-conference slate and a reasonably difficult Big East schedule, the Cardinals went 8-4, got massacred by both media and fans for terrible underachievement, and probably ended up limping through a tighter-than-expected Pinstripe Bowl versus a mid-level Big 12 team like Iowa State or Oklahoma.

In Sample A, however, the same team, with comparable schedule strength, went 12-0 and most assuredly reached the mythical BCS championship game.

"Every result is really part of a range of results," Brian Fremeau says, and he's right. Similarly, every season is really part of a range of results.

For instance, Alabama's 32-28 win over Georgia in the 2012 SEC Championship game could have gone a lot of different directions with just one extra bounce of the ball. "Really, Alabama did enough to score between 24 and 38 points or so, while Georgia scored between, say, 20 and 31," Fremeau says.

Meanwhile, a team's season as a whole could be defined more accurately (and less in less satisfying fashion) by describing a range of results. Because of luck and timely turnovers, Notre Dame only went 8-5 in 2011 despite playing like what, on average, would have been a 10-win team. Meanwhile, the Irish were probably only about a 10- or 11-win team in 2012 but won 12 games and reached the BCS title game because of similar breaks in the opposite direction.

In other sports, these breaks even out a bit over the course of a lengthy schedule. That's never going to be an option in football. Granted, we seem to add an extra game to the regular season every couple of decades in college football (and a playoff could certainly add another game to the docket); and granted, the NFL has yearned for a longer regular season for a while. But no matter what, we aren't going to get a big enough schedule to change this sample problem[76]. Nor should

---

[76] To C.J. Schexnayder, "No matter how far back you get with data, no matter how detailed you get, you're victim to Heisenberg's Uncertainty Principle," which, in physics, discusses the generally limited accuracy with which a given particle can be measured, and how the particle is affected by the way we go about measuring it.

we. Football is a dangerous enough sport with the number of games we already play.

The small sample, of course, will inevitably lead to some rankings that seem curious to the naked eye. In 2012, Louisville's football team went 11-2, upset Florida in the Sugar Bowl, and finished 13th in the AP Top 25. The Football Outsiders F/+ rankings, on which we will expand in a future chapter, ranked them 28th. Meanwhile, Oklahoma State and Michigan State, who went 8-5 and 7-6, respectively, and lost a combined eight games by a touchdown or less, ranked 12th and 15th. The high rankings could be explained by talking about near-misses, tough schedules, bad breaks, et cetera, but the casual football fan would still raise an eyebrow at this.

In 2011, another two teams ranked in the F/+ Top 15 despite at least five losses. Their iffy seasons could be explained almost fully by extraordinarily bad breaks and timely mistakes. They were No. 13 Notre Dame (8-5) and No. 15 Texas A&M (7-6). Needless to say, they were seen as rather legitimate the next year; Notre Dame ranked seventh, went 12-1, and reached the BCS title game. Texas A&M, meanwhile, ranked third, went 11-2, and knocked off eventual national champion Alabama on the road. Obviously there were some factors the 2011 F/+ rankings didn't know about – each would start a redshirt freshman quarterback in 2012 (Everett Golson at Notre Dame, Heisman winner Johnny Manziel at Texas A&M), a player who obviously had nothing to do with the 2011 season; plus, A&M hired a new head coach, Kevin Sumlin, in the offseason. Still, the strange-looking 2011 rankings hinted at two teams that were really close to accomplishing something much greater. And in 2012, each team indeed accomplished something much greater[77].

---

[77] In a strange twist, this same accuracy that added legitimacy to the F/+ rankings would have almost certainly prevented these rankings from ever being included in any sort of BCS formula. During the BCS era, when the computers said something with which the humans disagreed, the humans just changed the formulas.

There is one other issue, of course, when it comes to the prevalence and acceptance of football stats: We simply got a later start. *The Hidden Game of Football* came out more than a decade after Bill James began publishing his *Abstracts*. The establishment of Football Outsiders in 2003 has closed the gap a lot, but here's how Bill Barnwell put it on Grantland in August 2012, "Football statistics are about where Bill James was in 1986, just with additional computing power. There are still reams of data to be compiled, stunning concepts to be proven, and a billion arguments to be had. Even then, though, football has far fewer discrete events and games than baseball does. Our collective knowledge of football through numbers is going to improve, but it's never going to catch up."

Whatever inroads have been made in football, by the Aaron Schatzs (Football Outsiders) and Brian Burkes (Advanced NFL Stats) of the world, have been made mostly at the NFL level. College football is still uncharted wilderness. But that's okay. As *The Hidden Game*'s John Thorn puts it, "That's what the Wright Brothers in the bicycle shop were all about. There weren't that many others trying to figure out how to get aloft." These things take time. But we've come a long way in just the last few years.

****

There is plenty of naked ambition at Sloan, plenty of hungry people simply looking for an opportunity to exploit to get into the business of sports. To put it another way, I'm the only person here without a business card. Still, for so many of us in the Convention Center, the origin of our desire to make this trip to Boston came a couple of decades ago, maybe more, in relatively innocent, nerdy settings. There is a fraternity[78] of adults – some at Sloan, some not – who grew up analyzing the

---

[78] "Fraternity" is used for a pretty specific reason: We're talking mostly about males here.

numbers on the back of Strat-O-Matic player cards[79], or tinkering with ideas on clipboards for their own entertainment, coming up with ways to find breakthroughs for their rotisserie league team, or looking for ways to make predictions.

For Aaron Schatz, who grew up a bigger fan of baseball (and, naturally, the works of Bill James) than of football, it began, simply, with reading the *Hidden Game of Football*, realizing he had more questions he wanted to ask, "pasting every play from the 2002 NFL season into a spreadsheet, creating stats, and starting to do some analysis." He started Football Outsiders the next year.

For Bill Barnwell, fantasy sports actually played a huge role in his desire for statistical analysis. "I was playing in fantasy leagues as a proxy, in a joint team effort with my father since I was, honestly, six or seven years old. That sort of instilled a love for numbers in me." Things have obviously grown since he was blowing away his father's friends in the early 1990s, but "there's still something there for me." He joined Football Outsiders as an intern in 2005, became a full-time writer three years later, and carries the "Football Stats" banner as well as anybody in the writing world at Grantland[80].

For Brian Fremeau, it began in the early 1990s, when he and his brothers came up with a formula to use in picking brackets for the NCAA basketball tournament. "We had this idea that we could win a pool in our high school because we had this statistical advantage." Fremeau was always good at math, and he had taken a math theory class in his freshman year at Notre Dame (with the thought that he would pursue a major in it), but "they didn't apply the theory to anything

---

[79] The intro chapter to Jim Albert's and Jay Bennett's *Curve Ball* (2003) takes a look at the world of baseball probabilities through tabletop games. It is wonderfully done.

[80] More Barnwell: "Fantasy football has probably also led to overvaluation of touchdowns. There is nothing absurdly more difficult about crossing the goal line versus crossing the 2-yard line. And we don't care whether a guy gained 60 yards in the fourth quarter of a blowout or on a couple of key drives that determined the game."

tangible," and it stopped being interesting to him. He moved on to become a communications major, but he never stopped tinkering with his formulas.

A single game, however, changed his outlook in regard to statistics: Boston College 14, Notre Dame 7. November 2, 2002. "Notre Dame was off to an 8-0 start that year, and a 'return to glory' was happening. Everyone was excited. But Notre Dame turned the ball over five times and gave up a fumble return for a touchdown. They kicked field goals from distances they shouldn't have attempted, they went for it on fourth down deep in Boston College territory when they probably should have kicked field goals, and they lost by seven points.

"Notre Dame statistically dominated – they outgained Boston College by a couple hundred yards, and I don't think Boston College crossed the 50 with its offense the entire game. I was watching it unfold, and I just remember articulating to a friend of my brother, 'You know, if we could measure *that* [the way the drives finished], maybe we could measure the decision-making process of [then Notre Dame coach] Tyrone Willingham in these situations. I wonder how many times this decision-making has happened this year.'

"This data existed, but nobody was collecting it," Fremeau says. "All we have is the box score to tell us This Team gained this many yards and lost, while This Team gained this many yards and won. I was just very interested from that point forward in, 'Well, if this doesn't exist, then I need to be collecting it myself. I want answers to questions. I want to know how efficient teams are.'"

At first, he wanted to collect this data for a stat based on momentum and teams stringing together "successful" drives – How much is "doing a good thing three times in a row [making a stop, scoring, and making a stop, for example]" worth? But in the process of collecting drive data, he eventually created the Fremeau Efficiency Index (FEI) based on drives' expectations versus drives' actual results. In 2006, he introduced FEI to the mostly NFL audience at Football Outsiders.

For Bob Stoll, a statistics major at California, it started with some innocent tinkering with numbers. "I was taking a time series analysis class," Stoll says, one based around weather patterns. "I decided to do it on an NFL team, the Raiders; I was a huge Raiders fan, and I was wondering if there was any pattern to the way the Raiders played." He entered three years' worth of scoring data to see if there were patterns or randomness. "It turned out there was some predictive quality to the way teams performed. I started to use this stuff for a pool I was in, and I started doing pretty well." There were some picks he felt more strongly about than others, and a friend got him in touch with a bookie. One thing led to another, and now he's "Dr. Bob," one of the most successful sports handicappers on the market[81]. Stoll has found his greatest success spotting patterns in college football and making a very good living off of it.

My own experience with sports and stats has been, shall we say, rather circular. I, too, found early success in fantasy football (that was primarily because I had both Miami quarterback Dan Marino and Miami receiver Mark Clayton, and they went off). I, too, tinkered with numbers and spreadsheets behind closed doors. I, too, ended up a communications major (which seems to be a strange but effective first step toward writing for Football Outsiders). But

---

[81] More from Stoll: "What I'm doing now, I was doing 15 years ago. The guys starting out now in the stats world have much better tools, but I think I can see the forest for the trees better." His picks are successful, in part, because his statistics are only the starting point. For instance, when an important player is hurt, he makes manual adjustments to both the players' teams and the teams' opponents based on which version of the team they faced. Examples from 2012 might include Arkansas quarterback Tyler Wilson or Tulane quarterback Ryan Griffin; each of their respective teams were light years better when they were healthy than when they were not. "My adjustments make my model good," he says. Well, that, and "I think I'm better at factoring in various schedule strengths than anybody else."

it took a while for me to either acknowledge or establish my path.

As my parents tell it, I learned to read baseball cards and record albums (like, actual LP albums) at a young age. I obsessed over sports even though I wasn't great at many – solid hand-eye coordination doesn't make up for a complete and total lack of physical prowess – and I could figure out any game to play given two dice and a clipboard. Bill James was a bit over my head (I was probably about 6-8 when my father bought a James *Abstract*), but numbers, percentages and sports always worked in unison in my head.

I was always good with numbers, and my social fate was sealed pretty early on: I was taking third-grade math in first grade, clinching that I would be known for that all the way through high school. For years, I rebelled against what I was good at, yearning to be known for something *other* than being good at math. I came to the University of Missouri both because I was a fan (my father had gotten his doctorate there) and because I decided journalism was for me. I was the sports editor of my high school paper, and I stayed afloat early on in an honors English class at Mizzou, but it only took about one semester for me to realize that the other J-school students were much, much more into journalism than I was. My heart wasn't in it, so I flipped to communication pretty early.

Not quite knowing what I wanted to get out of my degree, I did the sane thing and stayed in school longer. I entered the Mizzou MBA program in 2001, graduated in 2003, and still really didn't know what I wanted to do. I took a job as a data analyst for the State of Missouri and picked up a lot of neat Excel and database tricks along the way. I had forever maintained what a friend and I called The Spreadsheet, my obsessive effort to track basketball stats, baseball stats, and every football player Missouri was recruiting over about a five-year radius. I tinkered with ways to rate the minor league players in my chosen team's system (the Pittsburgh Pirates),

testing out every new baseball rating and formula I could find[82]
I also kept writing long, meandering posts about football and
basketball on a Missouri message board called Tigerboard.

By about 2006, Tigerboard had seen the same shifts that
most popular message boards do: More readers means more
posters. More posters means more Crazy Internet People[83].
The Crazy Internet People outscream everybody else,
rendering almost any message board unreadable after a while,
and the site I frequented far more than I probably should have
became mostly unbearable for me. So I started a Google group
with some friends. And a year later, I started a blog.

There's one certainty in starting a blog about your
school of choice: The offseason is terribly boring. I didn't
know what to write about in the months between spring sports
and football season, so I figured I would survey the territory of
college football statistics. It was always my sport of choice, and
I only basically enjoyed baseball in spreadsheets, and not on
television (and that's only partially because I'm a Pirates fan),
so why not see what's out there? What are the primary
advanced college football stats? How do we measure
efficiency? Are there ways for me to prove that Iowa State
linebacker Alvin Bowen isn't very good?[84]

I didn't quite find what I expected to find. I found
almost nothing, actually. I had heard of Football Outsiders by
that point, but the only college measure on the site was

---

[82] Hey, when it comes to the Pirates, you seek out hope wherever you think you
can find it. Next Year is usually the earliest place to start.

[83] It's like an equation. Even if the ratio of crazies stays the same – say, 1 in 100
regulars – it only takes a few crazies to drown out everybody else.

[84] Poor Alvin Bowen. He has no idea that he was the impetus for a lot of my
stat obsession. In 2006, Bowen recorded 123.5 tackles (92 solo, 63 assisted), a
rather absurd 18 percent of Iowa State's overall tackles. He also had a decent
five tackles for loss and four passes defensed. He was clearly a capable player,
but the fact that he was garnering all-conference or All-American buzz because
of gaudy tackle totals – when the only reason he had that many tackles was that
nobody else on his mostly awful defense could bring anybody down – drove me
crazy. My obsession with tamping down his awards buzz led me down the road
I am still traveling. I should both thank him and apologize to him.

Fremeau's drive-based FEI. Being that baseball stats were where my intuition was based, I wasn't ready to wrap my head around that. I wanted to see advanced play-by-play stats, and none existed. So I decided to create my own.

But we'll come back to that.

****

We live in a world of algorithms, for better and for worse. The 2013 Sloan Sports Analytics Conference is, in the end, a place to see how far the analytics world has come and how far it still has to go. The ideas are flowing fast and furious. The computer power grows. The nerds are finding their place in the sports world. But where we do we go from here? I'm not sure an algorithm exists that can give you the answer to that one.

5. We Meet Again, Mr. Wizard

In the 2010 regular season, Oregon averaged 538 yards and 49 points per game[85]. Take out a near-miss at California[86], and those averages rise to 561 yards and 52 points. The Ducks beat 11 of 12 opponents by at least 11 points, eight by at least 20. They won at Tennessee by 35, at USC by 21 and at Oregon State by 17. They beat eventual Orange Bowl champion Stanford by 21. And my numbers hated them.

Well, perhaps hate is a strong word, but the numbers weren't as impressed by Oregon's fast pace and gaudy totals (against weak opponents) as the eyeballs were. It got bad enough that, with Oregon ranked 29th in S&P+ in late October, I had to cry on basketball wonk Ken Pomeroy's shoulder for a while for a column at Football Outsiders.

> BC: Even post-adjustment, Oregon still ranks only 29th in the current S&P+ rankings. As you

---

[85] Adapted from a piece that appeared at SB Nation on August 3, 2012.
[86] Oregon won a 15-13 slog, gaining just 317 yards as Cal went to great lengths to slow the game down to a crawl.

have tinkered with your formulas and approaches over the years, how have you tended to react to situations like this, where a team or small handful of teams just doesn't seem right? And what is the most egregious example you can recall, where a team ranked strangely high or low in your basketball rankings?

Pomeroy: I can challenge the Oregon case. In 2006, Gonzaga was thought to be a Top 10, maybe even a Top 5 team by the experts, and they were ranked in the 40s and 50s most of the season in my ratings. Even the casual fan remembers the scene with Adam Morrison crying on the court (actually before the game was completely decided) after Gonzaga lost in the Sweet 16 to UCLA in what could only be described as an epic collapse after the Zags dominated the Bruins for 38 minutes. At that point, I was crying, too. At least on the inside, because Gonzaga's run revealed a fatal error in my system.

There's strong evidence that in college basketball, there is little fundamental difference between a one-point loss and a one-point win when it comes to indicating a team's strength relative to its opponent. Therefore, my system doesn't treat those outcomes much differently. Gonzaga was different though – they repeatedly coasted against weaker competition only to pull out a close win late. Normally, the system sees this as luck, but in Gonzaga's case it probably wasn't. The thing is, I have not changed my system since then. Gonzaga was a tremendously interesting exception, but an exception nonetheless. Every tweak I made in the offseason to put Gonzaga in its rightful place made the system as a whole worse. That's the thing about making tweaks — I always rerun the system on past seasons, and when I did that with Gonzaga changes, it made the Zags predictions better, but the predictions were worse for all other games.

At some point late that season (or perhaps it was after the season was over), I came to accept three simple facts:

1. Statistics don't tell you everything, no matter how close we try to come with them.

2. Neither do scoreboards.

3. Sometimes scoreboards and other numbers are simply going to disagree.

When you're dealing with a 12-game sample size, crazy things will happen. They just will. Needless to say, this was a comforting line of thought as I was catching flak from Kansas State fans in 2011.

In 2011, Kansas State was Oregon minus any sort of offensive explosiveness. In one of the most offense-friendly conferences in the country, the Wildcats barely cracked the Off. F/+ Top 50 (44th) or the overall F/+ Top 30 (29th) [87]. If it were possible to perfect a bend-don't-break offense, the Wildcats did so in 2011. But guess what: They just kept winning. There is an advantage to be gained when you give up the illusion of style points and simply try to do whatever it takes to win games.

K-State barely even opened up the offensive playbook in a 10-7 win over Eastern Kentucky. Hell, since that game wasn't televised, they may have quick-kicked on every first down for all I know.

They needed a late goal line stand to win at Miami.

---

[87] We will go into great detail with F/+ in the Advanced Stats Class chapter.

They played rope-a-dope against Baylor, surviving a first-half offensive onslaught and calmly making every play in the fourth quarter of a 36-35 win.

They picked off a pass on the first play of the game versus Missouri (which quickly led to an early lead), gave up three points on Missouri's first four trips inside the KSU 35, built a big lead, then held on to win by seven.

They were outgained by Texas Tech by 241 yards but won, 41-34, almost entirely with special teams.

Following a blowout loss to Oklahoma, they gave up 575 yards to Oklahoma State while allowing just 19:11 of possession but, thanks to more good special teams, a pick six, and quarterback Collin Klein's long legs, they almost won anyway.

They were outgained by 71 yards by Texas A&M and trailed by 10 points with under six minutes remaining, but behind five Klein rushing touchdowns and one beautifully timed bomb to Chris Harper for 53 yards in the fourth quarter, they came back and eventually won in quadruple overtime.

They gained 121 yards at Texas ... and won.

They were outgained by Iowa State at home, for god's sakes. But they won by seven anyway, of course.

When all was said and done, some combination of Klein's legs, perfectly-timed late-game magic, and head coach Bill Snyder's wizardry led the Wildcats to one of the least likely 10-win seasons in college football history. They went 2-2 in games decided by more than a touchdown ... and 8-1 in games decided by eight or fewer points. This isn't supposed to happen. In the final F/+ rankings, K-State finished behind four teams it had beaten (No. 15 Texas A&M, No. 21 Texas, No. 22 Missouri, No. 26 Baylor), and it even kind of made sense.

Even though it made my numbers look questionable to some, was it bad that I kind of wanted them to do it again in 2012?

Here's what I said about the Wildcats in my 2011 SB Nation preview:

> Honestly, it's hard to know what to make of this team. A high-quality running back is replaced by a more highly-touted, less-accomplished back of similar stature. An athletic receiving corps with higher potential than in recent years will be taking passes from a quarterback who was completely untrustworthy last year. Passing downs defense that was poor last year might get worse (okay, that's really not possible), and standard downs defense that was solid might get better. Your guess is as good as mine. [...]
>
> Anything between a 4-1 and 2-3 start is possible, and it is hard to figure out what is more likely given the newcomers (especially those named Brown[88]) upon whom the Wildcats will be counting. Initial projections have K-State hovering around the .500 mark for basically the seventh consecutive season. One wonders if Snyder has another run in him at some point; with underclassmen at several key positions, KSU fans can look to the 2012-13 window for said run, if it exists.

"Anything between a 4-1 and 2-3 start is possible." Or, you know, 5-0.

"KSU fans can look to the 2012-13 window for said run if it exists." Or, you know, 2011.

The more I look into it, the more I realize that close wins are not entirely random and are actually tied somewhat to your quarterback. That was good news for Kansas State heading into 2012, obviously, because Klein was returning for his senior season. The brand of football they played had no

---

[88] The Brown brothers – Arthur and Bryce – were both five-star high school recruits out of Wichita, and both transferred back to Kansas State after stints at Miami and Tennessee, respectively. Arthur became one of the Big 12's best linebackers, while Bryce, a running back, barely played before quitting the team.

margin for error whatsoever, but with Klein behind center, they could get away with it. Can they with Klein and defenders Arthur Brown and Nigel Malone gone heading into 2013, however? That might be a different story. Or, hell, maybe not. Why question Bill Snyder at this point?

I honestly had no idea how to gauge success for Kansas State in 2012. A team that wins 10 games one year probably sets the bar around 10 wins again the next. A team ranked 21st in the preseason coaches poll (with five conference mates ahead of them), as Kansas State was, is probably looking at between seven and nine wins. A team projected 47th (yes, 47th) in the *Football Outsiders Almanac 2012* would probably looking at something closer to six wins. So I was basically willing to just hedge my bets and say that if K-State was ranked at the end of the season, despite a brutal conference schedule (which included trips to Oklahoma, West Virginia, TCU and Baylor), they would have succeeded. I thought anything between five and 10 wins was a possibility.

Naturally, then, KSU went 11-1, won the Big 12 and found itself briefly ranked No. 1 in the country in mid-November before a loss at Baylor. And the Wildcats actually looked good doing it this time around, winning just two games by six or fewer points.

Bill Snyder has nothing left to prove. In the 1990s and early 2000s, he led one of the most intimidating defenses and explosive offenses around, and his Wildcats won 11 games in six of seven seasons and at least nine games in 10 of 11. (This is a program, by the way, that went 4-50-1 from 1985-89 and had experienced minimal success over the last century.) In 2011, he had neither an intimidating defense nor an explosive offense, and he won 10 games anyway. At SB Nation, we jokingly (sort of) called him a wizard approximately 1,403 times in 2011. His teams had no margin for error and didn't care.

At this point, if K-State goes 2-10 for every year between now and when Snyder retires, it won't change anything. Snyder will still have been one of college football's greatest coaches, one of its most accomplished magicians. He took over a program with nothing – literally, nothing – going for it in 1989 and turned it into a national power, then he came back and won 10 games twice more just for old time's sake. That said, it's safe to say that he doesn't think he is finished.

The head (and the numbers) think that repeating the success of 2011-12 is probably too much to ask without Klein and company.

The heart, though? Different story.

Are you willing to bet against Bill Snyder at this point? Didn't think so.

6. Coaches vs. Stats

It is yellowing a bit at this stage, but the ink is still perfectly clear. Its lines were clearly marked using a ruler or, more likely, a yardstick. It is both enormous and enormously detailed.

It is called the "1992 Defensive Quality Control" chart. Alabama head coach Gene Stallings used it to track his team's progress (of which there was plenty) over the course of his national title season with the Crimson Tide. He learned it from Dallas Cowboys coach Tom Landry, for whom he worked as defensive backs coach for 14 seasons between head coaching jobs. "Coach Landry was an engineer by schooling, and he had such an analytical mind," Stalling says. "He was always big into quality control. When the game is over, Coach Landry knows exactly what happened just by looking at the board." (His use of present tense is endearing, conclusive proof that once you become a coach, you are always a coach, long after your actual coaching days end, even long after you pass away.)

My only exposure to this chart was through a random picture passed along to me on the Internet. I cannot see all of the categories, which drives me crazy. It was no longer on display at the Bryant Museum in Tuscaloosa when I visited in September 2012. But with a single picture, I see enough. There are three groups: Goals, Philosophy, and Quality. For Goals, Stallings listed things like Points Allowed/Game (goal: 17.0), Turnovers (36), Pressure QB on Passes (35 percent), Cause Fumbles (two per game), and Yards Per Attempt—Run (3.0). ("Nobody runs against my team[89]," he says. And he's right; they didn't.)

For Philosophy, things go micro. Pass Situation Big Pass Play (allowing big plays on passing downs; goal: 1 for every 9). Run Situation Big Pass Play (goal: 1 for every 11). Average Per Pass Attempt, 2nd & 10 (goal: 5.0). Average Per Pass Attempt, 3rd & 13-17 (goal: 7.5). Rifle Force (when a strong safety comes up and forces a run outside; goal: 3.0). Pistol Force (containing an end run with a cornerback; goal: 3.5). Box Force (containing an end run with an outside linebacker; the chart cuts off, so I can't see the goal for that one, nor can I see any of the Quality guidelines below it).

Microsoft Excel hadn't quite caught on by 1992, so this was all done painstakingly by hand. For each week, there was a game column and a season-to-date column. If Alabama failed to meet a goal in a given game, or fell behind for the season, the box was shaded in red. "I can look at that board, and I can tell that something's getting off-kilter rather than waiting till the end of the year. If you see just a whole lot of red, and you've got present game and total games, you can see problems developing as it's happening."

The 1992 Alabama defense was one of the best in semi-recent memory. The Tide allowed just 122 points and 660 rushing yards in 13 games, forced an absurd number of

---

[89] More from Stallings: Did he approach defense differently at Alabama (1990-96) or Texas A&M (1965-71) than he did when he was head coach of the NFL's St. Louis/Phoenix Cardinals (1986-89)? Not really, he says, though even by the mid-1980s you were forced to build your defense more around stopping the pass.

turnovers, and scored almost as many touchdowns via return (special teams and turnovers) as opponents did via pass. All-American bookend ends John Copeland and Eric Curry combined for over 20 sacks and pressured the quarterback nearly 50 other times. Corners George Teague and Antonio Langham combined for over 20 passes defensed (intercepted or broken up), and two blocked punts. Linebackers Lemanski Hall, Michael Rogers, Derrick Oden and Antonio London combined for nearly 30 tackles for loss, more than 10 sacks, and more than 10 passes defensed.

This unit didn't exactly have to worry too much about red boxes, in other words. The Tide 'only' forced two turnovers and picked off one pass in the second game against Southern Miss (a meager 17-10 win), and when they 'only' forced three combined turnovers against Tennessee and Ole Miss, they briefly fell behind schedule for their 36 overall takeaways. But then, after what were probably some contentious, "go get the damned ball" practices, they forced 11 against LSU, Mississippi State and Auburn. That catches you up in a hurry. While they occasionally struggled (relatively speaking) in allowing more yards than preferred on first downs (5.1 per attempt against Arkansas, 6.8 versus Ole Miss, a whopping 9.0 versus Auburn), they allowed just 4.8 for the season.

Tracking stats for such a dominant team might not seem as worthwhile as doing it for a more borderline unit, but the goals for this unit were rather extreme. Stallings knew he was going to have a great defense, and he set the bar high. "Your goals come from what you did the year before," he says. The 1991 defense had been excellent – 11.9 points per game, 300.3 yards per game – and returned a ton of talent, so Stallings set expectations accordingly.

We tend to use statistics for answers: Where does Team A rank? How many yards per game is Team B allowing? That's fine for crafting narratives, but it doesn't help coaches too much. For coaches, it's not about the answers; it's about finding the right questions to ask. Stallings' pursuit of questions, and Landry's before that, led to the Quality Control Chart, something every coach in the country should be creating[90].

The head coach of a college football team is basically a CEO. He has his hand in every aspect of the game, but his responsibilities also extend to fundraising, amateur psychology, et cetera. Stats are a useful tool, one it would be at least somewhat irresponsible not to pursue. If they can teach you more about yourself and your opponent, and if your opponent is using them in great detail to get a read on you, you should probably keep up in that regard. If other programs are subscribing to STATS, LLC's detailed charting service or employing their own charters/stat analysis people, shouldn't you?

"Sometimes measurement can substitute for a higher level of thinking," says *The Hidden Game of Football*'s John Thorn. "You come up with an answer that you can deal with, that is rational, explicable, maybe even repeatable – you hope so – but there is a higher level of thinking in coaching, beyond measurement, that is in the realm of philosophy. Your best coaches, your Vince Lombardis, weren't doing a lot of measurement."

For Stallings, the goal was not to figure out how good your run or pass defense was from a 20,000-foot view. It was to keep minute track of cracks, breakdowns and trends. If opponents are gaining a few too many yards on 2nd-and-10, you can focus your film study on a small selection of plays to figure out potential problems. If your pass defense is strong in passing situations but iffy in run situations, does that mean you're biting too much on the run? If your Rifle Force is not sufficient, then what is your strong safety doing wrong? He pared this list down to the categories that meant the most to

---

[90] Why don't more coaches do it? "We coach the ways we know," says Stallings. If you weren't taught to do it by others, you might not think to do it yourself.

his own defensive philosophy, and he tracked his stats religiously.

There are others. Back in his days as a receivers coach for the Baltimore Ravens and the University of San Diego Toreros, Stanford head coach David Shaw created a points system for his players. "I tried to track what most clearly affects wins and losses, and then I created a points system: Drops were negative, 15-yard catches were positive, blocks that led to touchdowns were positive. I wanted to inspire guys to do the things that lead to wins. I'm going to reward you individually for doing these things." He did the same a few years later as Stanford's running backs coach, rewarding things like yards after contact.

Even if coaches don't track stats with this amount of zeal, almost every football coach in the country, at almost every level, is coming up with some way to track the tendencies of both opponents and, in most cases, his own team. That always makes for a fascinating exchange when a coach is presented stats by the media or fans.

****

Following the departures of record-setting quarterback Brandon Weeden and two-time Biletnikoff Award winner (for the best receiver in college football) Justin Blackmon the previous year, Oklahoma State still found itself averaging a gaudy 56 points and 659 yards per game early in the 2012 season, numbers that actually exceeded the pace the Cowboys had set a year earlier (49 points, 546 yards). But that came mostly from wins over Savannah State and Louisiana-Lafayette (combined score: OSU 149, opponent 24). The offense shot itself in the foot repeatedly in losses to Arizona and Texas, and at 2-2, offensive coordinator Todd Monken wasn't too interested in discussing the "stats" being presented to him.

"You can't carry over points, you can't carry over yards," Monken told the *Daily Oklahoman*. "Stats are, really, for losers.

You don't want to be 600 (yards) one week and 200 the next, because you're going to lose that game. ... Most of the time, statistics and numbers are all there just to make yourself feel better."

It was a rather harsh (and humorous) way to put it, but it's not like he was alone in that sentiment. "'Stats are for losers' is one of those old coaching adages," says Wake Forest head coach Jim Grobe. "It's almost a coaching axiom." Coaches have been defensive about stats for decades; one gets the impressions that younger coaches, who are perhaps a little bit more stat-inclined than their older peers, are hesitant to admit such a thing in public.

"I just don't believe that [coaches] are as dumb as they make themselves out to be," says *USA Today*'s Paul Myerberg. And they aren't. But in the week-to-week grind of the season, the per-game stats we lean on for our narratives don't do much for them.

Of course, "you can say stats aren't very important," says Grobe, "but by the end of the year you'll see a lot of correlation between the numbers and whether you're good or bad. We get so caught up in all this stuff that we can't see the forest from the trees."

As John Thorn reminds us, legendary Baltimore Orioles manager Earl Weaver "decried the stat heads but kept rigorous index cards [with notes on matchups and stats]." Coaches probably know how they're doing, but a) they don't care about the same stats we do, and b) they don't care to talk to us about it. The latter point is key. In the end, stats are one of the many things that creates a divide between coaches and fans. When things are going poorly, fans have the tendency of complaining about the wrong thing[91]. And make no mistake, coaches field a ton of complaints.

"There are not a lot of jobs in the country where you are questioned on what you do every day by the media," says

---

[91] Other reasons for the coach-fan divide: salaries, hurt feelings from losses, and coaches' refusal to call the "touchdown play" more often.

Steven Godfrey, writer for SB Nation. "Politicians, coaches, and that's about it. They don't admit it out loud, but coaches' biggest asset is to be vague. The one thing they hate is having something thrown back at them. That's why these mantras are so vanilla. It's a cat-and-mouse game as to what they actually disclose[92]." When you're winning, you can get away with saying bland things like "We do what we do." It's confident and a bit badass. But if you're losing, it is proof of stubbornness and/or just being an ass[93].

****

Okay, so let's just assume that, behind closed doors, with the shades drawn and the lights turned down, coaches tinker with stats of some sort. What are they doing?

"On Sunday, one of the first things I'm going to do is look at the overall picture of the opponent: strengths, weaknesses, et cetera," says Ball State head coach Pete Lembo. "It puts you in a better state of mind when you look at the video. You have a background heading into the video."

---

[92] More from Godfrey: "It's funny how, when coaches have personalities and demeanors that match their system – if you have a guy like Mike Leach, who has an unorthodox system and an unorthodox personality – people like that. There's symmetry, and it's easy to write about. When you see the hard-nosed fiery guy, like [Georgia defensive coordinator] Todd Grantham, and he's running a cocky, aggressive 3-4 defense, and he's kind of a dick in the media, we almost embrace that. Georgia fans like Grantham, but so many of them hated [offensive coordinator] Mike Bobo, whose personality is quieter and more reflective of [head coach] Mark Richt's. And some of them still do, no matter how good Georgia's offense has been recently." It's the same with former Missouri offensive coordinator David Yost, who was a little weird and introspective and was never accepted by Missouri fans, even when the offense was just fine.

[93] As new Cincinnati head coach Tommy Tuberville told Godfrey in March 2012, "I understand the media, to a degree. Of course, we've kind of brought it on ourselves with all the money that's in it, the money that we make, the money that's in all of our sports, how things have changed. And we all look for that sense of wanting people to be interested in what we're doing. ... College football is great, but when something goes wrong, you've got to take the criticism."

Count Stanford's David Shaw, meanwhile, as a member of the "film first" camp. "I always start with the film. It's your résumé, it's who you are. After I watch a couple of games or cut-ups, I can look at the stats to see if they're backing up what I'm seeing. Stats have become a significant part of our game-planning, but we'll make subtle changes based on what we're seeing."

This is something Mitch Tanney of STATS, LLC, confirms. "Teams see something on film, and they can use the data to bounce it against their hunches. And sometimes you can use data to drive your video analysis."

It is a circular relationship, but that is okay. As Gene Stallings would say, you coach the ways you know. And you probably go about things in a similar way that you did as a no-name assistant.

"We're not any different," Wake Forest's Grobe says. "We look at every stat known to man. Break down game film ad nauseum. We know what you're doing on downs, field zones, hashes. For just about every situation you can possibly imagine, we've got it on a stat somewhere. But how do you manage all of those stats? How do you pull it together in a game plan that makes sense?"

"The approach hasn't changed through the years," says New Mexico head coach (and former Notre Dame chief) Bob Davie. "We look at it first from a defensive perspective. Every team, every offense is unique. That's different from the pros. Every week you're starting on Sunday, and the first thing you do is figure out what that offense does in frequency. What do they do the most of? What do they do the best? You don't formulate a defensive plan until you figure that out."

UL-Monroe head coach Todd Berry, meanwhile, almost goes in the opposite direction. "We tend to use stats more as an affirmation rather than trying to discover things. We're using them to ask, 'Is what I'm seeing accurate?'"

Regardless of the approach, film study is everything in football – you just aren't going to get the information you need about formations, tendencies, et cetera, without it – but stats are wonderful for setting the table. And, of course, film study itself has shifted dramatically through the years.

"What you do hasn't changed," says Davie. "What *has* changed is the volume of things people do. The resources you have to do more things from a breakdown standpoint – it was so elementary, and now it's so advanced."

In his first job as a graduate assistant under Johnny Majors at Pittsburgh, "the first prerequisite was taking the 16-millimeter film [of opponents], tearing it, hanging it by category, and splicing it. We used to have hangers all across our meeting room." That isn't so much a necessity in an age where graduate assistants can cut, splice and organize video clips in minimal time on a computer.

Sonny Dykes, head coach at California, places heavy scouting emphasis on stats. But you have to know what you're looking for. "What we try to do is look at all the types of variables that impact a football game. What's important? What impacts our style of play?" And for different schools, different stats are of variable importance. For Dykes, a disciple of pass-heavy Air Raid master Mike Leach (among others), time of possession means very little. For Davie, who operates a run-heavy system and is still in the process of building his team's talent base, it is vital.

"Statistics can – I'll never say they lie, but they can give you a version of the truth that isn't quite right," says Shaw. You have to understand the context involved, and you have to know what's important to you. For instance, "a team that rushes for a ton of yards might just be playing with the lead because of their great defense," he says. At the higher level, Shaw says the following stats are most important to his team's philosophy: first downs per game, first-down efficiency and the resulting third-down conversion rate, and red zone touchdown percentage[94].

---

[94] Finishing drives is incredibly important. In fact, there's an entire chapter about it later in this book.

For Air Force's Troy Calhoun, the list has a few differences, but not too many: turnover margin, third-down conversion rate, yards per carry, explosive plays (he defines this as runs of 10 or more yards and passes of 15 or more yards), negative-yardage plays (sacks, tackles for loss), penalties [95], opponent's starting field position, red zone touchdown percentage, fourth-down conversions. To maximize opportunities he goes for it on fourth down more than anybody else in the country[96].

If you surveyed every coach in the country, however, you would probably sense one major theme: "The number one thing is always turnovers," Dykes says. "Very seldom did we win the turnover battle and lose the game."

There is quite a bit of luck involved in turnovers, which has to be maddening to coaches who try to control every aspect of preparation and execution. But considering the impact turnovers can have – on average, I have found that turnovers are worth about five points when you take into account the field position the offense lost and the field position the defense gained – they are very clearly important. You can't control the way the ball bounces, but coaches very much try to control the number of fumbles they force (and commit) and, in some cases, the number of passes they bat down.

"A year ago [in 2011], we only batted down two balls at the line," says Colorado head coach Mike MacIntyre, who came to Boulder after three years at San Jose State (2010-12). "Last year [in 2012], it must have been 35. We practiced it

---

[95] A typically outmanned program like Calhoun's Falcons simply cannot afford the same number of self-inflicted setbacks that other programs can, so penalties might mean more to a team like Air Force than to other FBS teams.

[96] Calhoun also has a checklist for special teams (no blocks allowed, net punting average over 38.0 yards, average punt distance over 43.0 yards, opponent kick returns under 19.0 yards, punt returns over 11.0 yards, et cetera), but he uses these stats in a different way than Stallings did with his Quality Control Chart. There aren't many prescriptive changes to come of these things, only reminders of what you're doing well and poorly.

every day. We told the defensive line that if they get held up, get those hands in the air and tip it. There's luck in where it gets tipped, but there's also skill. Learning where the quarterback moves and where to rush so you're in the passing lane is something you can do[97]."

****

No matter how you are using stats, of course, the ridiculous range of a team's level of competition at the FBS level, in both non-conference play and, in some cases, conference play, is significant. It is one of the key differences between looking at football stats at the pro and college level. If you aren't adjusting for the opponent at hand when you are using college football statistics, then you are missing vital context.

Take Mississippi State, for instance. In 2012, Dan Mullen's Bulldogs went 8-5 and reached a bowl game for the third straight year. In the SEC West, that is a pretty impressive accomplishment on its face. But they pulled off this record while ranking just 62nd in the Football Outsiders F/+ rankings. They benefited from some turnover luck, but they also benefited from the most pillow-soft schedule possible.

Mississippi State's 2012 season began with a visit from FCS program Jackson State, then featured games versus Auburn (final 2012 record: 3-9, 105th in the F/+ rankings), Troy (5-7, 78th), South Alabama (2-11, 118th), Kentucky (2-10, 112th) and Tennessee (5-7, 57th).

On October 20, the Bulldogs moved to 7-0 with an easy win over Middle Tennessee (8-4, 96th) and reached 13th in the AP Poll. Their terribly easy non-conference schedule had allowed them to pile up a gaudy record, as had the fact that they drew Kentucky and Tennessee for their two games versus

---

[97] More from MacIntyre: "We look at where a quarterback completes his balls and his completion rate to the right or left. It helps us determine whether we should try to flush him one way or another."

SEC East teams instead of, say, Florida (11-2, fourth) and Georgia (12-2, sixth). Because of their luck of the draw, their visit to No. 1 Alabama on October 27 became a marquee game, a battle of two undefeated SEC teams. "The line for that game should have been 31 points," says "Dr. Bob" Stoll. "I had Mississippi State ranked 33rd heading into that game. People kept telling me that couldn't be right; I said, 'Believe me. Trust me. By the time the season's over, you'll understand.'"

Indeed, the schedule eventually caught up to MSU. The Bulldogs lost at Alabama by 31, to Texas A&M (a team advanced stats pinpointed as a Top 10 team very early on) at home by 25, at LSU by 20, and at Ole Miss by 17. They lost four of five to finish the season, but their schedule still allowed them to win eight games despite ranking below two 5-7 teams from the SEC East, Tennessee and Missouri.

Coaches might not use opponent-adjusted statistics as a rule[98], but they do feel the need to take the schedule into account. "Ohio's out-of-conference games versus Western Michigan's in a given year, it can be completely different," says Lembo. "That will skew your stats. MAC teams play Army a lot, and of course that's going to skew your rushing statistics. I have a laminated chart on my desk that has all of the MAC schedules on it. I want to know not only who teams are playing, but in which order."

In 2011, for example, Ball State played South Florida, Army, Oklahoma and Temple, four incredibly physical teams of varying quality. By the time they got to Temple, Lembo says "Temple might as well have been Alabama at that point because of the games we'd played previously and the physical toll it took." (Ball State lost to Temple, 42-0.) Meanwhile, after a 2012 season opener against Penn State, Ohio took on New Mexico State, Marshall, Norfolk State, UMass, Buffalo and Akron, then had a week off before heading to Miami (Ohio). "There's a good chance you're getting through that stretch at

---

[98] Yet.

6-1 or 7-0, and you're pretty healthy getting to your bye week," Lembo says[99]. How your schedule unfolds will impact how a coach will scout you. Or, at least, it should.

****

Depending on your system of choice, scouting yourself might be as or more important than scouting your opponent. Bob Stitt, head coach at the Colorado School of Mines, runs his own unconventional version of the spread offense, and since teams play his school differently than everybody else, "film study doesn't necessarily produce a lot of value. We'll prepare for the top two or three defensive fronts and their major tendencies, of course, but for the most part we focus on our own team."

Self-awareness is vital. "Sometimes my defensive coordinator will walk in and say, 'I think I have a really good bead on these guys,'" says Lembo. If a team is not sufficiently aware of its own tendencies, it's like playing Tecmo Bowl on Nintendo: the defense simply calls Run 1, floods the play with defenders, and stuffs you for a loss. (You might get away with this if you have superior talent, and in college football, some teams are vastly superior in this regard.)

Coaches like UTSA's Larry Coker go to great lengths to get the same read of themselves that their opponents will derive, then adjust the game plan accordingly. "This is what opponents are going to have on us, but here are our tendency breakers."

---

[99] In the end, it is your overall quality that matters. In 2011, Lembo's second year at Ball State, his Cardinals weren't deep enough or far enough along in terms of program development to handle such a tough slate, but they did win three of four after the loss to Temple. And in 2012, Ohio managed to pull an upset of Penn State and move to 7-0, but narrow wins over awful UMass and Akron teams were harbingers to the Bobcats' eventual MAC doom. Thanks in part to injuries, they lost four of five to finish the regular season before rebounding to beat UL-Monroe in the Independence Bowl. But coaches scouting you don't care about the end result.

This is true at every level, of course. STATS, LLC's Mitch Tanney points out that, in 2012, from just about every formation, the San Francisco 49ers' run-pass tendencies were the same. "That means they have probably self-scouted quite a bit."

Meanwhile, at the high school level, offensive coordinators also have to reflect from time to time. Rob Paschall, offensive coordinator at Carrollton Creekview High School in Texas and an enlightening presence on Twitter, says that he and his staff are often picking up on cues they are giving opponents. "We'll find that, in this certain situation, we do a certain thing 90 percent of the time.[100]"

Of course, being aware of your own tendencies does not necessarily mean changing them, and knowing your opponent's tendencies doesn't dissuade you from going with your gut. "If you know what you want to do, and it's a good system, you don't care so much about what the defense knows or is aligned in," says Berry.

Berry gives an example from one of ULM's biggest wins of 2012. On the road against a hot Western Kentucky team, his Warhawks fought back from a 14-point, second-half deficit to send the game to overtime with a touchdown in the final seconds of regulation. In the first overtime period, WKU got the ball first and scored in two plays. It took ULM four plays to respond with its own score, but Berry decided to go for two points and the win. On the two-point conversion, "We knew what they were going to do," he says. "When it came down to the play-call, I changed the play. The design was not as effective as the other play, but I had more confidence in the quarterback and our players executing that one play. You're

---

[100] More from Paschall: What kind of halftime adjustments do you make? "It's too late! If you're waiting till halftime to make adjustments, it's too late. You're making adjustments all game. I have three guys up in the box working on very specific things. We have an idea for what the defense might do, and when they do it, we have our answers." But regarding adjustments, "figure out why something didn't work. If it's execution, keep at it. If it's because the opponent has a superior defender who blows it up, don't keep at it."

going to use stats in some degree, but you'll still end up playing your hunches a little bit.[101]"

As was frequently the case in 2012, Berry's hunches were correct. After executing a draw play left for a touchdown on the previous play, lefty quarterback Kolton Browning spun around a blitzing WKU defender, rolled right, and finessed a ball to receiver Rashon Ceaser in the end zone. ULM 43, WKU 42.

Self-scouting is interesting when it comes to teams that use a lot of different formations. In 2012 [102], West Virginia ran about seven percent of its charted plays from a no-back, spread formation, 53 percent with one back in the backfield, 35 percent with two backs in the backfield, and four percent with three backs in what is typically a variation of a diamond formation (one back behind the quarterback, two either even with the quarterback or ahead of him in something like a pistol/flexbone combination). With no backs in the backfield, the Mountaineers, like most teams out of the no-back, almost always threw the ball (86 percent of the time). With one back, they ran 41 percent of the time, with two, they ran 51 percent of the time, and with three, they ran 54 percent.

The success of WVU's run game was inversely correlated to how predictable the run was. Out of the no-back, with everybody expecting pass, the Mountaineers averaged 7.2 yards per rush[103]. With one back, 7.1. With two, 5.1. With three, mostly in power situations, 2.1. Some unpredictability might have helped, but this might have just been the nature of the beast. WVU was potentially just built to succeed with more

---

[101] You will occasionally hear of coaches even trying to plan their spontaneity, a la Diane Chambers in *Cheers*. In-game situations are stressful, man.

[102] West Virginia formation data comes from the eight games charted for the 2012 charting project at Football Study Hall, something described more fully in a future chapter.

[103] WVU also averaged 11.2 yards per pass from the no-back. The Mountaineers were built perfectly for that formation but didn't operate from that look nearly as much as you might have thought.

players lined up wide and not well-equipped to handle short-yardage situations.

In the end, calling a football game becomes a giant game of chess, albeit one in which the pieces have minds of their own (and don't always take directions well), and a third party called luck (bounces, officials, et cetera) can lay waste to even the best-laid plans. As Grobe puts it, "We've got what you do down to a science, but you know we've got it. It's a cat-and-mouse game. It probably boils down to how good your players are." I know what you're going to do, but you know that I know what you're going to do, and I know that you know that I know what you're going to do…

****

Every coach scouts opponents' tendencies, and almost every coach scouts his own. They look at film in much the same way, and they probably look at stats the same. But if you talk to enough coaches, you'll eventually find some unique examples and tendencies.

Gene Stallings broke everything down into "run situations" (first-and-10, second-and-5 or more, et cetera) and "pass situations" (second- or third-and-long). Because teams have different tendencies in such situations – in run situations, the offense has control because of the ability to run or pass, while pass situations shift the odds dramatically in the defense's favor – you have no choice but to coach the game differently[104].

Strategy and play-calling can certainly bleed into special teams, as well. ULM's Berry: "If we know we're facing a kicker who's marginal outside of a certain distance, that will impact

---

[104] When I told him I did something incredibly similar with Football Outsiders, breaking things down in standard downs (first downs, second-and-7 or fewer, third-and-4 or fewer) and passing downs (second-and-8 or more, third-and-5 or more), he corrected me: "No, not downs. Situations." Noted, Coach.

our decision-making. We'll take chances at certain areas of the field that we wouldn't elsewhere."

And perhaps most interestingly of all, Mack Brown initiated a long-term statistical study of what Berry calls "about 70-some-odd variables" to figure out what truly impacts the college game. The study revealed that big plays (and therefore yards per play) were enormous factors, even bigger than expected[105]. Third downs are also vital, while turnover margin might not be quite as impactful as it was once considered to be[106], time of possession is outdated, and plays per game (in both directions) can be quite telling. This study actually led to a change in philosophy for some; perhaps it is worth it to take risks and go for big plays despite the consequences?

The rate of big plays also matters. Stallings: "Saying a guy averages five yards per carry doesn't tell you anything. What percentage are you making at least five yards?" If a running back breaks off a 75-yard run but gains just 15 yards in his next 17 carries, he averaged a healthy five yards per tote, and his team probably lost[107].

****

Stats do have one other positive role to play in a coach's job, by the way. A good coach can use them to prevent his players from overthinking.

At Oklahoma, Trent Ratterree says that coaches would always preach a series of easy mantras for the offense, especially during the Sooners' run of dominance in 2008. And it helped tremendously. "When you're walking down the ramp at the Cotton Bowl, and the whole Texas team is behind you hootin' and hollerin', and the Texas fans are beside you

---

[105] As you'll see, our Football Outsiders research finds the same. It is one of the cornerstones of our work there.

[106] It's still huge.

[107] Here's where the Football Outsiders concept of efficiency, Success Rate, comes into play. It takes both efficiency and explosiveness to win, even if explosiveness is worth a hair more.

cussing and flipping you off, and you walk out and half the stadium's cussing you and half the stadium's rooting for you, you just had to remember certain things. If we run for positive yards, if we don't drop passes, we're going to win. All we've got to do is get that first first down, and we'll score." That probably wasn't *always* true, but it was true enough.

7. The New Box Score

As is typically the case with box scores, the way college football data is presented to us has not changed much through the years. And the changes that have come our way have been glacial.

Table 1 on the following page shows us what the typical newspaper box score looked like for Missouri's 21-14 win over Navy in the 1961 Orange Bowl. That Missouri won with a completion rate of 17 percent (in just six passes) is pretty damn impressive, but it was, to say the least, a little more common for that to happen in 1961. We don't know how many times each team attempted to run the football, but with just 29 total passes, it is safe to say this was your typical 1960s game: Run the ball unless you have to pass. (And since Navy was down for most of the game, it's safe to say the Midshipmen had to pass.) In all, however, this box score features a number of pretty familiar features: yards, first downs, passing line, turnovers, punts, penalty yards.

Table 1: 1961 Orange Bowl box score

	Navy	Missouri
First Downs	9	19
Rushing Yardage	-8	206
Passing Yardage	176	5
Passing	13-23	1-6
Passes Intercepted	1	4
Punts	7-35.4	4-30.5
Fumbles Lost	0	2
Yards Penalized	4	15

Table 2: 1930 Rose Bowl box score

	Pitt	USC
Total Yardage	285	454
"Yards from scrimmage"	199	167
Passing yards	96	297
First downs	10	14
Passing	4-19	8-16
Passes Intercepted	2	4
Avg. Yards for punts	37	40
Yards Penalized	55	65

Table 2 takes a look even further back, to the 1930 Orange Bowl between Southern Cal and Pittsburgh. Other than categorizing rushing yards as "yards from scrimmage," this one is pretty much the same[108]. In a couple of instances, you can also find the per-quarter scoring or the starting lineup, which was a bigger deal in the days of non-platoon football (and can still be found in the extended, official box scores at schools' websites).

Compare this to what we are presented in the basic box score today: first downs (perhaps with third- and fourth-down efficiency), total yards, passing yards, passing line, rushing yards, penalties, turnovers (fumbles and interceptions), time of possession. What is presented to us has barely changed in 80

---

[108] You can certainly find more differences in the recap articles than in the box scores. There was quite a bit more use of terms like "scampered" and "ran unmolested."

years. Think about how much the sport itself has changed in that time. In the 1930 Rose Bowl, the two teams combined to attempt 35 passes (more than I would have thought, actually), completing 34 percent of them for 32.8 yards per completion. Passes were desperate heaves. Hell, 31 years later, Missouri completed one of six pass attempts for five yards and *won*.

The game has changed dramatically since then, but our box score has not. "We continue to fight yesterday's war," says *The Hidden Game of Football's* John Thorn[109]. "We are looking at the game of today and measuring it by the way it used to be."

You have to go back to the pre-World War I days to see any significant differences in the way football data is presented; then, things were basically just presented like a soccer match: lineups, scoring, recap, and that's about it.

"For the most part, I dismiss the box score entirely," says Football Outsiders' Brian Fremeau. "It isn't giving me the data that's relevant to how the game is won. If it's available, I might skip to the drive summary and start there[110]; that gives me the clearest picture for how the game was played."

Now, make no mistake: There is a lot of information featured in the basic box score. And a lot of it is perfectly descriptive. Yardage is, on average, a better and more accurate evaluator of quality than even points or wins, and a lot of important basics like third-down conversions and turnovers are typically covered. The box score could be much, much worse. But it could also be better.

So let's start from scratch. Never mind what we've been presented, never mind basic box score conventions. If we're

---

[109] More from Thorn: Something like Total QBR from ESPN was a "move in the right direction. The NFL passer rating has been declared an abomination for about 35 years. It ignores completion percentages and compares touchdowns to interceptions as equals." It is akin to something like K/9 (strikeouts per nine innings) in baseball, he says. "Creating false ratios, like TD-to-INT – because it's statistical, it creates the illusion that you are measuring something real when you're not."

[110] Regarding the drive summary, Football Outsiders' Matt Hinton says, "Basically, I look at total yardage as 'This is how well you played.' And I use the drive chart to see how you screwed it up."

looking to create the most useful, telling box score possible, what should we include[111]? And how different would the end product actually be?

****

As I interviewed people for this book, I initiated a rather informal, one-question survey: Let's say you are busy watching/attending/covering a certain game, and you miss another pretty big game. You find that Team A beat Team B, 24-17 (or, since this is college football we're talking about, Team A more realistically won, 31-27). You have the basic box score pulled up on your computer. Where does your eye go first to figure out how exactly Team A went about winning this game?

Here were the results, the official poll rankings, so to speak: 1. Turnovers, 2. Total Yards, 3. Third Down Conversions, 4. Yards Per Play, 5. Total Plays (runs and passes), 6. Scoring Summary, 7. Penalties, 8. Pass Efficiency, 9. Fumble Recovery Percentage, 10. Explosive Plays.

Does your list look similar? Do you still look at time of possession? Do you go any further than yards or scores? Do you look at something completely different?

Here are some of my favorite answers from this survey:

Stewart Mandel: "I've come around to yards per play recently. Tempo-adjusted stats are important, and they haven't really caught on yet. On offense, I'm more concerned with yards and efficiency. On defense, I'm more concerned with yards, third-down conversions and explosive plays. For example, Virginia Tech's

---

[111] Note that in the next chapter, we will explore advanced concepts like success rates, leverage, et cetera. They could all play a role in the common box score. But this exercise is intended to solely emphasize the stats we already know and can glean from a play-by-play with relative ease.

defensive numbers were solid in 2012, but they allowed a ton of explosive plays, and it had an impact."

Paul Myerberg: "Go back and look at the win percentage for teams winning turnovers, third downs and total yardage. It has to be close to 100 percent, doesn't it?"

Matt Hinton: "Pass efficiency is reflective of the entire offense. It isn't perfect, but it's one of the better tools we have available."

Holly Anderson: My eyes go toward the weird stuff. Unusual scores in the scoring summary, turnovers … how close were we to something completely different?"

Steven Godfrey: "Older reporters will swear by total offense, by time of possession. That's what they've done their entire lives. My eyes go to places that I know are deceptive. The box score to me is a metaphor for being a reporter in 2012. I'm 31, and in journalism school they still taught us the freaking 'width of type' deals you had when you used printing presses. I had to use all this outdated crap, then teach myself how to do the new stuff."

This list was heartening in many ways in that it zeroes in pretty specifically on the areas advanced analysis tells you are most important. Generally speaking, college football people look at the right things in the box score. Now let's make it easier for them.

Below are some of the categories that absolutely must be accounted for in a new box score.

Tempo and yardage

Godfrey is right that many still refer to time of possession as an important statistic, and for some teams, perhaps it is. But looking at total plays tells you approximately the same story that time of possession does, and it tells it better. Plus, it gives you the denominator for any per-play calculations that follow.

Meanwhile, yardage tells you a lot. Yardage, accompanied by some more general information – total plays, total possessions, yards per play – tells you even more. In 2012 an FBS team playing another FBS team averaged about 404 yards, 74 plays, 5.5 yards per play, and 13 possessions per game. Any major variance from these averages tells you a lot about how a game played out.

Tempo quite obviously affects the way we judge an offense. If you run enough plays, you are simply going to end up with gaudy yardage totals the eyeballs cannot avoid. In 2012 under Sonny Dykes, Louisiana Tech averaged 578 yards per game, but the Bulldogs also attempted an equally astounding 88 plays per game. Their per-play average of 6.58 yards was certainly strong (12th in the country), but it wasn't the best by any means. An even better example: Marshall averaged 534 yards per game in 2012, third in the country. But the Thundering Herd averaged just 5.90 yards per play, which ranked 45th. Their positively absurd pace (90.6 plays per game) boosted their totals tremendously.

Of the 10 teams that averaged the most yards per play, only four ranked in the Top 10 for overall yards per game. Teams like Georgia (7.09 yards per play), Florida State (7.00), Alabama (6.95), Utah State (6.83), UL-Lafayette (6.77), Cincinnati (6.63), and USC (6.60) all ranked 76th or lower in plays per game, which distracted us a bit from their overall efficiency. In particular, Georgia's offense was absolutely devastating, despite the loss of a couple of impact receivers, but the Bulldogs flew under the radar a bit in this regard.

There is a clear, visceral draw to wanting to play fast. Yards and points are fun, yes? But while a particularly high pace can have a cumulative, tiring effect on opposing defenses, it could, at times, have the same effect on your own defense. If your offense runs a lot of plays, of course, your defense will probably face a lot as well. Of the top 10 teams according to plays per game, seven ranked among the bottom 25 teams according to plays per game faced by the defense. Arizona attempted 83.2 plays per game and faced 83.5. Baylor attempted 82.5 and faced 83.1. Meanwhile, a slow pace aided great defenses like Florida State's (the Seminoles faced only 65.9 plays per game) and Alabama's (the Tide faced a nation-low 59.8 plays). It also saved Utah State's defense from further pressure; the Aggies played a host of high-paced offenses like Louisiana Tech, but their own slow pace minimized fatigue.

Pace hurts defenses in another way, too: perception. For years, Big 12 defenses have had to face one high-octane offense after another. Even good defenses in this conference end up with pretty poor yardage totals. In 2012, only two Big 12 defenses ranked in the top 40 for yards per game allowed (TCU was 16th, Texas Tech 38th); that's one more than the conference managed in 2011 (Texas was 11th, and Oklahoma came in next at 55th).

Again, as a whole, yards are a pretty good measurement of team strength. But pace adjustments place everything on an even playing field.

Depending on the space available in the box score, you could also add an Explosive Plays row (and a corresponding Explosive Play Rate figure). You can find quite a few different definitions of that term, from anything over 10 yards to rushes over 12 and passes over 20. This gives you a nice, quick look at both how consistent an offense was (did they derive a good portion of their yardage from one or two big plays?) and how leaky a defense was. We will refrain from doing that in the examples below, but it is certainly an option.

Turnovers

One should never ever forget how random football can be. "Turnovers skew everything," says Stewart Mandel.

As mentioned earlier, I've found that a turnover is typically worth about five points in terms of the field position lost by the offense and the field position gained by the defense In 2012, FBS games saw, on average, about 3.5 turnovers per game; that means that somewhere around 17.5 points per game are being determined by the bounce of a pointy ball.

"You know luck is involved," says the *USA Today*'s Paul Myerberg, "because of those silly blooper reels with 20 guys diving for a bouncing ball." There is almost no skill involved in falling on the ball. You can certainly take steps to ensure you *don't* recover a high percentage of fumbles – if your other offensive players aren't following a play to its conclusion, for instance, you are less likely to have a guy available to fall on the ball – but there is so much randomness in this game no matter how well you coach your team to pursue the ball.

"That's the beauty of it," says Holly Anderson. "It's so wiggly."

It's not just luck, of course. Good ball security can limit the number of fumbles, though it won't prevent them entirely. "The only thing you have any control over is not losing the ball," says Myerberg.

Style plays a role in turnovers as well. In 2012, Houston featured both a flawed (and frequent) passing offense and a ridiculously aggressive defense; the Cougars committed 35 turnovers but forced 31. Their games featured 5.5 turnovers per game. On the flip side, Wisconsin rode a pretty safe offense into battle and couldn't hold on to an interception to save its life. Wisconsin games featured only about 1.9 turnovers per game.

Turnovers are one part skill, two parts luck, and they can change a game. They deserve a front row seat in the new box score. And if you have enough space, they deserve a little more detail than you typically see, as well. We typically get a "Fumbles-Lost" column, signifying the number of fumbles you committed and the number you lost. This is important, as it hints at whether one team was a little bit lucky in terms of fumble recoveries – if there were six fumbles in a game, and one team recovered five, they lucked out a bit. The ball could have bounced any number of ways, but it found their hands more often than it typically would.

There is another aspect of turnover luck, however, that we haven't talked about very much. Play-by-play data tracks both interceptions and what are called "passes broken up." Combined, they make up an overall "passes defensed" number.

On average, interceptions make up around 21 percent of all passes defensed. Just as you should be expected to recover in the neighborhood of 50 percent of your fumbles over a long period of time, you should also expect to regress or progress toward that mark when it comes to your interceptions as a total of overall passes defensed. The long term becomes especially important considering this is college football, and even if you have a ball-hawk defender with particularly sticky hands, he isn't going to be around for more than four years.

So if we're looking at the turnover category for information about both game-turning plays and luck, it would make sense to show you the number of interceptions compared to the overall number of passes defensed[112]. We'll do that below.

Rushing and passing

Obviously we are still going to need a breakout of total yards (and yards per play) into rushing and passing, even if it has been collected since the beginning of time. We will talk about different, more telling ways to categorize plays (into standard downs and passing downs), but for now, rushing and passing will suffice.

---

[112] This also offers you the chance to create a Pass Defense Rate of sorts, looking at the number of opposition passes you got a hand on. It's a nice, quick look at aggression that doesn't really exist anywhere. We don't do nearly enough with pass defense data.

One change, however: Sack yardage really, really needs to count against the passing totals. Sacks are, by definition, not "rushes." They are attempted passes that went awry. Counting them as part of a team's rushing total completely ruins the usefulness of rushing totals.

Take the 2012 Pittsburgh-Cincinnati game, for instance[113]. Pittsburgh lost, 34-10, despite being outgained by just 49 yards (464 to 415). Turnovers played a role in this (Pitt committed two to Cincinnati's none), but so did sacks. Cincinnati brought down statuesque (as in, he tended to move like a statue in the pocket) Pitt quarterback Tino Sunseri six times for 42 yards in losses. On second-and-10 from the Pitt 42 on the Panthers' second drive, Cincinnati's Walter Stewart both sacked Sunseri and stripped him of the ball; the Bearcats recovered at the Pitt 38, setting up a short, easy touchdown drive.

On the next drive, Sunseri was sacked on third-and-3 from the Cincinnati 38, ending a potential scoring drive. Late in the third quarter, with Pitt still somewhat within striking range (they were down, 24-3) and driving, Sunseri took a sack on third-and-7 from the Cincinnati 28, once again ending a potential scoring opportunity.

Sacks played a direct role in Cincinnati's easy win, both in ending a couple of scoring chances for Pittsburgh and creating one for the Bearcats. But the box score said that Pittsburgh rushed 42 times for 137 yards (3.3 yards per carry) and completed 24 of 37 passes for 278 yards, a touchdown, and an interception. That gives you the impression that rushing was the reason Pittsburgh couldn't move the ball; 3.3 yards per rush is pretty bad, while 7.5 yards per pass is perfectly decent. But Pitt's Ray Graham gained 103 yards in 19 carries (granted, 50 came in a single handoff); passing was the problem for the Panthers. Count sack yardage as part of passing, and you end up seeing that Pitt rushed for 5.0 yards

---

[113] You have your choice, really, of Pittsburgh games from 2011-12 with Tino Sunseri at quarterback. He got sacked a *lot*.

per carry (solid) and averaged just 5.5 yards per pass attempt (bad).

One added benefit to moving sacks back into the passing column: You don't have to worry about fans failing to understand it. Sacks are already counted in passing totals in NFL box scores.

Third downs

Third-down conversions are as important as everybody says they are. That said, your third-down conversion rate is usually caused by how well you *set up* third down, not how well you actually performed on it.

In 2012, Nebraska had a perfectly solid third-down offense, though the Cornhuskers faded late in the season in this regard. Midway through the season, they had converted 50 percent of their third downs, good for 19th in the country, but that was based entirely off of their ability to create third-and-short opportunities. After the games of October 6, they had converted 14 of 15 chances on third-and-1, six of seven on third-and-2, and nine of 12 on third-and-3. They were one of just six teams with a conversion rate of 85 percent or higher on third-and-3 or fewer. At the same time, they were below the national average from any other distance. With four to seven yards to go on third down, Nebraska had only converted 31 percent of its opportunities; with more than seven yards to go, the Huskers' conversion rate was a woeful 18 percent. If they didn't get at least seven yards combined on first and second down, they had a minimal chance of converting on third.

Then, you had a team like Washington State. At the same point in time, after October 6, Mike Leach's Cougars had been tremendous on third-and-8 or longer; they had converted 42 percent of their chances on such downs and an even 50 percent with eight to 10 yards to go. But their problems were twofold. First, they weren't that great on third-and-short. On

150

third-and-3 or fewer, they had converted just 44 percent. Second, even if you are a great third-and-long team, your conversion rates still aren't going to be as high, on average, as they would be on third-and-short.

To add proper context to third-down conversions, you have a couple of options. Really, you could go with either yards per play on first down or average yards to go on third down. We'll go with both below. Typically if a team had a good third-down conversion rate, it's because they weren't facing many long third downs. One small, extra piece of information is vital.

Field position

"Starting field position should be a conventional stat," says Matt Hinton, and I agree. It is so important that it gets its own chapter later on in this book. For now, just know that if your average starting field position was in the low 20s, you probably lost. If it was in the high 30s, you probably won. While the way you capitalize on your opportunities matters, the simple fact is, creating more opportunities through field position typically results in more points.

Special teams

This one is space-dependent. Special teams accounts for somewhere between about 10 and 15 percent of a game's outcome. Technically, average starting field position covers a good portion of the kicking and return games, but if there is space allotted, net punting, net kicking, and field goal stats (misses, makes) would be a reasonable addition. Why net punting and kicking? Because in one number, it summarizes both the distance of the kicks and the returns. If a punter averaged 48.0 yards per punt, that's impressive, but if he outkicked his coverage and created a lot of strong return opportunities, then 48.0 doesn't mean a lot. Net yardage is both a strong descriptor and a space-saver.

So what common stats *aren't* we including in this box score?

Not included: First downs

Typical box scores have led off with first downs since, almost literally, the beginning of football. And there is some value in this number – it hints at efficiency in a way that simple yardage (or yards per play) does not. But with the slight expansion of the third-down discussion to include first-down yardage, the first down totals become a little bit redundant. If you've got space, go ahead and include it. But it is not of as much value as what has been listed above.

Not included: Penalties

Generally speaking, penalties just do not correlate strongly to wins and losses. If we were to categorize penalties as either procedural or aggressive, we could get somewhere. Penalties like false starts are typically inexcusable to coaches, but a personal foul here and there signifies a level of aggressiveness that coaches are probably okay with encouraging.

Not included: Time of possession

Again, this can still be worthwhile for specific types of teams. But you get what you need to know from total plays. This just occupies real estate that could instead be filled by more useful numbers.

We aren't making drastic changes here – apparently we did a reasonably decent job of figuring out what was important almost a century ago – but there are enough changes involved that we should take a look at how this new box score takes shape.

Here is a look at the 2012 national title game using a new format.

Table 3: New Box Score – 2012 BCS Championship (Alabama 42, Notre Dame 14)			
		Alabama	Notre Dame
Basics	Possessions	10	11
	Plays	73	55
	Yards	529	302
	Yards/Play	7.2	5.5
	Yards/Possession	52.9	27.5
Rushing	Rushes	45	17
	Rushing Yards	265	48
	Yards/Carry	5.9	2.8
Passing	Comp-Att-Int	20-28-0	21-36-1
	Passing Yards	264	270
	Sacked-Yards	0-0	2-16
	Net Passing Yards	264	254
	Yards/Attempt	9.4	6.7
	Yards/Completion	13.2	12.9
Turnovers	Total Turnovers	0	1
	Fumbles-Lost	0-0	1-0
	Total Fumbles-Recovered	1-0	1-1
	Int-Passes Defensed	0-1	1-5
3rd Downs	3rd Down Conversions	8-of-13	2-of-8
	Avg. Yards To Go	5.8	7.8
	Avg. 1st Down Gain	5.8	4.5
4th Downs	4th Down Conversions	1-of-1	0-of-1
Field Position	Avg. Starting F.P.	23.2	19.5
Special Teams	Punts-Net Yards/Punt	4-43.8	5-42.6
	Kickoffs-Net Yds/Kickoff	7-45.9	3-46.0
	Field Goals	0-0	0-0

The typical box score at ESPN.com and similar sites features about 15 rows of data. This features just 26 and tells you almost everything you need to know about how a given game played out. You could easily pare it down to 15 by removing some of the lower-priority items: special teams (not a feature of the ESPN box scores), the rate measures (yards per play, yards per possession, yards per carry, yards per pass attempt and completion), fourth downs (of which there are rarely many), and the last two lines in the Turnovers section.

Table 4: Abbreviated New Box Score – 2012 BCS Championship			
		Alabama	Notre Dame
Basics	Possessions	10	11
	Plays	73	55
	Yards	529	302
Rushing	Rushes	45	17
	Rushing Yards	265	48
Passing	Comp-Att-Int	20-28-0	21-36-1
	Passing Yards	264	270
	Sacked-Yards	0-0	2-16
	Net Passing Yards	264	254
Turnovers	Total Turnovers	0	1
	Fumbles-Lost	0-0	1-0
3rd Downs	3rd Down Conversions	8-of-13	2-of-8
	Avg. Yards To Go	5.8	7.8
	Avg. 1st Down Gain	5.8	4.5
Field Position	Avg. Starting F.P.	23.2	19.5

When accompanied with the typical scoring summary and per-quarter scoring breakout, this tells you just about everything you truly need to know about the way this game played out. With the two sacks credited to the passing game, you see that Notre Dame averaged fewer than seven yards per pass attempt, that Notre Dame's average third down was a third-and-long, that the field position battle was a virtual draw (just imagine what might have happened had Alabama won that category, too), and that neither team was particularly lucky or unlucky in the turnover battle.

154

Of course, you expect relatively complete domination when you have a 42-14 final score. Statistically speaking, we probably don't need much clarification when it comes to understanding how Alabama beat the Irish. So let's look at other recent BCS title games, along with a wildcard from the 2012 season.

Table 5: New Box Score – 2011 BCS Championship (Alabama 21, LSU 0)		Alabama	LSU
Basics	Possessions	12	11
	Plays	69	44
	Yards	384	92
	Yards/Play	5.6	2.1
	Yards/Possession	32.0	8.4
Rushing	Rushes	33	23
	Rushing Yards	159	65
	Yards/Carry	4.8	2.8
Passing	Comp-Att-Int	23-34-0	11-17-1
	Passing Yards	234	53
	Sacked-Yards	2-9	4-26
	Net Passing Yards	225	27
	Yards/Attempt	6.3	1.4
	Yards/Completion	10.2	4.8
Turnovers	Total Turnovers	0	2
	Fumbles-Lost	0-0	3-1
	Total Fumbles-Recovered	3-1	3-2
	Int-Passes Defensed	0-4	1-2
3rd Downs	3rd Down Conversions	3-of-14	2-of-12
	Avg. Yards To Go	5.8	7.1
	Avg. 1st Down Gain	6.5	3.1
4th Downs	4th Down Conversions	2-of-2	0-of-1
Field Position	Avg. Starting F.P.	36.9	24.5
Special Teams	Punts-Net Yards/Punt	3-37.3	9-38.2
	Kickoffs-Net Yds/Kickoff	6-45.8	1-38.0
	Field Goals	5-7	0-0

Perhaps we should just skip the Alabama games? This one, as with Alabama-Notre Dame, was statistical domination.

Alabama's offense was reasonably similar in its effectiveness (5.6 yards per play in 2011's title game, 5.9 in 2012's), but LSU's offense was 25 percent less effective than Notre Dame's (2.1 yards per play to 2.8).

We also see that Alabama's biggest advantage came on first downs, where the Crimson Tide were consistently able to set up second-and-short for itself while almost always creating second-and-long for LSU. This was one of the focal points of the Bama game plan; quarterback A.J. McCarron consistently threw short, play-action passes to tight ends to keep LSU's aggressive defense on its heels. While Alabama scored just one touchdown and pretty consistently stalled out before the end zone (despite reasonably favorable yardage on third downs, the Tide were barely able to convert against the nasty LSU D), the first-down yardage helped to tilt the field in Alabama's favor. Starting field position, combined with Alabama's impenetrable defense, led to something truly startling: Of LSU's 44 plays (an incredibly low total), only four took place on Alabama's side of the 50. All four of those plays took place on one drive midway through the fourth quarter, and after advancing to the Alabama 32, LSU was pushed back to midfield and lost a fumble.

Table 6: New Box Score – 2010 BCS Championship (Auburn 22, Oregon 19)		Auburn	Oregon
Basics	Possessions	13	12
	Plays	85	73
	Yards	519	449
	Yards/Play	6.1	6.2
	Yards/Possession	39.9	37.4
Rushing	Rushes	48	30
	Rushing Yards	267	84
	Yards/Carry	5.6	2.8
Passing	Comp-Att-Int	20-35-1	28-41-2
	Passing Yards	265	374
	Sacked-Yards	2-9	2-13
	Net Passing Yards	256	361
	Yards/Attempt	6.9	8.4
	Yards/Completion	13.3	13.4
Turnovers	Total Turnovers	2	2
	Fumbles-Lost	2-1	1-0
	Total Fumbles-Recovered	3-1	3-2
	Int-Passes Defensed	1-4	2-6
3rd Downs	3rd Down Conversions	9-of-17	5-of-15
	Avg. Yards To Go	5.6	6.7
	Avg. 1st Down Gain	6.9	7.7
4th Downs	4th Down Conversions	0-of-1	2-of-3
Field Position	Avg. Starting F.P.	24.2	23.2
Special Teams	Punts-Net Yards/Punt	5-39.2	5-32.8
	Kickoffs-Net Yds/Kickoff	4-53.8	5-44.6
	Field Goals	2-2	1-1

This game gives us a look at what this box score can tell us about an actually *close* game. The two teams could barely separate from each other overall, and it shows throughout, from yardage to turnovers to field position.

This box score also shows us some limitations with the format. You get the impression that Oregon's offense was positively dominant on first downs, averaging nearly eight yards per play. But most of the Ducks' first-down yardage came on two plays: an 81-yard pass to Jeff Maehl and a 43-

yard pass to Lavasier Tuinei. Take those two plays away, and Oregon averaged a paltry 4.1 yards on first-down plays. This shows you where an additional first-down efficiency measure like Success Rate (which we will explore in the next chapter) can be of use.

That said, you still get a really good feel for how this game played out. It was close throughout, with neither team leading by more than eight points at any point, and the only separation Auburn was able to build came on third downs. Despite facing similar to-go yardage on such downs, the Tigers converted quite well; this, combined with Auburn's solid special teams advantage (Auburn averaged 6.4 more net yards per punt and 9.2 more net yards per kickoff), gave Auburn more margin for error.

For a good number of games, you can glean most of what you need to know simply from yardage and points. Most college football games aren't that close. But occasionally you come across something truly baffling. This was certainly the case on October 20, 2012, when Florida gained a total of just 183 yards and beat a highly-ranked South Carolina team by 33 points. That is very, very difficult to do, and the typical box score only begins to tell you how that may have happened.

		Florida	S.C.
Basics	Possessions	15	13
	Plays	65	66
	Yards	183	191
	Yards/Play	2.8	2.9
	Yards/Possession	12.2	14.7
Rushing	Rushes	45	22
	Rushing Yards	114	59
	Yards/Carry	2.5	2.7
Passing	Comp-Att-Int	12-17-0	17-40-1
	Passing Yards	94	155
	Sacked-Yards	3-25	4-23
	Net Passing Yards	69	132
	Yards/Attempt	3.5	3.0
	Yards/Completion	7.8	9.1
Turnovers	Total Turnovers	0	4
	Fumbles-Lost	0-0	4-3
	Total Fumbles-Recovered	4-3	4-1
	Int-Passes Defensed	0-2	1-8
3rd Downs	3rd Down Conversions	7-of-16	3-of-14
	Avg. Yards To Go	9.3	8.7
	Avg. 1st Down Gain	2.2	2.9
4th Downs	4th Down Conversions	0-of-0	0-of-0
Field Position	Avg. Starting F.P.	53.8	20.8
Special Teams	Punts-Net Yards/Punt	7-50.4	7-36.9
	Kickoffs-Net Yds/Kickoff	8-43.8	2-14.5
	Field Goals	1-1	3-4

Table 6: New Box Score – 2012 South Carolina at Florida (Florida 44, South Carolina 11)

The first thing you notice when something is this out of whack is turnovers, and South Carolina had quite a few. The Gamecocks turned the ball over four times to Florida's zero; you're almost never going to win a game with a minus-4 differential. Still, how exactly did Florida gain 183 yards and score 44 points? Field position. You will almost never see a team with a bigger field position advantage than what Florida derived here. The Gators began six of 15 drives in South

Carolina territory and three inside the Gamecocks' 12-yard line. They scored on touchdown drives of three plays and two yards, two plays and one yard, and three plays and 11 yards.

If you are generating 33 extra yards per possession in the field position battle, you are almost certainly going to win big, even if your offense is barely able to move the ball. Field position and turnovers earned Florida an unlikely, easy win. Hell, it nearly single-handedly earned Florida an 11-1 regular season record, as well.

****

Again, it is encouraging to see that the box score we have been leaning on for nearly a century is at least reasonably helpful; and it is great that the people who need to understand the box score the most – the sport's writers and analysts – look at the right things within the traditional box score. But with some relatively minor, easy-to-understand changes, we can add more dimension, more descriptiveness, and more usefulness to the box score.

8. Advanced Stats 101

"So much of modern statistical writing, in baseball and football both, is unreadable."

— John Thorn

I have attended two Sloan Sports Analytics Conferences, and I have already heard the same refrain an infinite number of times: Communication is key. Depending on who you are trying to communicate with, be it executives, coaches, or fans, you have to figure out how to describe and deliver your point – your measure, your theory, your Player-A-versus-Player-B conclusion – with extreme clarity. And make no mistake: That is pretty damn difficult. It is also pretty easy to mock. An SB Nation colleague of mine, Andrew Sharp (now at Grantland), was also in attendance at Sloan in 2013, and he got a kick out of what skeptics could see as a "We're never wrong, we just don't communicate the idea well enough" approach.

Since the moment I began to tinker with numbers and come up with my own measures in the summer of 2007, I have fought the communication issue. There is difficulty in communicating sometimes complicated ideas in a couple of succinct sentences; plus, there is the inherent language barrier between English and Stat. Sometimes you come across somebody who simply doesn't want to understand what you are attempting to explain and never will.

Though this book obviously isn't meant to discuss only stats, I felt it was important to talk about the things we've done with advanced stats in college football to date. Instead of simply rehashing old Football Outsiders columns, however, to talk about where we are with advanced stats in the sport of football right now, let's try a different approach. Let's assume the role of a coach looking to improve his scouting and self-scouting abilities. What would he need to know[114]?

****

The Basics

Let's start by talking about the principles of the advanced stats universe. What are some of the concepts that lead us to (perhaps arrogantly) call our stats "advanced?" How do these numbers differ from the yards-per-game and third-down-percentage world in which we are used to living? Coaches know to use numbers, but if they were to dive into these, what are some of the concepts they might need to

---

[114] The stats discussed below are mostly my own. I hope you enjoy them and find them useful, but it bears mentioning that quite a few others have taken the college football stat mantel and run with it in the last few years. Brian Fremeau at Football Outsiders has done lovely things with drive data and visualization. Brett Thiessen, who goes by "The Mathlete" at Brian Cook's MGoBlog Michigan site, has established a cool win probability model (one that can give us a look at the plays that most directly influence the probability of a team winning a given game), and Justin at Tempo Free Gridiron is developing his own, similar model. Ed Feng at The Power Rank is great from a visualization standpoint (and his picks are better than mine, I'm pretty sure). Et cetera. There are quite a few of us out there, pecking away in Excel (or something more advanced), and we aren't that hard to find. Googling "advanced college football stats" will produce far more results now than it did when I tried that six years ago.

understand ahead of time? Here are some of the basics (and obstacles).

Rates

Over the past few seasons, as teams like Oklahoma, Oregon, Houston, and Baylor have found great success in running teams ragged with no-huddle attacks, the concept of pace has become more well-known, even if it has a long way to go in terms of overall acceptance. For decades, we have evaluated baseball pitchers on wins, basketball teams on points per game, and college football teams on points or yards per game. We do it because it is easy, and because big numbers are sexy, even though they sometimes lead us to awkward conclusions.

In 2012, Houston averaged 3.02 plays per minute of possession, and Oregon averaged 2.83. At the same time, Alabama averaged just 2.02, and Navy averaged 2.07. This adds up. Think about if both Houston and Navy had finished a game with exactly 30 minutes of possession time. On average that would result in about 91 plays for Houston and 62 for Navy. If both teams averaged 5.0 yards per play, then Houston would have gained around 450 total yards, Navy 310. Houston gets credit for gaudy totals (and its opponent gets dinged for giving up a lot of yards), while Navy's totals relegate it to the middle of the per-game yardage totals.

If you are looking for an accurate method for evaluating an offense or defense, then, you absolutely must use per-play, or at least per-possession, rates instead of totals.

This has begun to catch on more in a sport like basketball, where pace adjustments and per-possession averages are becoming commonplace. In football, though, we are still a bit behind. Even though we know what pace can do to yardage totals, we are still rather distracted by big, shiny numbers.

Rates are perhaps even more important when breaking out offensive or defensive stats by run and pass. Teams that are ahead are almost guaranteed to run more and face more passes; teams that are behind a lot are going to pass more than they intended to and face a lot of rushes. A Big 12 team is probably going to pass more (and face more passes) than a service academy, or even a team from the Big Ten. That's just how the game goes, and we frequently get distracted by this[115].

This bias shows up most with the passing stats. Every year, we hear about how "BCS Conference Team A's pass defense has been a major liability, they rank [some awful ranking] in pass defense!" In 2008, amid a spread offense explosion, Oklahoma ranked 99th in passing yards allowed per game, and Texas ranked 104th. This was seen as a major liability for each team.

Meanwhile, New Mexico State ranked third that season, and Tulane ranked 14th. Whose pass defense was actually better, that of a Texas team that nearly made the national title game, or that of a New Mexico State team that went 3-9? Precisely[116].

Opponent Adjustments

Most advanced stats pit output versus expected output in some way. There are countless ways of gauging expected output, but it is an outright necessity because, to put it simply, it matters who you play.

In college football, schedule strength differs dramatically, and you really need to account for that in some

---

[115] On the flipside, teams that are either ahead or in the Big 12 (or both) are all but guaranteed to look great in terms of rushing yards allowed per game, not only because teams are attempting a lot of passes, but also because sacks in college football count toward rushing yardage totals.

[116] By the way, in 2009, the No. 1 team according to passing yards allowed per game was 0-12 Eastern Michigan. Yes, Pass Efficiency defense is a step in the right direction compared to passing yards per game, but even that measure fails to take opponent into account.

way. In a previous chapter, Ball State head coach Pete Lembo talked about keeping a list of teams' schedules on his desk. That's the right idea, though schedule adjustments are one of the tenets of advanced stats.

You have probably gotten used to saying "Yeah, but..." when looking at gaudy offensive totals. In 2012, the top five teams according to yards per game were Louisiana Tech, Baylor, Texas A&M, Oklahoma State, and Oregon. Marshall came in sixth, Nevada eighth, and Troy 11th.

You look at this list and immediately say, "Yeah, but Louisiana Tech's, Marshall's, and Troy's schedules were much weaker, so their offense probably wasn't as good as Baylor's or Texas A&M's." You also probably say, "Yeah, but A&M did that in the SEC West; they should get extra credit for that," and rank A&M first in your mind even if they were third overall.

Opponent adjustments do the yeah-butting for you. We will soon talk about the Offensive F/+ rankings, what they are and what they mean; well, in this schedule- and pace-adjusted measure, the top five offenses in 2012 were Texas A&M, Alabama, Baylor, Georgia, and Oregon. Louisiana Tech was 14th, Nevada 30th, Marshall 31st, and Troy 53rd[117]. If you play weak opponents and operate at as fast a pace as you can maintain, you are going to end up gaining a lot of yards. Adjusting for those things gives us a much, much more accurate view of quality.

For most of my own measures, I have, as a nod to the baseball stats that influenced me, chosen to indicate opponent adjustments with a "+." For instance, we will define the S&P concept below. S&P itself is raw and unadjusted for opponent; S&P+, however, is adjusted.

---

[117] While we're at it, let's go back to those 2008 pass defense rankings referenced above. When adjusting for pace and opponent, Oklahoma's pass defense ranked sixth in the country in Passing S&P+, Texas ranked fifth, Tulane ranked 63rd, and New Mexico State ranked 75th.

Garbage Time Adjustments

A game changes when the score is out of reach. The winning team starts to run the ball a lot more, the losing team probably goes all-in on the pass (or gives up), and eventually the second- or third-stringers enter a game. It's called "garbage time" because the stats produced for that period in the game are basically, yes, garbage. The goal of the game for one team has changed from winning to making the game end as quickly as possible.

If you are looking at per-play or per-drive rates for a game, instead of simply the final point and yardage totals, you can create an even more effective measure by removing garbage time from the equation altogether[118]. The game is, in effect, over, and what happens after garbage time begins is no longer truly evaluative of the teams at hand. If you are leading 35-0 heading into the fourth quarter, your backups give up three quick touchdowns to your opponent's starters, and the game ends at 35-21, then the final score is in no way indicative of what happened when your starters took the field against theirs. Again, you might know to "Yeah, but..." this in your head; but a good measure will do that for you.

Outliers

Garbage time and its effects have led to what has long been a major complaint of mine in regard to the BCS

---

[118] We all have different methods of garbage time adjustment, and really, as long as the logic behind them is sound, we are more or less all correct in our own methods. Here's mine: I eliminate all plays and possessions in which the scoring margin is higher than 28 points in the first quarter, 24 in the second, 21 in the third, and 16 in the fourth. These are pretty aggressive; if you jump out to a 35-0 lead in the first quarter, you still probably won't put in your backups until the second half. You also probably won't put in your backups if you're up by only 17 in the fourth quarter. But these are the numbers that resulted in the strongest correlation between my measures and strong prediction/evaluation. Loosening up these requirements gave me a less effective measure.

standings. In order to solve an abstract problem in the BCS formulas, we created a concrete one.

The original version of the BCS formula was odd and overthought but, in comparison to the current-day formula, rather effective. The original formula consisted of an average of the AP and *USA Today* polls, an average of the Jeff Sagarin, Anderson & Hester, and *New York Times* computer rankings, a strength-of-schedule figure provided by the NCAA, and a losses penalty. After the first season, more computer rankings were added: Richard Billingsley's, Richard Dunkel's, Kenneth Massey's, David Rothman's, and the Scripps Howard rankings.

Now, the strength-of-schedule component was redundant, as the computer rankings were almost certainly taking that into account in some way. And some of the computer rankings involved are relatively sketchy in their methods. Plus, the losses penalty was probably not entirely necessary but was at least an acceptable response to the fact that a lot of computer formulas could conceivably rank a two-loss team with a great schedule ahead of an undefeated team with a terrible schedule.

Still, considering the sport had never used something like this before, the people in charge of the BCS rankings went with a method that was a lot more intriguing than simply averaging the human polls with some sort of RPI-esque figure[119].

In the 2000 season, the BCS rankings produced a result a lot of people disliked: It chose Florida State over Miami. The Seminoles began the season second in the country and finished 11-1, but their lone loss had come on the road, 27-24, to a

---

[119] The RPI is a computer rankings system championed by Jerry Palm for use in college basketball. Its formula is transparent – 25 percent of your rating is derived from your win percentage, 50 percent is from your opponents' combined win percentage, and 25 percent is from *their* opponents' combined win percentage – and it has become well-accepted in the college basketball universe; it is also not predictive in any way and provides little more than a resume-at-a-glance look at a given team. Granted, it is also probably more effective than a couple of the computers used in the BCS model.

Miami team that *also* finished the season with a single loss (34-29 at then-No. 15 Washington). The Hurricanes had been No. 2 in the AP polls, behind only undefeated No. 1 Oklahoma, since early November, but the computer rankings boosted Florida State, No. 3 in the polls, ahead of them. Five of the chosen formulas – Dunkel, Massey, the *New York Times*, Sagarin, and Scripps Howard – had FSU ranked No. 1. *"This cannot be right,"* said an outraged American populace (and media) to these results, especially after Oklahoma beat Florida State, 13-2, to win the national title. "Miami beat Florida State, therefore Miami was better!" Changes quickly followed.

The *New York Times* and Dunkel rankings were scrapped in favor of Peter Wolfe's formula and the Colley Matrix. Why? Because the BCS had begun to decide that rankings that include margin of victory should be marginalized[120]; we don't know if the results of 2000 played directly into this, but it bears mentioning that Florida State had beaten teams by scores of 63-14 (North Carolina), 59-7 (at Maryland), 58-14 (at No. 21 N.C. State), 54-7 (No. 10 Clemson), and 30-7 (No. 4 Florida). We were encouraging teams to run up the score, and that was unsporting! We must not reward bullies! Scripps Howard and Rothman were dumped a year later for the same reason. To remain in the mix, Jeff Sagarin had to produce a new, less accurate set of rankings that eliminated margin of victory.

Look at those scores again, by the way. Florida State had beaten the No. 10 team in the country by 47 and the No. 21 team (on the road) by 44. That is damn impressive, indicative of a great team. It is sometimes easy to mock the process-versus-outcome mantra, but let's review what happened here: Because of an outcome that didn't feel right to us, we changed the process and eliminated one of the most telling pieces of basic information we have.

---

[120] The other change was sensible if perhaps unnecessary: A 'quality win' component was added. If you beat a Top 15 team in the BCS standings, you got bonus points.

In 2003, the BCS standings produced a matchup of LSU and Oklahoma in the title game. USC, No. 1 in the polls but third in the computer rankings because of a weaker strength of schedule, was left out. *"This cannot be right,"* said an outraged American populace (and media), and changes quickly followed. This time, the (intentionally less-accurate) computer rankings were further marginalized, given less weight in favor of human polls.

In the BCS era, every time the computers spit out a ranking the humans don't like, the humans minimize the effect of the computers in the BCS rankings. If that was going to be the case, it is difficult to find justification for using computers at all. In 2006, UC Irvine professor Hal S. Stern called for a boycott of the BCS from the statistical community. Bill James agreed, calling the BCS' formula "nonsense math."

In the grand scheme of things, communication between a numbers person and a chosen audience is key. But so is the simple fact that numbers reach conclusions that often seem counter-intuitive. We don't tend to react well to this.

As mentioned previously, in 2011, the Football Outsiders F/+ rankings placed an 8-5 Notre Dame team at 13th overall, just ahead of 10-4 Georgia, and had 7-6 Texas A&M – a team that collapsed down the stretch of games and blew second-half leads in nearly every loss – at 15th, ahead of an 11-2 Arkansas team that had taken the Aggies down, via late comeback, on October 1. Our numbers drew the conclusion that both Texas A&M and Notre Dame were both built on a rock-solid foundation, but that some combination of bad luck and untimely poor play had held them back.

When you are breaking things down at a per-drive or per-play level, instead of simply looking at results and yardage, you are going to find that results sometimes don't give you an accurate view of quality. If Team A has a 1-in-10 chance of beating Team B, then that team is going to win 10 percent of the games between the two teams even though Team B is, on average, the much better team. For Texas A&M and Notre

Dame, luck and timing were not on their side; the two teams combined to go 4-8 in games decided by one possession and 11-3 in games decided by more.

In 2012, luck turned a bit. The two teams went 8-2 in one-possession games and 15-1 in games decided by more. Both the Aggies and Fighting Irish truly got better with younger quarterbacks, deeper squads, and in A&M's case, a new head coach. A&M went 11-2 and finished fifth in the final AP poll, and Notre Dame went 12-1 and finished fourth after losing to Alabama in the BCS title game. But their improvement was not as drastic on paper as it seemed in the win column. The two teams shored up some weaknesses and were kissed by some good luck this time around; but Notre Dame only improved from 13th to seventh in the F/+ rankings, while A&M improved from 15th to third.

The numbers told us that both Texas A&M and Notre Dame were hinting at greatness in 2011; in 2012, both teams proved it. This was a solid example of process versus outcome. The process for determining our 2011 rankings was sound (which, to an extent, was proven the next year), even if the immediate outcomes seemed odd. But can you imagine if the F/+ rankings had been a part of the BCS standings? Let's put it this way: "Notre Dame and Texas A&M being ranked as high as they were in 2011 would have disqualified F/+ from ever being used by the BCS," says my Outsiders colleague Brian Fremeau. We use numbers, in part, to see which pieces of conventional wisdom are faulty; but if the numbers stray from conventional wisdom, they are often rebuffed for that very reason.

From a conventional wisdom perspective, then, nothing is more difficult for computers to overcome than the transitive property, the simple rule that says if Team A beats Team B, Team A is better than Team B. It makes perfect sense that we would lean on this from a logic perspective; it is clearly, infinitely easier to compare two teams when they're on the same field at the same time. When they are playing each other, we don't find ourselves thinking "If these two teams played 10 times, Team B would probably win seven," so much as we think "Team A is winning. Team A is better."

"Head-to-head results are terribly overrated," says Football Outsiders' Matt Hinton. "Look at Georgia and Florida in 2012. Georgia beat Florida, but Florida was more consistently strong.[121]" Computer rankings look at every game each team has played. Maybe they give different weights to different games; if you wanted to put heavier emphasis on games against better teams, or if you wanted to add a recency factor and weight later games more heavily, then you could pretty easily come up with justification for doing so. But you're still not going to give one specific game all of the weight.

In our hearts, we know that the transitive property doesn't really tell us much. In 2012, Alabama beat LSU, LSU beat Texas A&M, and Texas A&M beat Alabama. Washington beat Stanford, Stanford beat Oregon, and Oregon massacred Washington. South Carolina whipped Georgia, Georgia beat Florida, and Florida whipped South Carolina. But when two teams are really close together in the polls, humans are going to weight a head-to-head matchup much stronger than computers do. Good analytics and opponent adjustments can give us a better way of judging teams based on a full, 12- or 13-game schedule. But our lyin' eyes are going to disagree sometimes, and those numbers can just be so damned anti-social…

Scouting

In 1962, Steve Belichick published *Football Scouting Methods*, one of the seminal books for the wonky side of the football world. Belichick is probably known best for the accomplishments of his son, Bill, a three-time Super Bowl champion as the head coach of the New England Patriots. But

<hr/>

[121] Florida ranked fourth in the season-ending F/+ rankings; Georgia, propelled by a late surge, finished sixth.

Steve was a bit of a scouting savant; he bounced around from job to job following the end of World War II – he was the head coach at Hiram College for three years and a backfield coach for Vanderbilt for four years and North Carolina for three. But beginning in 1956, he began a long tenure as a scout for Navy. His son was famously helping him analyze film starting at the age of 10, but *Football Scouting Methods* would more or less immortalize him among football coaches.

Football Scouting Methods outlines the job of a scout, provides examples of charting worksheets, teaches you how to understand what defense a team is running (and how to understand the role of each position on the field), and goes into great detail about pulling together a scouting report on both sides of the ball. For anybody looking to better understand both the game of football and the job of a scout, this book is invaluable.

The work of a scout in this regard can never be replaced. It can, however, be enhanced. As discussed earlier, the numbers can help in any number of ways. You can find answers to questions your scouting process has unearthed, find new, better questions to ask, set the table with an at-a-glance view of your opponent on Sunday, and evaluate yourself after each game and season. At this point, a lot of coaches understand this, and some are perhaps even willing to dip a toe into the pool of advanced stats, at least if the concepts are both intuitive and clearly communicated. So let's talk about where we are in terms of football stats, and how it can help a given team in its scouting process.

In chatting with coaches, I found some common, and pretty obvious, themes when it came to the statistics they most commonly track. A given coach's list was likely to include some combination of explosiveness stats (i.e. yards or yards per play), efficiency stats (first downs, et al), third-down conversion rates, and turnovers. Some coaches go much further down Gene Stallings Boulevard than others, but if they are looking at numbers, they are looking at the ones that give them information about the above categories. Leaving turnovers out of the discussion for now[122], let's use those as a jumping-off point.

Explosiveness[123]

EqPts Per Play (PPP): An explosiveness measure derived from determining the equivalent point value of every yard line and, therefore, every play of a given game. Each yard line is given a point value based on the average number of net points a team can expect to gain from that spot on the field.

As referenced in an earlier chapter, Mack Brown once organized a statistical study of common variables. "It was about a 10-year study," UL-Monroe head coach Todd Berry tells me. "He took 70-some-odd variables to see what truly impacted the college game. The No. 1 thing in his study was explosion plays. That had the highest correlation between winning and losing. We had to go back and redraw some boundaries because of the spread offenses and the up-and-down nature of the game."

Coaches have caught on through the years: It is really difficult to sustain a drive over the course of 10, 12 or 14 plays. It is doubly difficult when you are relying on players between 18-22 years old to go that many plays without making a drive-killing mistake. The bend-don't-break defense is viable because the more plays you can force an offense to attempt, the more likely the offense is to eventually trip up.

Mack Brown's study was correct. Big plays are the most important single thing in college football. Make more big plays than your opponent (however you go about defining that), and you are probably going to win. From an advanced stats

---

[122] It's difficult to statistically "scout" turnovers much, other than looking at the frequency with which teams are breaking up passes (and how) or fumbling.

[123] These definitions were pulled from two websites: Football Outsiders and Football Study Hall.

perspective, the best measure I have derived for evaluating explosiveness is PPP, as defined above. EqPts Per Play takes the easy-to-understand yards-per-play concept and adjusts it based on expected points.

The idea behind EqPts ("Equivalent Points") is easy: For each yard line on the field, you can assign a point value based on your criteria of choice. The authors of the *Hidden Game of Football* used the concept of "the next scorer," as in which team would score next when one team had the ball at a given yard line. For the college game, I have found accuracy in looking simply at the average number of points a team is likely to score on a drive from a given yard line, and the average number of points its opponent is likely to score on the next one. So if you have the ball at your 1-yard line, your opponent is more likely to score on its next drive (a punt and a short field might lead to points) than you are on this one, so the net point value of the 1 is negative.

"The net points in *Hidden Game* were based as much in the 1910 view of field position as anything else," says co-author John Thorn, "the idea that the changes in possession were multiple, and a given yard line was not worth simply whatever it was worth on that drive." For my own use, I tweaked that theory based on the logic that teams score a lot more points in college football in 2013, and the return-on-investment for a given yard line doesn't take very long to present itself.

Here was the resulting table for net point values[124]:

---

[124] One odd finding: I found more accuracy simply using a single point total for each yard line even though common sense would suggest that taking down and distance into account would make things even more telling. First-and-10 from your 1 is likely to produce a more positive outcome than third-and-15 from your 1, right? But the extremes in point values in this method led to some extreme outliers. Keeping things simple, in this case, was both easier and more accurate.

Table 1: Equivalent Net Point Values							
Yard Line	Net Pts.	Yard Line	Net Pts.	Yard Line	Net Pts.	Yard Line	Net Pts.
1	-1.39	26	0.08	51	2.05	76	4.52
2	-1.34	27	0.15	52	2.14	77	4.63
3	-1.29	28	0.22	53	2.23	78	4.74
4	-1.24	29	0.29	54	2.32	79	4.85
5	-1.19	30	0.36	55	2.41	80	4.96
6	-1.13	31	0.44	56	2.51	81	5.08
7	-1.08	32	0.51	57	2.60	82	5.19
8	-1.03	33	0.58	58	2.69	83	5.30
9	-0.97	34	0.66	59	2.79	84	5.42
10	-0.92	35	0.73	60	2.88	85	5.53
11	-0.86	36	0.81	61	2.98	86	5.65
12	-0.80	37	0.89	62	3.08	87	5.77
13	-0.75	38	0.96	63	3.17	88	5.88
14	-0.69	39	1.04	64	3.27	89	6.00
15	-0.63	40	1.12	65	3.37	90	6.12
16	-0.57	41	1.20	66	3.47	91	6.24
17	-0.51	42	1.28	67	3.57	92	6.36
18	-0.44	43	1.37	68	3.68	93	6.49
19	-0.38	44	1.45	69	3.78	94	6.61
20	-0.32	45	1.53	70	3.88	95	6.73
21	-0.25	46	1.62	71	3.99	96	6.86
22	-0.19	47	1.70	72	4.09	97	6.98
23	-0.12	48	1.79	73	4.20	98	7.11
24	-0.05	49	1.88	74	4.31	99	7.24
25	0.01	50	1.96	75	4.41	100	7.36

You'll notice that the net values go pretty far beyond seven points at the end of the field. This is simply based on the fact that I used a regression equation to come up with these values. For years, I used averages, and it resulted in some odd bumps in the field that I felt were inaccurate and in need of smoothing. Using this setup produces the most accurate results I could find, even if the thought of a 99-yard touchdown pass actually being worth 8.75 points a little off-putting.

As you can see, the slope changes as you advance down the field. A one-yard gain is worth just 0.05 to 0.06 equivalent points when you are pinned inside your 20, but the same gain is worth twice that when you have advanced inside your opponent's 20. So basically, the PPP concept divvies out extra credit for gaining yards in the areas of the field where it is tougher to gain yards.

Using PPP, the definition of "explosiveness" changes as you get closer to the end zone. Equivalent points tells us that gaining 18 yards from your 1 to your 19 (which is worth about 1.01 equivalent points, subtracting the point value of the 19 from the point value of the 1) is worth about the same as gaining nine yards from your opponent's 19 to its 10 (1.04).

Points per play takes everything you get from yards per play and adds an extra, relevant variable. It is a wonderfully useful measure for what is one of the most important concepts in college football. Of course, per-play measures can be a little bit misleading. If you gain 80 yards in one play and none in the next 10, you probably aren't going to succeed. Explosiveness matters the most, but efficiency still belongs in the equation as well.

Efficiency

Success Rate: A common Football Outsiders tool used to measure efficiency by determining whether every play of a given game was successful or not. The terms of success in college football: 50 percent of necessary yardage on first down, 70 percent on second down, and 100 percent on third and fourth down.

S&P: Success Rate and PPP combine to form S&P.

Line Yards: A statistic that attempts, even to a small extent, to separate the ability of a running back from the ability of the offensive line. Line Yards begin as a measure of average rushing yards per play by running backs only, adjusted in the following way:

- *0-4 yards: 100% strength given to the offensive line*
- *5-10 yards: 50% strength*
- *11+ yards: not included*
- *runs for a loss: 120% strength*

Opportunity Rate: The percentage of carries in which the offensive line "does its job," so to speak, and produces at least five yards of rushing for the runner.

Power Success Rate: The percentage of runs on third or fourth down, two or fewer yards to go, that achieved a first down or touchdown. Also includes runs on first-and-goal or second-and-goal from the two-yard line or closer.

Stuff Rate: The percentage of runs in which the runner is tackled at or behind the line of scrimmage.

Sack Rate: Sacks divided by pass plays, which include passes and sacks.

For all intents and purposes, PPP can be seen as a Slugging Percentage for football stats. Slugging Percentage (the number of total bases divided by the number of at bats) is quite a useful baseball measure; it gives us an easy-to-understand view of a player's or team's power and explosiveness. But it is made more useful when combined with On-Base Percentage (OBP, which is the number of hits and walks divided by the number of plate appearances, or at-bats and walks) to create OPS, a measure that at once evaluates both efficiency and explosiveness.

For football purposes, the closest thing we have to OBP is Success Rate, a play-for-play look at how frequently an offense keeps the ball moving forward as planned. Like OBP, it basically deems every play a yes-no success, as defined above.

To succeed at the highest level offensively, a team must register some level of both efficiency and explosiveness. If you gain five yards on every single play, your success rate is going to be off the charts, but it will take you about 15 plays to drive the length of the field; in college football, that is a recipe for stalled drives. At the same time, if you bust a couple of big plays per game and gain three yards per play the rest of the time, your per-play averages will likely look stellar, but your success rates will suggest plenty of three-and-outs[125].

The S&P equation around which I have based a lot of my work, then, is basically a football version of OPS: Success Rate plus PPP[126]. With S&P, you can gauge an offense (or defense) exactly like you would a batter in baseball. An offense like Navy's, with five-yard precision and, often, little explosiveness, is a .280 hitter who slaps nothing but singles. Meanwhile, an offense like Miami's, with big-play ability and little consistency, is your customary .230 hitter with good power. There is some value in both of these players in baseball, but the ones who both get on base and hit for power are going to be far more valuable.

Using the S&P measure and the concepts of opponent adjustments referenced above, I have been maintaining S&P+

---

[125] Ed Feng of The Power Rank has another statistical idea for measuring the type of consistency and efficiency that is required of an offense: "There's this idea called 'bagging.' You essentially take a set of plays, and they go into your rankings. And you randomly sample certain plays. Some plays you use twice, some you use zero times. You pick randomly, and you run it through your algorithm, then you do it again and again, and over time your estimate – whatever it is that you're estimating – gets better. And my intuition tells me that if we were to use something like this for play-by-play data, we'd get to a place that rewards consistency. And there is value in having a consistent offense, having, say, an 80 percent chance of gaining five yards per play. Quantifying that is difficult, but huge plays can really skew your yards per play, and this [bagging] approach would dock you if you are too reliant on them."

[126] For the greatest evaluative accuracy, the equation needs to be about 60-40 in favor of PPP, but this combined measure is still much more indicative of success than PPP alone, or any raw stat like yards or yards per play.

as my 'official' rating of record for a while. Combined with Brian Fremeau's drive-based Fremeau Efficiency Index (FEI), we have also created a combined measure called F/+, which, as referenced above, serves as the official college ranking of Football Outsiders. F/+ rankings are broken out into an offensive rating, a defensive rating, and a special teams rating.

At Football Outsiders, you can find F/+, S&P+, and FEI ratings going back to the 2005 season. While S&P+ is primarily a play-by-play rating, the overall S&P+ ratings include a drive efficiency rating for accuracy purposes[127]. But perhaps the greatest usefulness in this measure is not simply in the overall measure but in its situational use. You can break S&P+ out into rushing versus passing, standard downs versus passing downs, red zone versus the rest of the field, per-quarter, per-down, et cetera. That can be of specific help to coaches. Simply knowing you rank 22nd in Offensive F/+ is nice, but knowing where you might be going particularly right or wrong is infinitely more useful. This harkens back to the "Stats are for losers" truism; coaches are typically confronted with stats – "You rank Xth in Broad Category Y" – for which they have no use.

As listed above, we have other tools for dialing in on where you're going right or wrong, as well. Football Outsiders line measures like Line Yards, Sack Rate, Opportunity Rate, Power Success Rate, and Stuff Rate are as helpful as anything for evaluating line play, and when combined with S&P+ and Success Rate, making a general diagnosis gets a lot easier.

Third Downs

Standard Downs: Any first down, second-and-7 or fewer, third-and-4 or fewer, or fourth-and-4 or fewer.

---

[127] As we'll discuss in a future chapter, finishing drives seemingly requires a different set of skills, and including drive efficiency, i.e. how well you turn field position into actual points, made it a better overall measure.

Passing Downs: Second-and-8 or more, third-and-5 or more, or fourth-and-5 or more.

Leverage Rate: Percentage of a team's plays that take place on standard downs.

It seems almost every coach tracks third-down conversion rates. That's a good thing, of course: It's a very important measure. But third down conversions are an outcome, and coaches are going to get the most use out of stats if they are more closely following the process that leads to the outcome. As we discussed in the last chapter, third-down conversion rates are actually dictated mostly by the yardage you gain (or allow) on first and second down. Some teams are better than others at converting third-and-long situations, while some are more prone to allowing such conversions; generally speaking, though, if you are gaining plenty of yards on first and second down — if you are staying "on schedule," so to speak — then your chances of converting on third down are strong.

To elaborate on this point, let's take a couple of the concepts discussed above for a test drive. Here is a look at the Success Rate and PPP data for second- and third downs based on distance:

Table 2: Second- and Third-Down Success Rates and PPP by distance (2012 FBS games)						
	Second Down			Third Down		
Yards to Go	Success Rate	PPP	S&P	Success Rate	PPP	S&P
1	72.5%	0.43	1.159	73.5%	0.39	1.126
2	65.0%	0.48	1.134	59.3%	0.47	1.063
3	55.2%	0.48	1.029	53.5%	0.49	1.020
4	58.5%	0.51	1.095	46.1%	0.48	0.946
5	48.6%	0.47	0.955	42.0%	0.49	0.914
6	43.9%	0.53	0.968	39.2%	0.52	0.915
7	43.6%	0.54	0.979	35.2%	0.52	0.872
8	38.2%	0.52	0.902	32.7%	0.53	0.856
9	33.7%	0.55	0.886	30.3%	0.55	0.849
10	34.3%	0.54	0.880	27.2%	0.55	0.823
11	29.6%	0.49	0.786	25.7%	0.57	0.823
12	25.2%	0.51	0.761	21.3%	0.49	0.698
13	23.1%	0.48	0.716	20.7%	0.55	0.756
14 or more	18.4%	0.53	0.719	13.0%	0.58	0.708

The first thing you may notice is that PPP doesn't change very much based on distance. In fact, it goes up a bit as the yardage-to-go goes up. Since Equivalent Points are not down-and-distance specific, this makes sense. A gain of eight on third-and-13 would be worth a decent Equivalent Points total, but it would be worth a big, fat zero in the Success Rate column.

Through the years, there has been a reasonably stark drop-off in success between second-and-7 and second-and-8 and between third-and-4 and third-and-5. It has been a rather natural cut-off point between what I call standard downs and passing downs.

The idea behind standard downs and passing downs is simple: On standard downs, the offense has the advantage. The defense cannot load up to attack the pass because the offense can still legitimately gain necessary first down yardage via ground or air. But on passing downs, the advantage shifts to the defense. The offense almost has to pass to get the first down, and the defense knows it. On standard downs, teams run nearly 60 percent of the time; on passing downs, teams pass nearly two-thirds of the time.

Table 3: Standard- and Passing-Down Success Rates and PPP by run and pass (2012 FBS games)				
Category	Plays	Success Rate	PPP	S&P
Standard Downs	81,752	47.9%	0.52	0.999
– *Rushes*	*48,616*	*47.8%*	*0.44*	*0.922*
– *Passes*	*33,136*	*48.2%*	*0.63*	*1.111*
Passing Downs	36,952	30.8%	0.53	0.841
– *Rushes*	*12,399*	*26.7%*	*0.48*	*0.749*
– *Passes*	*24,553*	*32.9%*	*0.56*	*0.887*

As we see in Table 3, the difference in success between standard downs and passing downs is stark. So unless your quarterback is Colt McCoy[128], to consistently succeed on offense, you probably need to avoid passing downs as frequently as possible, yes?

That's where Leverage Rate comes in handy. Leverage Rate is simply a ratio (standard downs to total plays) that allows you to see how well a team is staying "on schedule," so to speak. It gives you what you think you're getting from third-down conversion rates. In the last chapter, we discussed how telling it could be to add measures like yards per play on first down or average yards to go on third down to the typical box score. Well, Leverage Rate basically gives you both of those numbers in one.

---

[128] Sometimes, a team is able to bail itself out of passing downs situations; those teams typically have a pretty fantastic quarterback. One of the best examples of this is with Texas' offense in McCoy's junior and senior seasons. In 2008, Texas ranked just 25th in Standard Downs S&P+ but was seventh in Passing Downs S&P+; in 2009, Texas ranked 23rd and third. The Longhorns were actually almost *better* on third-and-7 than on third-and-3.

Table 4: 2012 win-loss records for teams in a given Leverage Rate range (FBS games)		
Leverage Rate Range	Record	Win %
85-100% standard downs	12-2	85.7%
75-84% standard downs	231-71	76.5%
70-74% standard downs	248-169	59.5%
65-69% standard downs	214-233	47.9%
60-64% standard downs	96-207	31.7%
55-59% standard downs	30-117	20.4%
Under 55% standard downs	5-37	11.9%

If at least three-quarters of your plays take place on standard downs – first downs, second-and-7 or fewer, third-and-4 or fewer – then on average, you are going to win well more than three-quarters of the time. Obviously, some passing downs magic can go a long way, and while it's important to stay out of passing downs, it's also important for your defense to *force* passing downs. But consider this proof that "You've got to stay on schedule" is one cliché that is a cliché for a reason. (We'll get to more in future chapters.)

Problem Solving

So we have these tools. Let's use them. The best way to figure out how they might aid in scouting or self-scouting is to find a real-world example.

In 2012, Arkansas stunk in the red zone. Despite a solid pitch-and-catch combination of Tyler Wilson to Cobi Hamilton, and despite the presence of big running back Knile Davis in the backfield, Arkansas was rather unsuccessful close to the goal line. The Razorbacks scored on just 71.4 percent of their red zone trips (116th in the country) and scored touchdowns on just 46.9 percent of trips (118th). Those are atrocious numbers for a team that was otherwise decent at moving the football; Arkansas ranked ninth in the play-for-play component of the S&P+ rankings but only 33rd in the drive component. What can the numbers tell us about where they went wrong?

First, the Hogs ranked 68th in the opponent-adjusted Red Zone S&P+. That's not great, but if there's that large a difference between raw rankings (116th) and opponent-adjusted rankings, that tells us that schedule had a role to play in the problems. The Hogs indeed played six teams with defenses that ranked in the top 40 for Defensive Red Zone S&P+: Alabama (No. 7), South Carolina (No. 11), Rutgers (No. 19), Mississippi State (No. 24), Auburn (No. 36), and Ole Miss (No. 36); even a good red zone offense would have failed a few times along the way against this slate.

Second, Arkansas ranked 48th in Red Zone PPP+ but 91st in Red Zone Success Rate+[129]. That tells us the problem was one of efficiency, not explosiveness. Dialing in further, the Hogs ranked 65th in Red Zone Rushing Success Rate+ but 90th in Red Zone Passing Success Rate+. Considering they passed 52 percent of the time in the red zone (much higher than the national average of 40 percent), we can start to figure out the problem. Arkansas was a pass-first team in all areas of the field, including the red zone. You can certainly find examples of pass-heavy teams succeeding close to the goal line, but Arkansas was not one of them. The Razorbacks didn't do a good enough job of finding easy passes in that area of the field, likely because their passing game was pretty aggressive overall. Quarterback Tyler Wilson averaged 13.6 yards per completion, but the lack of go-to short passes appeared to hurt.

Now, saying Arkansas should have thrown shorter passes or run more really isn't much of a diagnosis. But again, stats aren't necessarily intended to give a final answer but to focus your line of questioning. That Arkansas was inefficient in its pass selection tells you where to begin looking at the film.

You can find countless examples like this, of course.

Vanderbilt was a great short-yardage team that couldn't run the ball very well on standard downs; a closer look shows

---

[129] Remember, the "+" means the number is opponent-adjusted.

us that Vandy's Stuff Rate ranked 112th in the country, suggesting that while the Commodores could mow you over on third-and-1, they were quite leaky and easy to penetrate on first-and-10. Meanwhile, Toledo's defense saw the same issues: fourth in Power Success Rate but 107th in Opportunity Rate. That meant the Rockets could attack the line well on third-and-1 but were easy to push around on first down.

Kent State's defense was strong early in halves (23rd in First Quarter S&P+, 56th in Third Quarter S&P+) but faded late (94th in Second Quarter S&P+, 121st in Fourth Quarter S&P+); that would prompt a series of questions about either potential depth issues or the predictability issues that came when opponents adjusted to what was clearly a strong game plan. Temple's offense had the same problem: 69th in the first quarter and 32nd in the third, but 101st in the second and 118th in the fourth.

And when you look at sack rates, you see teams that pinned its ears back well but couldn't generate a pass rush with just its front three or four in run-or-pass situations. Texas A&M ranked fourth in Passing Downs Sack Rate but 83rd in Standard Downs Sack Rate. Meanwhile, the Fresno State offense was 14th on standard downs and 99th on passing downs, meaning it handled a four-man rush pretty well but completely broke down in the face of a blitz (or in the face of men named Margus[130]).

Other Fun Tools

There are a lot of other measures we've developed through the years for the purposes of either evaluating a team or simply figuring out what sets them apart from others (better or worse). Which teams tend to play their best against the best

---

[130] In the 2012 Hawaii Bowl, SMU defensive end Margus Hunt thoroughly emasculated members of the Fresno State offensive line, piling up three tackles for loss, two sacks, two forced fumbles, and three quarterback hurries as the Mustangs, heavy underdogs, destroyed the Bulldogs, 43-10.

opponents? Use a tool like Covariance to compare weekly performances to F/+ rankings.

Which running backs have the best explosiveness independent of the quality of the line in front of them? Try Highlight Yardage, a look at the yards gained by a running back beyond the Line Yards listed above.

Which teams move the fastest (or slowest) between plays? Try a run- or pass-independent tool[131] like Adjusted Pace instead of simply plays per game.

Which defenses are most prone to a bend-don't-break style? Compare success rates to PPP to find a malleability ratio of sorts. Teams with iffy success rates and great PPP averages are willing to give up shorter gains in the name of preventing the longer ones; teams with great success rates and leaky PPP averages are more aggressive and prone to both making and allowing big plays.

And it probably goes without saying that if you're looking for information on receivers, simply finding catches and yards isn't enough – you need target data and catch rates.

Explore the archives at Football Outsiders and Football Study Hall; you'll find some pretty fun things there.

****

So what's next? We've been wringing every ounce of relevant data out of the box score and play-by-play for a few years now, even if people are still only beginning to notice. Where else might we take advanced college football stats?

For starters, we are starting to get somewhere with charting data. At the pro level, with no more than 16 games in a given week, Football Outsiders and others are able to chart games for extra information about formations, distance of

---

[131] Since a lot of passes fall incomplete and stop the clock, teams that run the ball a lot are naturally going to eat up more time of possession. Adjusting a figure for run-pass ratio takes us a lot further down the road of figuring out which teams are operating at the zippiest pace.

186

passes (in the play-by-play, all we know is how far the play went, not how far the actual pass traveled in the air), broken tackles, blitzing, etc. But charting takes time, and there are many, many more college games than pro games in a given week. Logistically, it has been an impossible task, but as you will see in the next two chapters, with just a couple of interns we were able to get somewhere with charting data in 2012. The goal is to take things further with each passing year[132].

NFL nerds also got the benefit of All-22 data this year. The NFL began to make this valuable film, which gives an end zone view of the entire field and all 22 players, available online, and while college football will almost certainly never be able to legislate something like this (that whole "no central governing body" thing is a hindrance at times), it is a pretty good sign that this is the direction football analysis is going. There is more of a demand for charting data, and it will likely only grow in future years[133]. And as the tools become available – if they become available – then we could even move toward the type of location tracking data (recording a player's positioning on the field from play to play) that has become popular in soccer.

If charting data isn't the holy grail for college football stats, then player projections are. College is a pivot point from high school to the pros, and while we have begun to get somewhere in terms of projecting college stats to the pros, projecting the high school-to-college path has been nearly impossible to date. The reasons are both obvious and in high

---

132 Through STATS, LLC, a lot of this data is already available – the number of defenders on the line and in the box, shotgun/pistol/under-center data, number of pass rushers, formation, blown blocks, participation data, defensive targets, etc. "With STATS data, you can look at offensive line personnel groupings to gauge effectiveness," STATS manager of football products Mitch Tanney tells us. But you have to pay quite a bit for it. Teams might be willing to do that, but random fans probably can't afford it. As time progresses, our goal is to get further with charting data in an open-source sense.
133 Grantland's Bill Barnwell notes that there is added benefit to All-22 film as well. "More exposure to it will give casual fans a better sense of coverage in the secondary." And besides, "most fans have played [EA's] Madden [NFL video game], anyway, so we're totally used to that angle."

volume: There aren't many plays in a high school game. A lot of the offenses are beyond primitive. And even on great high school teams, most of the players on the depth chart aren't going to even sniff a college football field. Oh yeah, and any stats you can find are sketchy at best. (High schools aren't exactly known for having enormous athletic departments, nor should they.) But it has always struck me as conceivable to come up with a rough model that takes into account a given school's district (or, to put it another way, the size and quality of the schools in the district) and basic stats. Perhaps it only works with skill position players. Perhaps it also requires some basic combine-type data. Perhaps it is a pipe dream on which progress will never be made. But we need to aim high. We need pipe dreams. That one's mine.

9. College Football's Curveball

Football is, by nature, a sport based on bursts[134]. Only the craziest, oddest plays are going to last more than about 15 seconds, and when the play is over, you'll get at least about 20-30 seconds to recover from it. Boom, lull, boom, lull. It's not baseball in this regard, but it's not exactly a never-avert-your-eyes sport like hockey or soccer can be.

In this sense, the no-back formation is football on crack Not only do you know something is probably going to happen in a short amount of time; you know that something's probably going to happen within about 1.2 seconds. There are few fakes, there are few slow-developing plays; there is just a snap and nearly immediate action.

When an offense lines up in the no-back set, you know that in most instances you're either going to see a short, quick pass or a quarterback sneak. Sure, you can throw in a slow-developing jet sweep at times (when it comes to charting, if the jet sweep recipient is already in the backfield when the ball is

---

[134] Adapted from a piece that appeared at Football Study Hall on February 14, 2013.

snapped, it counts as one back in the backfield), and if your offensive line is better than the opponent's defensive line, perhaps your quarterback will have enough time to look downfield. But really, an offense lining up in a no-back set is basically admitting that it is going to do something immediate, and usually predictable, with the ball. It seems no offense is confident enough to run a no-back full-time, perhaps because of that predictability, but as we'll see below, if a team needs to gain seven yards on a specific play, it has no problem leaning on the no-back.

In 2012 at Football Study Hall, SB Nation's two research and analytics interns – Mike Nixon and Chris A. Brown – spent the college football season charting college football games. They charted 109 games; this is not a representative sample for all FBS teams by any means, but it was not intended to be. It is still healthy and robust, and it still gave us a lot of information about how college football was played in 2012.

In this 2012 Charting Project, we ended up with 15,504 plays with a listed formation (i.e. number of backs in the backfield at the snap, number of receivers lined up wide). Table 1 gives us a breakout of backs in the backfield.

Table 1: Backs in Backfield (2012 Charting Project Data)		
Backs	Plays	% of All Plays
0	836	5.4%
1	9,380	60.5%
2	4,580	29.5%
3	700	4.5%
4+	8	0.1%

Football has changed through the years, but it really hasn't changed *that* much. Ninety percent of all plays are run with either one or two players in the backfield with the quarterback; I'm pretty sure those numbers wouldn't have been much different if this were 1997 or 1989 (though obviously the further back you go, the more the numbers would skew toward two backs instead of just one). So despite the prevalence of the spread offense (with which the no-back is often frequently associated), we are talking about a formation that still only shows up once per every 20 plays or so.

Table 2: Frequency of No-Back Usage by Down (2012 Charting Project Data)	
Down	Frequency
First Down	3.8%
Second Down	4.8%
Second-and-5 or fewer	*3.2%*
Second-and-6 or more	*5.5%*
Third Down	9.5%
Third-and-2 or fewer	*1.8%*
Third-and-3 or more	*10.9%*
Fourth Down	10.4%
Fourth-and-2 or fewer	*5.9%*
Fourth-and-3 or more	*14.3%*

That said, the no-back is used almost twice as frequently in "we've got to move the chains right here" situations.

With run options basically limited to "QB up the middle," this formation is built for quick passing. And it is the perfect formation for the spread ethos, which is often to peck you to death with seven-yard passes and hope you eventually miss a tackle that springs a big play. If your quarterback is good at reading defenses and determining exactly what he is going to do pre-snap, you can kill a defense with this formation. But as the much-higher-than-normal 7.8 percent sack rate would suggest, hesitation is deadly.

When a no-back formation is employed, the quarterback isn't the only one making something of an automatic read. The defense is likely doing the same thing. Mike Nixon, former Arizona State linebacker, says that the Sun Devil defense would have an automatic call when the offense showed no-back, and it was usually a blitz of some sort. Perhaps that call would change as a given game progressed, but knowing that a quick read was coming, a defense would fall back on its own quick read.

Table 3: No-Back Run-Pass Splits (2012 Charting Project Data)		
Type	% of Plays	Yards/Play
Pass	78.0%	6.3
Run	22.0%	5.3

In my head, the no-back is an automatic blitz situation, especially considering it's often used on shorter passing downs, such as third- or fourth-and-medium. I was a little bit surprised, then, to see the data in Table 4 on the next page.

Taking into account the fact that we had 3.5 percent of both three- and four-man rush situations documented as zone blitzes, that means that opponents only blitz against the no-back 25 percent of the time, choosing instead to rush four and react to the quarterback's quick read. Considering the results – blitzing results in 4.5 yards per play, not blitzing results in 6.2 – this appears to be a generally faulty approach.

Table 4: Pass Rush on No-Back Passing (2012 Charting Project Data)		
No. of pass rushers	Frequency	Yards/Play
2	0.6%	4.8
3	20.2%	8.1
4	56.8%	6.3
5	16.9%	4.5
6	5.5%	4.6

Not everybody takes the approach Arizona State did in the last part of the last decade, but perhaps they should. If a quarterback has time to find an open receiver, there are five of them running around for him to find. That's a lot to ask of a secondary.

So where *does* the quarterback throw when he has a chance to get the pass off?

Table 5: No-Back Pass Distribution (2012 Charting Project Data)		
Category	**Percent of passes**	**Comment**
Behind the line of scrimmage	14 percent	Quarterbacks threw what we will call catchable balls (passes that were either caught or dropped, but either way hit receivers in the hands[135]) 91 percent of the time on these passes. Passes of this distance were completed 85 percent of the time, defensed just one percent of the time, and marred by a poor throw (i.e. an uncatchable ball that wasn't intentionally thrown away) five percent of the time[136].
0-3 yards from line of scrimmage	15 percent	Quarterbacks threw catchable balls 77 percent of the time at this distance, with a 72 percent completion rate. These passes were defensed six percent of the time, and 16 percent of passes were poor throws.
4-6 yards	28 percent	The rate of catchable balls at this distance was 70 percent, with a 64 percent completion rate. These passes were defensed nine percent of the time and fell victim to a poor throw 16 percent of the time.

[135] We could include passes defensed as "catchable balls" as well, but that introduces the slight possibility that the ball was catchable only by the defensive player, which misses the point of catchability. Yes, "catchability" is now a word.

[136] These numbers do not add up to 100 percent because they do not take into account either passes that were thrown away or had no data of this type listed in the charting file. There was no data for about three percent of all passes.

7-10 yards	15 percent	Quarterbacks threw catchable balls 66 percent of the time for this range, with a 61 percent completion rate. Passes were defensed 13 percent of the times, and quarterbacks made poor throws 13 percent of the time.
11-16 yards	14 percent	Here's where we begin to see a drastic drop-off in the quality of passes. Quarterbacks threw catchable balls just 53 percent of the time at this distance, with a 46 percent completion rate. Opponents defensed just nine percent of passes, but quarterbacks made poor throws 26 percent of the time.
17+ yards	14 percent	The numbers here are similar: quarterbacks threw catchable balls just 50 percent of the time, with a catch rate of 44 percent. Defenders defensed 11 percent of these passes, and quarterbacks made poor throws 32 percent of the time.

The general appeal of the no-back is at least partially because it offers quarterbacks both easy reads and easy throws. About 57 percent of the time, a quarterback's pass is traveling fewer than seven yards away from the line of scrimmage. The completion rate for such passes is dramatically high; for passes thrown behind the line of scrimmage (typically a bubble screen or something similar), there is an 85 percent completion rate. And if you include drops and, in this case, defensed passes, a quarterback is going to throw semi-accurately on a behind-the-line pass about 92 percent of the time. For passes between zero and 10 yards from the line of scrimmage, the percentage is about 80 percent, though obviously a defender is more likely to make a play on the ball the further you get from the line.

One can understand, then, why these formations might be popular on third-and-5. (Personnel obviously also plays a role here, too; these are the most reliable plays in the playbook as long as you know the pass catcher is actually going to catch the pass.)

So who most effectively utilized this formation in 2012? Remembering one key point – that we are not working from a full, representative sample of games – let's take a look at the teams in our data set that succeeded the most from the no-back.

Table 6: Teams Averaging Better than 10 Yards/Play in No-Back Formation (2012 Charting Project Data)				
Team	No-Back Plays	% of All Plays	Yards/No Back Play	Games Charted[137]
Arizona	11	3.4%	15.9	4
USC	12	2.5%	13.7	7
Notre Dame	62	17.8%	11.2	5
Tulsa	10	10.6%	11.2	1
West Virginia	43	7.3%	11.2	8
Oregon State	16	5.4%	11.0	4
Arizona State	22	14.7%	10.4	2
Miami	21	16.9%	10.4	2
Northwestern	22	30.1%	10.3	1

Despite Arizona coach Rich Rodriguez's spread-'em-out tendencies, he does not go to the no-back well that often. In the four Arizona games we charted, the Wildcats only used the formation 11 times – once against Oregon (on fourth-and-12 from the Oregon 20), once against Oregon State (second-and-10 from the 25), seven times against USC and twice against Nevada. In these plays, quarterback Matt Scott rushed three times for 33 yards and completed four of eight passes for 78 yards. The Wildcats' averages were skewed dramatically because of a single 60-yard bomb from Scott to Austin Hill on third-and-22 against USC. (This was indeed a bomb – it

---

[137] The full list of games charted in this sample can be found at Football Study Hall.

traveled 29 yards in the air, and Hill took it another 31 yards after the catch – and not a dink pass with a broken tackle.)

Really, the team that combined no-back frequency with effectiveness the best might have been Notre Dame. The Irish were known mostly for their defense, but even against the strong defenses listed in the above sample (Michigan State, Stanford, and Alabama), they were tremendously effective from the no-back set. Quarterback Everett Golson was just 14-for-32 passing for 178 yards overall versus Michigan State, but from the no-back he was 9-for-14 for 122. (That means he was 5-for-18 for 56 otherwise.) In the first half versus USC, Golson was 7-for-13 for 115 yards from this look. Hell, even against Alabama, he was more successful in the no-back (5-for-8 for 71) than he was in other formations (16-for-28 for 199).

The no-back formation is a wonderful curveball for a football offense. If you use it sparingly, it can be terribly efficient; as we see, it is quite useful when you absolutely need a small handful of yards. But coaches seem to think that if you use it too much, defenses will tee off on it. While an offense like Notre Dame leaned on it often, the Irish still used *other* formations four-fifths of the time. It is a formation that doesn't cater to one specific type of offense — a spread team like Texas A&M used it a ton, while Washington State, led by Mike Leach, one of the spread's most influential coaches, used it less frequently than even Alabama. It was an extreme rarity for Oregon, too, but Florida used it much more than one might have guessed.

Few major league pitchers are capable of leaning on the curveball to great success, but if you've got it in your arsenal, your offense could benefit greatly from it.

10. QBs and The Passes They Throw

One of the most useful, relevant, and interesting pieces of information that your normal play-by-play data does not provide is the distance a pass travels in the air[138]. For example, a bubble screen that a receiver catches at the line of scrimmage and takes 50 yards for a touchdown looks the same in the box score as a perfectly-thrown, play-action bomb that a receiver catches in the end zone 50 yards downfield.

For the 2012 Charting Project at Football Study Hall, then, one of the most exciting pieces of data we brought in was air yards, the distance a pass actually travels. Since so many passes in college football are basically extended handoffs counting them the same as a deep ball when it comes to completion percentage just seems odd, especially considering how much we lean on completion percentage as a relevant, important measure.

One of the things STATS, LLC, looks at with its charting data is the idea of a "real completion percentage,"

---

[138] Adapted from a piece that appeared at Football Study Hall on February 28, 2013.

basically a look at how a quarterback would have done throwing the same passes as everybody else. They have more charting data than we do, but I thought it would be interesting to look into the same idea with our data[139]. Below, we'll look at some pretty detailed data about pass distance for the 43 quarterbacks for whom we charted at least 50 passes in 2012[140].

So who is throwing what kind of passes? Below are some general tidbits from our sample[141]:

Baylor doesn't believe in moving backwards.

Despite the perception of the spread as an offense that frequently uses passes as extended handoffs, Baylor quarterback Nick Florence threw just six percent of his passes behind the line of scrimmage. Meanwhile, he threw 54 percent

---

[139] Before we move any further, a perpetual disclaimer: The data below comes only from the games we charted. For some teams – the Alabamas and LSUs of the world – we charted almost every game. For others, it was minimal. That, and not everybody has the same receiving corps, obviously. While this data represents a step forward in terms of the level of analysis we can do, it is still not exactly context-independent. In this case, the data below should be used more for conversation than bold, concrete conclusions. Actually, in most cases that is how it should be.

[140] Here is the list of quarterbacks in this sample: David Ash (Texas), Matt Barkley (USC), Tajh Boyd (Clemson), Trevone Boykin (TCU), Tyler Bray (Tennessee), Teddy Bridgewater (Louisville), Kolton Browning (UL-Monroe), Derek Carr (Fresno State), Rakeem Cato (Marshall), Clint Chelf (Oklahoma State), Seth Doege (Texas Tech), Jeff Driskel (Florida), Cody Fajardo (Nevada), Nick Florence (Baylor), Kiehl Frazier (Auburn), Everett Golson (Notre Dame), Connor Halliday (Washington State), Kevin Hogan (Stanford), Brett Hundley (UCLA), Landry Jones (Oklahoma), Collin Klein (Kansas State), E.J. Manuel (Florida State), Sean Mannion (Oregon State), Johnny Manziel (Texas A&M), Marcus Mariota (Oregon), Taylor Martinez (Nebraska), Andrew Maxwell (Michigan State), A.J. McCarron (Alabama), Zach Mettenberger (LSU), Braxton Miller (Ohio State), Stephen Morris (Miami), Aaron Murray (Georgia), Ryan Nassib (Syracuse), Josh Nunes (Stanford), Keith Price (Washington), Tyler Russell (Mississippi State), Matt Scott (Arizona), Connor Shaw (South Carolina), Geno Smith (West Virginia), Dylan Thompson (South Carolina), Jeff Tuel (Washington State), Bo Wallace (Ole Miss), and Max Wittek (USC)

[141] The full Football Study Hall post, linked above, features extensive pass distribution charts.

of his passes between zero and nine yards from the line. Even pro-style quarterbacks like Alabama's A.J. McCarron (15 percent behind the line) and LSU's Zach Mettenberger (12 percent) threw horizontally more frequently than Florence. Baylor's formations spread out as wide as anybody's in the country, and this allows the Bears to build in easy throws that still move forward at least a little bit.

On the flip side, West Virginia's Geno Smith threw a full one-third of his passes to targets behind the line, along with another 38 percent within nine yards. As we will cover, Smith also threw a nice deep ball; but with over 70 percent of his passes serving almost as extended handoffs, his completion rate had no choice but to be awfully high.

South Carolina quarterback Connor Shaw is old-school.

If you do not cover the dink-and-dunk, South Carolina's injury-prone No. 1 quarterback will kill you with it. In the sample, he did throw 38 percent of his passes within four yards of the line of scrimmage. But he also went deep more frequently than anybody else on this list. A full 20 percent of his passes traveled at least 30 yards[142]. Granted, throwing deep isn't quite the same as *successfully* throwing deep, and Shaw was below average on those passes, but has a style all his own, especially considering how well he can also run with the ball (when healthy). "Old-school" might not be the right way to describe Shaw – he runs quite a bit more frequently than Sammy Baugh did, for instance – but slinging downfield is certainly a less-frequently-used option than it used to be in the days of all-or-nothing passing games.

When Shaw was injured, he was replaced by Dylan Thompson, who took a completely different approach. Only three percent of Thompson's passes traveled 30 yards, though

---

[142] Others who threw deep relatively frequently: Baylor's Nick Florence (13 percent of passes 30 yards or more), Oklahoma State's Clint Chelf (12 percent), TCU's Trevone Boykin (10 percent).

he did focus heavily on more intermediate routes – 60 percent of his passes traveled between five and 19 yards, and only 26 percent were shorter than that. This is almost certainly part personality, part play calling.

Stanford quarterback Kevin Hogan was mature for a redshirt freshman.

Midway through its eventual 2012 Pac-12 title campaign, Stanford switched quarterbacks. The Cardinal started then-junior Josh Nunes at the beginning of the season; he beat out then-sophomore Brett Nottingham for the job. Nunes struggled, but it wasn't for lack of aggressiveness. He threw 50 percent of his passes between 10 and 24 yards from the line of scrimmage. He wasn't effective enough, however, and eventually lost his job to Hogan.

Hogan was infinitely more willing to take what the defense gave him – 76 percent of his passes were within nine yards of the line, while only 18 percent were between 10 and 24 yards. Conservatism isn't inherently a good thing, but in this case, it was. In his five starts, Hogan and the Cardinal beat No. 13 Oregon State (at home), No. 1 Oregon (in Eugene), No. 15 UCLA (in Los Angeles), No. 17 UCLA (at home in the Pac-12 Championship game), and Wisconsin (in the Rose Bowl). The next loss Hogan suffers will be his first in the cardinal and white.

USC quarterback Max Wittek played from Matt Barkley's playbook.

Both South Carolina and Stanford featured quarterbacks with entirely different personalities. But when USC's Matt Barkley went down late in the 2012 season, his replacement, Max Wittek, threw basically the same passes in Barkley's absence. For Barkley, 41 percent of his passes were within five yards of the line of scrimmage; for Wittek, it was 43 percent.

For Barkley, 39 percent went between five and 14 yards; for Wittek, it was 37 percent. Et cetera.

This type of data tells us a little bit about the personality of different teams' passing games. With former Mike Leach assistant Dana Holgorsen pulling the strings, West Virginia's Air Raid threw 71 percent of its passes within 10 yards of the line of scrimmage; but Leach's Washington State offense threw about 62 percent that distance. The Clemson spread looked downfield a bit more (34 percent of Tajh Boyd's passes were between 10 and 24 yards downfield), while Baylor loved the five- to nine-yard routes. With Connor Shaw in the game, South Carolina went either very short or very long; with Dylan Thompson, there was a lot more intermediate passing.

Barkley really did not have a very good 2012.

A former blue-chip recruit who started for most of four seasons at USC, the Trojans' golden boy simply did not do enough with the luxurious weapons at his disposal. His completion percentages were below average on all passes shorter than 15 yards – he completed just 83 percent of his throws behind the line of scrimmage (UCLA's Brett Hundley completed 93 percent), 64 percent from zero to four yards (Connor Shaw completed 86 percent), 58 percent from five to nine yards (Texas Tech's Seth Doege completed 79 percent), and 50 percent from 10-14 yards (Oklahoma's Landry Jones completed 72 percent). These poor percentages came despite the presence of perhaps the best 1-2 receiver combination in college football: sophomore Marqise Lee and junior Robert Woods.

Kansas State quarterback Collin Klein, meanwhile, was a much more effective passer than his reputation would suggest.

Klein, Kansas State's lumberjack quarterback who built more of his reputation with his legs than his funky delivery, was above average on all passes under 25 yards. One-third of his passes were between five and nine yards, and he completed a healthy 67 percent at that distance. He was at 56 percent or better on all passes under 25 yards, and he actually had a healthy percentage (albeit with a small sample size) on passes over 30 yards. His delivery is funky and slow, and it is up to others to determine whether he has any chance of performing as an NFL quarterback; but these numbers give him more credibility than one may have imagined.

West Virginia's Geno Smith had quite a bit to offer.

The biggest doubt I saw regarding the former West Virginia quarterback as an NFL prospect was in regard to his arm strength. This data brings to the table both confirmation and doubt about that. He throws an absolutely gorgeous deep ball, and he was pretty good at completing them – 50 percent from 30-34 yards, 67 percent from 35-39, 43 percent from 40+. And yes, he had help from a pair of fantastic receivers in Tavon Austin and Stedman Bailey.

But while he was acceptable on the shorter passes that he threw frequently, he was mediocre to poor on intermediate passes: he completed 33 percent from 20-24 yards and 40 percent from 25-29, both well below the national average. Those passes are considered to require the most zip, and it was a potential weakness for him. But his numbers suggest that his fantastic 71 percent completion rate wasn't solely due to throwing short. It had an impact on the numbers, but he still showed solid passing ability with most longer throws.

Alabama's A.J. McCarron is good.

The Alabama quarterback, and two-time national champion, was slightly below average on throws behind the line of scrimmage (86 percent completion rate) and throws of 10-14 yards (48 percent), but he was above average in every single other category. He was also perhaps the most effective passer in the country on deeper passes: 64 percent from 20-24 yards, 56 percent from 25-29, 40 percent from 30-34, 86 percent from 35-39, and 57 percent from 40+. Yes, he had an amazing freshman receiver in Amari Cooper, and yes, Alabama's devastating run game opened up the play-action, but percentages that high are not guaranteed against air. McCarron played some role in that and proved that his awful performance late in the Texas A&M game (which we will discuss in a future chapter) was the outlier, not the norm.

Texas A&M waterbug/quarterback Johnny Manziel has room for improvement.

The 2012 Heisman winner is absurdly elusive in the pocket and was perfectly fine on most shorter passes, but his completion percentages on the rare 20+ yard passes were spotty and, for the most part, below average (30 percent from 20-24 yards, 46 percent from 25-29, 17 percent from 30-34). His accuracy is fantastic, but the arm strength is lacking a bit.

E.J. Manuel and Landry Jones weren't asked to show off their arms much.

Both quarterbacks – the starters at Florida State and Oklahoma, respectively – were accurate from 15 yards in, but in our sample of games, they neither threw, nor completed, many balls over 20 yards.

Some other tidbits:

- Georgia's Aaron Murray completed 77 percent of his passes from 15-19 yards and 60 percent from 20-24 but was average or below in most other ranges.

- LSU's Zach Mettenberger was outstanding against Alabama, but he left a lot to be desired for the season as a whole; he was below average under 15 yards and was only average from 15-29. Of course, his raw receiving corps might have had something to do with that.

- Ohio State's Braxton Miller was not asked to do much — two-thirds of his passes were within 10 yards of the line of scrimmage — but he was good to great on those passes. He was a bit dicey after that, but with his outstanding running ability, the shorter throws were usually enough (as they were for Johnny Manziel).

- Nebraska's Taylor Martinez completed a robust percentage of shorter passes (91 percent from 0-4 yards, 75 percent from 5-9) and an egregious percentage of anything further (50 percent from 10-14, 10 percent from 15-19, 17 percent from 20-24).

So what if all of these quarterbacks threw the same percentage of passes to different lengths? With the charting data at hand, we can come up with our own approximation of STATS, LLC's Real Completion Percentage. For fun, I'll call it a QB's Adjusted Completion Percentage. You know, to be different.

Table 1 shows us the adjusted completion percentages for quarterbacks' passes if they all threw passes at the following rates: 17.8 percent of passes <0 yards, 21.4 percent 0-4 yards, 24.3 percent 5-9 yards, 14.0 percent 10-14 yards, 8.9 percent 15-19 yards, 4.9 percent 20-24 yards, 3.1 percent 25-29 yards, 2.3 percent 30-34 yards, 1.8 percent 35-39 yards, and 1.6 percent 40+ yards.

Table 1: Adjusted Completion Percentages for quarterbacks based on 2012 Charting Project data	
Range	Player
70% or better	Teddy Bridgewater, Louisville (70.2%)
	Clint Chelf, Oklahoma State (70.0%)
65-70%	Rakeem Cato, Marshall (69.7%)
	Collin Klein, Kansas State (69.0%)
	E.J. Manuel, Florida State (68.5%)
	A.J. McCarron, Alabama (68.5%)
	Nick Florence, Baylor (68.4%)
	Marcus Mariota, Oregon (67.6%)
	Johnny Manziel, Texas A&M (66.8%)
	Geno Smith, West Virginia (66.6%)
	Landry Jones, Oklahoma (66.5%)
	Taylor Martinez, Nebraska (65.1%)
60-65%	Jeff Tuel, Washington State (64.5%)
	Jeff Driskel, Florida (64.5%)
	Kevin Hogan, Stanford (64.0%)
	Tajh Boyd, Clemson (63.0%)
	Braxton Miller, Ohio State (62.9%)
	Matt Barkley, USC (61.7%)
	David Ash, Texas (61.4%)
	Sean Mannion, Oregon State (61.3%)
	Aaron Murray, Georgia (61.1%)
	Ryan Nassib, Syracuse (60.6%)
	Zach Mettenberger, LSU (60.1%)
	Seth Doege, Texas Tech (60.0%)
	Brett Hundley, UCLA (60.0%)

55-60%	Kolton Browning, UL-Monroe (59.6%)
	Cody Fajardo, Nevada (59.4%)
	Tyler Russell, Mississippi State (59.0%)
	Everett Golson, Notre Dame (58.8%)
	Derek Carr, Fresno State (58.0%)
	Matt Scott, Arizona (57.6%)
	Connor Shaw, South Carolina (57.6%)
	Kiehl Frazier, Auburn (57.0%)
	Tyler Bray[143], Tennessee (55.9%)
	Bo Wallace, Ole Miss (55.6%)
	Keith Price, Washington (55.4%)
	Dylan Thompson, South Carolina (55.0%)
55% or lower	Connor Halliday, Washington State (54.6%)
	Max Wittek, USC (52.4%)
	Trevone Boykin, TCU (52.1%)
	Josh Nunes, Stanford (50.8%)
	Stephen Morris, Miami (48.8%)
	Andrew Maxwell, Michigan State (48.7%)

One fun aspect of this list: looking at the bunching. Manuel, McCarron, Florence, Mariota, Manziel, Smith and Jones are all within two percent of each other, and then there is a bit of a cascade down toward the middle, where Barkley, Ash, Mannion, Murray, Nassib, Mettenberger, Doege and Hundley are also bunched together.

Charting data allows us to evaluate a passer while stripping away some of the context that clouds the normal passing data. And even this data-limited look tells us some things we might not have already known.

---

[143] No quarterback was hurt by the sample size more than Bray, whose two charted games were against Alabama and Florida, the teams that finished No. 1 and No. 2 in Def. F/+ in 2012. His adjusted percentage is really low, especially considering he was working with a solid line and two NFL-caliber receivers (Cordarrelle Patterson, Justin Hunter), but at least part of that can be explained by the competition.

11. Sometimes Clichés Are Clichés for a Reason

On September 27, 2008, Tim Tebow gave a short speech that would create his legacy. The Florida quarterback, already a contributor to a national champion in 2006 and the 2007 Heisman Trophy winner, had just laid an egg, or at least his version of it. Against unranked Ole Miss at home, he had completed 24 of 38 passes for 319 yards and a touchdown (13 of 16 for 189 yards to Percy Harvin, who also rushed 10 times for 82 yards), but he was sacked three times, rushed for just 40 non-sack yards, lost a fumble, and was stuffed on fourth-and-1 from the Ole Miss 32 with just 41 seconds left. With assistance from a blocked PAT attempt and an 86-yard bomb from Jevan Snead to Shay Hodge with about five minutes left, the Rebels pulled a stunning 31-30 upset of Tebow's fourth-ranked Gators.

To reporters after the game, a defiant Tebow delivered a speech that would end up on a plaque outside Florida's football complex: "To the fans and everybody in Gator Nation I'm sorry. I'm extremely sorry. We were hoping for an undefeated season. That was my goal, something Florida has never done here. I promise you one thing: A lot of good will come of this. You will never see any player in the entire country play as hard as I will play the rest of the season. You will never see someone push the rest of the team as hard as I will push everybody the rest of the season. You will never see a team play harder than we will the rest of the season. God bless."

The speech didn't specifically promise a national title, but four months later, Florida indeed took the BCS Championship with a 24-14 win over Oklahoma. Tebow went from star to legend. He became the most well-known college football player of the decade. A simple post-loss rant became "The Promise."

And if Oklahoma had been able to finish a couple of drives in the second quarter, history might have played out in an entirely different way. For all intents and purposes, Florida won the national title game with Tebow on the sideline.

In 2008, Oklahoma had perhaps the greatest "screw you" offense of all-time. The Sooners all but copyrighted the term "video game stats[144]." They scored 54 points per game in the regular season and put up at least 58 in six straight games. Offensive coordinator Kevin Wilson, now the head coach at Indiana, found a rhythm every person who has ever decided to become an offensive coach strives for (and almost never achieves), and he rode it for the final two months of the season.

"All he would ever say is, 'I just watch,'" says Trent Ratterree, then a redshirt freshman for the Sooners. "He was utilizing the philosophy of the hurry-up offense, but there was a lot of him in it, too. He spent a lot of his time watching the other team. If he noticed they were trying to sub, he would slow it way down to the point where they're calling two or

---

[144] That has become the go-to term for ridiculous offensive statistics, stemming from how fun it is to put a college football video game on Junior Varsity mode and run up 112 points and 1,100 yards in a game.

three fake snap counts before calling a play. And he would sub players in and out just to mess with the other team."

Wilson certainly had plenty of talent at his disposal in 2008, but looking at the names on the depth chart, you wouldn't necessarily presume this was a team averaging nearly 60 points per game. There was certainly some elite talent: Tight end Jermaine Gresham would eventually become a first-round draft pick and Pro Bowler in the NFL, and Lord knows quarterback Sam Bradford, the No. 1 overall pick in the 2010 draft, was great. And the line kept Bradford upright at all times; in the regular season, opponents managed just 11 sacks and five quarterback hurries. That's absurd.

Still, the running backs were Chris Brown, DeMarco Murray and Mossis Madu, not Adrian Peterson. And the wideouts were Juaquin Iglesias, Manny Johnson, Quentin Chaney, and a still-raw Ryan Broyles. There was undeniable talent with this unit, but Oklahoma always has talent. What Wilson had in his favor in 2008, perhaps more than anything else, was versatility. Once he caught on to the other team's substitution patterns, it was over. He would bring in big personnel – extra tight ends, et al – and line them up wide. He would go with power in one look and pure spread in another. "People weren't ready for that," says Ratterree. "He was just screwing around with the other coaches the whole time."

Plus, he had a team full of attitude. It gave Wilson an incredible, justifiable amount of confidence. And that confidence would bite him in the national title game.

For most of the first half of the BCS Championship, Oklahoma was in control. The Sooners advanced into Florida territory on every first-half drive and got inside Florida's 10 on each of the last three. They also had Tebow confused. Nic Harris picked him off on Florida's first possession, and defensive tackle Gerald McCoy baited him into another pick on a zone blitz midway through the second quarter.

After McCoy's interception, Oklahoma took over at the Florida 26 with 7:29 left in the half. Chris Brown immediately ripped off a 17-yard run off left tackle to the Gator 9, then got five yards wide right on first-and-goal. To that point, he had nine carries for 78 yards. On second-and-goal he picked up three more yards off right guard to the Florida 1.

On third-and-goal, Wilson elected to run Brown again, this time to the left, and with good reason. Not only had Oklahoma been running the ball incredibly successfully to that point in the game, but the left side of the line, with 6'8, 337-pound All-American Phil Loadholt at tackle and 6'5, 335-pound All-American George Robinson at guard, was perhaps the strongest piece of OU's offense in 2008. But sophomore defensive tackle Torrey Davis held up against Robinson and brought Brown down for no gain on third down.

On fourth down, Wilson had a choice to make. A field goal was off the table – this team didn't kick 18-yard field goals, not with this offense. (You could certainly make the case that no team should *ever* attempt an 18-yard field goal unless it's to win the game in the final seconds.) But how would Wilson choose to attack? He could attempt a play-action pass, perhaps to Gresham, an incredible red zone threat. He could attempt a run to a different part of the field. Or he could say "Screw you," and run the same play again. He chose the latter. And Davis sliced through the line and stopped Brown for a two-yard loss.

Florida flipped the field with a long run by Percy Harvin, but with 2:32 left in the half, Oklahoma got the ball back at its 20-yard line and immediately worked its way back down the field. Bradford found Iglesias for 17 yards, completed a series of short passes, found Broyles for 12 yards to the Florida 17, then found Gresham for 11 to the six. Oklahoma called timeout with 10 seconds left in the half; the Sooners had a chance for probably one more play before attempting a field goal. With two players lined up to his left and one to his right, Bradford fired to a well-covered Manny Johnson at the goal line, and Joe Haden broke it up. The ball deflected into the air, and Florida safety Major Wright came down with the interception.

In terms of expected points based on field position, Oklahoma should have been up by at least 10 points at halftime. Instead, the game was tied at 7-7. Florida would go on to block a 49-yard field goal in the third quarter and eventually find its offensive rhythm. The Gators would win, 24-14, fulfilling The Promise, but if Oklahoma had taken advantage of the opportunities Florida had given it, Bradford very well might have taken Tebow's title ring.

"I saw Coach Wilson after the game on the beach at about six in the morning," says Ratterree. "He was walking around with a whiskey and Coke, looking like a lost puppy. It was the saddest thing I've ever seen. I've never seen somebody take losing as hard as he did that night." But you can't blame Wilson for going into shock a bit. It had been a while since his offense had failed.

In the first 13 games of the 2008 season, Oklahoma entered its opponent's 40-yard line 117 times, not including two end-of-game, clock-killing drives versus Kansas and Texas A&M. In those trips, the Sooners turned the ball over on downs five times (four times between the 27 and 39, once at the 1), punted four times, attempted 12 field goals (they made eight), somehow turned the ball over just twice, and scored 94 touchdowns. Points per trip: 5.7. That is an absurd average, one that is better than the 2008 national average for trips inside the *20* (5.4).

In 99 trips inside an opponent's 10, that Oklahoma team failed to score a touchdown just five times (four field goals, one turnover on downs). But in the most important game of the year, the Sooners scored just seven points on three first-half trips.

Finishing drives is everything. Sometimes a coaching cliché is a cliché for a reason. But from a statistical perspective, it isn't something we look at that often. Or if we do, we look at the wrong statistic: red zone scoring percentage[145].

Table 1: 2012 FBS vs. FBS possession data			
	Average	Winner	Loser
Points per game	28.3	36.7	19.9
Points per possession	2.2	2.8	1.5
Points per trip inside 50	3.6	4.1	3.0
Points per trip inside 40	4.2	4.7	3.6
Points per trip inside 20	5.4	5.7	5.0
Points per trip inside 10	6.1	6.3	5.8
Points per trip inside 5	6.5	6.6	6.3

On the most basic level, football comes down to two things: creating opportunities and capitalizing on them. It takes both to win games. Table 1 gives us some possession data from the 2012 season[146]. Generally speaking, a winning FBS football team averaged nearly twice as many points per possession as its vanquished foe. This was mostly a case of a superior team both creating and capitalizing on opportunities better than its over-matched opponent.

But if we hone in on just the games that ended up close (Table 2), we start to notice a few things. First, wow, can decimal points make a huge difference. College football is not college basketball, where averaging 1.1 points per possession instead of 1.0 can result in a loss becoming a semi-comfortable win. We're dealing with tens of possessions, not more than 100. But in tight games, the team that averaged 2.3 points per possession (say, three touchdowns, three field goals, a turnover, and six punts) won, and the team that averaged 2.0 lost. The teams created about the same number of opportunities for

---

[145] What's wrong with red zone percentage? For one, it doesn't tell you whether teams are scoring touchdowns or kicking field goals. As Stanford head coach David Shaw so aptly puts it, "You win more games by scoring touchdowns." At the very least, we should be looking at some sort of "points per trip" statistics, but we rarely see that.

[146] The table looks only at the 732 games that featured FBS teams taking on other FBS teams. Games versus FCS competition were filtered out.

themselves, but the winning team made basically one more play – maybe forcing a key turnover, or scoring on third down instead of kicking a field goal, or forcing a field goal (one that the offense may have missed) with a big stop.

Table 2: 2012 FBS vs. FBS possession data (Games decided by 8 or fewer points)			
	Average	Winner	Loser
Points per game	27.7	30.0	25.4
Points per possession	2.1	2.3	2.0
Points per trip inside 50	3.5	3.6	3.4
Points per trip inside 40	4.2	4.3	4.0
Points per trip inside 20	5.4	5.4	5.3
Points per trip inside 10	6.1	6.1	6.0
Points per trip inside 5	6.5	6.6	6.3

Second, we notice that the difference between winners and losers in points per trip inside the 5 and inside the 40 (0.3 points) is the same as the overall per-possession difference. On average, the winners and the losers in these close games create about the same number of scoring opportunities for themselves. The team that better turns minor scoring opportunities into points, and deep trips into touchdowns, wins.

On 104 different occasions in 2012, a team created more scoring opportunities[147] than its opponent but lost, in part, because the opponent averaged more points in its own scoring opportunities. Washington State lost four such games, while Air Force, Florida International, Hawaii, New Mexico, TCU, Troy, and Western Michigan each lost three[148].

In a demoralizing loss in the Hyundai Sun Bowl, USC made six trips inside Georgia Tech's 40 and scored just seven points.

---

[147] We'll define "scoring opportunities" as trips inside the opponent's 40.
[148] On the flip side, Ohio State *won* four such games, while Middle Tennessee, Navy, Oregon, Stanford, and UCLA all won three.

Duke created 11 scoring opportunities versus Cincinnati in the Belk Bowl but averaged just 3.0 points per trip; Cincinnati averaged 5.9 points per trip and pulled away late to win by 14.

On November 23, Arkansas could have pulled an upset of LSU and salvaged, to some small degree, an otherwise terribly disappointing season. But in seven scoring opportunities, the Razorbacks scored just 13 points. LSU scored 20 in four opportunities and won.

On October 27, Oregon State's undefeated season was wrecked when the Beavers averaged just 2.8 points in six scoring opportunities against Washington; Washington averaged 5.0 points in four trips and pulled a 20-17 upset.

We didn't know it at the time, but Texas A&M lost a potential national title chance on October 20 when the Aggies scored just 19 points on seven trips inside LSU's 40 and lost, 24-19. And Florida State may have lost a similar opportunity on October 6 when the Seminoles turned six scoring opportunities against N.C. State into just 16 points, leaving themselves vulnerable to a late Wolfpack charge and a 17-16 defeat.

And in perhaps the most impressive (in a bad way) feat of the season, Hawaii created 12 scoring opportunities to Colorado State's four on October 27 and outgained the Rams by 102 yards, but *lost*, 42-27. The Warriors lost three turnovers (at the CSU 30, 31, and 33), punted twice (at the CSU 39 and 40), attempted three field goals (missing one), and turned the ball over on downs at the 2. And one of the three turnovers, an interception, was returned for a touchdown.

Okay, so finishing drives matters. How do coaches coach that? The answer varies dramatically.

Take Bob Stitt and Sonny Dykes. In terms of general offensive philosophy, the two are generally considered rather similar. Stitt, the head coach at Division II's Colorado School of Mines, has crafted a funky, unique, underdog-friendly spread offense, mostly out of necessity. Because of rigorous academic standards[149], the Orediggers are rather overmatched physically; but in 13 seasons, Stitt has gone 90-57, 69-41 in the RMAC, thanks mostly to an explosive offense that combines the West Coast principles he learned as a graduate assistant at Northern Colorado with spread formations he built through experimentation. His teams throw a lot – 57.5 times per game in 2012 [150] – but they also take major pride in being able to punch the ball into the end zone when they get the chance.

"We practice red zone situations three times per week," Stitt says. While the conventional wisdom is that a pass-first team is going to struggle near the end zone because the field shrinks and defenders don't have to worry about getting stretched vertically, Stitt thinks the opposite.

"Simply being a run-first team does not mean being a good red zone team," Stitt says. "I was watching Georgia Southern play North Dakota State [in the 2012 Football Championship Subdivision (FCS) semifinals], and Georgia Southern's percentage of touchdowns was really, really low. And they run the heck out of the ball, they're fantastic running the ball with the option. But once they get close to the goal line, it's really tough on them. Defenses don't have to fear play-action. You have to be a good passing team to score touchdowns in the red zone."

That said, he has found value in jumbo sets, short-yardage formations with extra size in the form of extra linemen, fullbacks, or defensive players-turned-fullbacks.

---

[149] According to Stitt, for every 10 players his competitors recruit in the Rocky Mountain Athletic Conference (Adams State, Black Hills State, Chadron State, Colorado Mesa, Colorado State-Pueblo, Fort Lewis, New Mexico Highlands, Western New Mexico, Western State), he will only be able to go after a couple of them because of admissions standards.

[150] Mines ranked fifth in Division II in passing yards per game. The other four teams in the Top 5 (Merrimack, Shippensburg, Henderson State, and New Mexico Highlands), averaged just 45.6 passes per game. Of course, part of CSM's passing volume was due to the fact that the Orediggers suffered a catastrophic series of injuries at running back; still, they also threw an above-average 42 times per game in 2011.

"I think the size really helps you when you get inside the 5-yard line," he says. "We'll go to a package where I'll steal a couple of guys off the defense and put them in the backfield. We'll go double-tight [end], three backs [in the backfield], and just pound 'em." This differentiates him from a lot of other spread offense gurus.

Stitt also goes out of his way to preach the importance of touchdowns over field goals, especially in the college game, where place-kickers are often less than automatic.

"We've been a really good red zone scoring team, but we're an even better red zone touchdowns team. I just really don't like leaving things in the hands of a kicker[151]. It kills me when those kids have put in so much work year-round, and then you end up putting it in the hands of a kicker."

Mines attempted just 12 field goals in 2012, making 10. The Orediggers attempted only seven field goals of under 30 yards[152]. "That's what I want. That's right where I want to be," he says. If they could sniff the end zone, they were probably going for the touchdown.[153]

Dykes also fancies the forward pass. He grew up in college football – his father, Spike, was Texas Tech's head coach for 14 years, from 1986-99. Sonny is an Air Raid disciple who became a graduate assistant for offensive innovator Hal

---

[151] He left dramatic pauses after "just," "really," and "don't."

[152] Both of CSM's misses came in the same game. The Orediggers' kicker missed two field goals of under 30 yards against New Mexico Highlands in a five-point loss. One was a 27-yard attempt on fourth-and-goal from the 10, the other a 29-yard attempt on fourth-and-6 from the 12. If Stitt didn't believe in minimal field goal attempts *before* that game, he most certainly did afterward.

[153] Another fun thought about place-kicking, from *The Hidden Game of Football*'s John Thorn: Why haven't we abolished points after touchdown by now? "It seems to me something well worth getting rid of. It ought to be mandated. If a play is to mean something, it ought not be automatic. It is completely vestigial, and it is almost a silent tribute to the game in the 1890s, when the game was called 'football' because the foot was the primary thing about it." FBS kickers made 96.5 percent of extra point attempts in 2012; the percentage is typically higher in the pros. "Anything that is going to work out 95 percent of the time or better needs to be adjusted on an institutional level," Thorn says. "There should not be that high an expectation of success in anything you do in life."

Mumme at Kentucky in 1997, then followed Mumme's right-hand man, Mike Leach, to Lubbock when Leach was named Spike's successor. Sonny served as Texas Tech's receivers coach for five seasons (2000-04), then became offensive co-coordinator in 2005. He moved to Arizona in 2007 to lead head coach Mike Stoops' offense, then he took the head coaching job at Louisiana Tech in 2010. After three seasons and a 17-8 record in 2011-12, Dykes took the head job at California.

In 2012, Dykes' Louisiana Tech offense averaged 5.1 points per trip inside an opponent's 40-yard line, the sixth-best average in the country. The Bulldogs averaged 6.6 points per trip inside the 10 (ninth). They did this despite running just 59 percent of the time in the red zone, slightly below the national average of 60 percent. They ran more in the red zone than out of it, but Dykes does not believe in going jumbo when the end zone is within sniffing distance.

"I don't think people attack the field horizontally as well as they should," he says. "Defenses will play off of you a bit, and you can get more catch-and-run opportunities." And what about sticking a defensive tackle in the backfield as a fullback? "There are a lot of creative ways to create misdirection, leverage defenders, and do the things a fullback would do."

There is no single correct answer here. There never is. Dykes' philosophy is pretty simple, really: "Just get the ball to your best players, and run the plays you can execute the best. Don't come up with new schemes, new stuff – just do the stuff you do the best."

Simplicity is naturally a common sentiment. For Ball State head coach Pete Lembo, "things don't really change for us until we get to about the 10 or 12-yard line. Things start getting compacted at that point, and you have to get different play calls ready." They don't save plays or change their philosophy, though: "There are just certain pieces of your package that you will emphasize more."

Simplicity sounds great in theory, but it is difficult to avoid overthinking when there are points on the line. "Some spread guys undergo an identity crisis when they get down there," says Smart Football's Chris B. Brown. It might take more practice time for a pass-first team to succeed near the end zone, but there are certainly enough examples to show it can be done.

Brown offers another interesting possibility, however. Georgetown (Kentucky), an NAIA powerhouse, operates mostly out of a run-and-shoot look. But head coach Bill Cronin, operating an insanely efficient offense he adapted from small-school legend Red Faught, switches to what is basically a Delaware Wing-T near the goal line. Georgetown will pass frequently out of this formation – the shovel pass is particularly effective – but this is a run-first look. Still, it is built around misdirection and angles, which isn't that far from the approach of the run-and-shoot.

A lot of offenses get run-happy near the end zone. It would make sense, then, that teams that operate from run-friendly formations like the Wing-T or Flexbone might not have to change much in scoring situations. Former Air Force head coach Fisher DeBerry is a Flexbone disciple who won 169 games in 23 seasons coaching the Falcons (1984-2006), won eight or more games in a season 11 times, and finished two seasons ranked in the AP Top 15 (eighth in 1985, 13th in 1998). DeBerry saw clear benefit to his option offense. "Your play-calling never changes, whether you're at the minus-1 or the plus-1 yard line. We're going to call what we call regardless. Maybe your play-calling is impacted by the time remaining on the clock, but it never has to change based on field position."

It stands to reason, then, that option teams are also more apt to go for it on fourth downs. In 2012, the three teams that attempted the most fourth-down conversions were Air Force (43), Army (41) and Georgia Tech (37). All three run option offenses, and all three were among the nation's top five in run frequency. "When we ran the football really well, we were big on going for it on fourth-and-1, fourth-and-2," says Wake Forest head coach Jim Grobe. "Our mentality was, if we're not good enough at getting a yard or two, especially on the ground, we don't deserve to win[154]. You are probably more apt to go for it on fourth-and-1 from the 15 if you're a running team." The numbers certainly back that up.

Grobe also believes that passing gets infinitely more difficult near the goal line. "The closer you get, the more your throw lanes are being restricted. If you're not good at running the ball, you end up with more field goals." But on the flip side "you have more big-strike potential from outside the end zone. There's a coach for every viewpoint[155].

There are other factors at play, too, when it comes to one's philosophy in scoring opportunities. "We were extremely aggressive [in 2012]," says UL-Monroe head coach Todd Berry "We knew we were going to have to score points because our defense was pretty immature. We'll revisit how aggressive we'll be on offense [in 2013] based on that." A team like ULM went for broke frequently; meanwhile, a team like Michigan State, with a fierce defense and a flawed offense (thanks in part to a brand-new quarterback), tried just 11 fourth-down conversions all year and attempted a whopping 32 field goals, making 23 [156]

Berry is known as a particularly aggressive offensive coach. His definition of aggressiveness might differ from others. "We look at points-per-trip stats a lot. You're robbing yourself of points in some situations. Our red zone scoring

---

[154] Safe to say, Kevin Wilson probably thought something very similar on the evening of January 8, 2009.

[155] To further the "coach for every viewpoint" meme, try this out: Pass-happy Bob Stitt is also a huge proponent of going for it on fourth downs. In 11 games, his Orediggers attempted 36 fourth-down conversions in 2012 (they converted a reasonably healthy 21 of them, or 58 percent) despite running the ball only 28 percent of the time and rarely actually running the ball well.

[156] Michigan State also lost five games by four or fewer points. It is easy to correlate aggression and success – "State clearly should have gone for it more," or "State played scared, and it cost them" – but you can't just go for it on fourth downs. You also have to convert. State's offense did not lend much optimism there.

percentage might not be as high as others', but I bet our points per trip are high because we forego field goals a lot." He's right: ULM averaged 4.9 points per trip inside the opponent's 40, 11th-best in the country. His Warhawks also averaged 6.0 points per trip inside the 20, 10th-best.

"A lot depends on who you're playing," he says. "Against an SEC team, you can't outrun somebody," which means your ability to stretch defenses horizontally near the end zone might be minimized. "It changes a bit based on that, but once we cross the 50, we know that we're in four-down territory. We have an extra shot. And once we hit the 25-yard line, I don't want to leave the area without taking a shot at the end zone."

That's something even a run-heavy coach can buy into. Troy Calhoun, Air Force's head coach, sees his philosophy change once his team reaches the 30. "Between the 18- and 30-yard lines, that sector, there's a chance to have some big plays, some scoring plays." And if that doesn't work, "you've just physically got to be able to jam the ball forward when you need to."

An unsuccessful shot at the end zone could result in a turnover, a sack, or simply an incomplete pass. In the red zone, negative or neutral plays can be particularly costly. Even if you are going to continue attempting to throw the ball near the end zone, passing downs can be devastating for all the reasons conventional wisdom suggests. There is benefit to stealing whatever yardage you can. "If you can keep averaging even four yards per play or carry down there, you're getting second-and-mediums and staying in run-or-pass situations," Stanford's David Shaw says. "To keep getting positive yards is so important."

For every reward, there is a risk, and for every philosophy, there is a coach.

****

If you are looking for further reasons to be aggressive in scoring opportunities, and the statistical importance of touchdowns over field goals doesn't necessarily do it for you (or you don't have much confidence that you *will* score touchdowns), there is another factor that should keep your foot on the gas pedal: Even if you fail, your opponent probably isn't going to get good field position out of the deal. And "Field position matters" is every bit as important an old-school cliché as anything related to finishing drives.

As discussed in an earlier chapter, average starting field position is one of the most underrated, and underused, statistics in football. It is free yardage. As we see in Table 3, if you start your possessions, on average, just four to eight yards ahead of your opponent, you win more than two-thirds of the time. And if you tilt the field drastically in your favor (12 yards or more), you might even be able to afford some missed opportunities; in the end, you'll create (and prevent) enough to win nine times out of 10.

Table 3: 2012 FBS vs. FBS Positive Average Starting Field Position Margin			
	Wins	Losses	Win%
+0 to 4 yards	115	116	49.8%
+4 to 8 yards	147	59	71.4%
+8 to 12 yards	104	30	71.6%
+12 to 16 yards	89	8	91.8%
+16 yards or more	62	2	96.9%

The impact of field position is obvious, of course. "If your opponent has to go 80 yards, that's hard to do," Grobe says. In the 732-game, FBS vs. FBS sample from 2012 that we've been referencing, there were 6,028 possessions in which the offense started at its 20 or worse. These possessions produced, on average, 1.5 points. Only 1,137 of the possessions (19 percent) resulted in a touchdown, and only 1,514 (25 percent) resulted in any points. Meanwhile, 1,473 (24 percent) resulted in a three-and-out and punt.

As Table 3 shows, however, while it's easy to understand why field position can impact winning and losing, building separation of any kind in the field position battle is difficult. Almost one-third of FBS vs. FBS games in 2012 saw a near-stalemate (zero to four yards) in this battle. Four of every five games saw a margin of fewer than 12 yards. The range of starting field position just isn't that large.

A team's average starting field position was worse than 24.0 (i.e. the team's 24-yard line) in just 14.1 percent of the 2012 FBS vs. FBS games. It was better than 36.0 just 15.7 percent of the time. In most games, teams were trying to average in the 32-36 range (win percentage in this range: 66 percent) instead of the 24-28 range (win percentage: 32 percent).

These aren't huge numbers. On average, a team got 13 possessions in a given game; the total difference between an average start of 26.0 and an average start of 34.0 is just 104 yards (13 possessions times 8.0 yards). One turnover could mean a difference of about 40 yards. One field-flipping punt that bounces past the punt returner and rolls a while could mean 25 yards. One huge stop on a kick return could mean 15 yards. A sack on third-and-long, instead of a short completion, could mean 15 yards. A third-down conversion that simply extends a drive from three-and-out to six-and-out could mean 10 yards. And just like that, you're at 105 yards, and you've gone from likely loss to likely win.

That is a bit of an extreme example with a significant special teams impact, but one can see how smaller plays, particularly third downs, can add up quickly. And almost nothing is more devastating to your field position cause than a three-and-out, especially if a drive involves a sack or negative play on third down. Never mind the impact such a series might have on momentum; that's significant enough. It can have an even larger impact in the field position battle.

Table 4: 2012 FBS vs. FBS 3-and-Outs*			
3-and-outs	W-L	Win%	Avg. Margin
0	64-32	66.7%	+9.8 points
1	170-100	63.0%	+7.8 points
2	204-155	56.8%	+3.7 points
3	140-147	48.8%	-1.0 points
4-5	119-222	34.9%	-7.6 points
6-7	35-67	34.3%	-12.2 points
8 or more	0-9	0.0%	-22.4 points

* For these purposes, 3-and-outs refer only to drives that ended in punts, not turnovers. As you would guess, turnovers are higher up on the devastation list.

As Table 4 shows, in 2012 you were basically limited to two three-and-outs, max, in your 13 or so possessions. If you stayed under three, you had about a 60 percent chance of winning. With three or more, however, the combination of wasted possessions and field position opportunities you were creating for your opponents put you behind the 8-ball.

And what kind of "field position opportunities" might we be talking about? On average, a drive that ended in a punt resulted in a field flip (the difference between the starting field position of one drive compared to the opponent's starting field position on the next) of about 46.8 yards in 2012. On three-and-outs, the flip was only about 39.8 yards. As we saw in Table 3, seven yards can add up.

Three-and-outs are still better than turnovers, of course. Never mind the potential points that could result from a fumble or interception return; the average flip on drives that resulted in turnovers was only about 26.5 yards. In other words, there's a reason why you see so many teams all but forfeiting third-and-long situations by running a draw play or short pass, and there's a reason why, as Grobe puts it, "I know guys who won't let their coordinators open it up until they get to at least the 40-yard line." It makes an enormous difference in the field position battle.

In fact, field position is so important that you almost wonder why coaches don't go to even greater lengths to protect themselves in this regard, at least when they don't have a clear offensive advantage.

"[Former Georgia Tech head coach] Bobby Dodd used to talk at clinics and say that when you're backed up in your own territory, don't be afraid to punt on third down," Grobe says.

The quick kick used to be a common option in the game of football. The thought of passing, especially on second- or third-and-long, when the defense knows you are going to pass, was terrifying to generations of coaches[157] and was almost a no-win situation, so teams would frequently just punt when they fell behind schedule. "Can you imagine what your fans would do if you tried that today?" Grobe asks. "You'd get run out on rails!"

Table 5: 2012 FBS vs. FBS 6-and-Outs*			
6-and-outs	W-L	Win%	Avg. Margin
0-1	77-25	75.5%	+14.7
2	128-64	66.7%	+9.9
3	147-121	54.9%	+4.0
4	134-121	52.5%	+0.6
5	106-122	46.5%	-2.3
6	73-120	37.8%	-6.7
7-8	56-120	31.8%	-10.4
9 or more	11-37	22.9%	-20.1
* For these purposes, 6-and-outs refer to drives that lasted six or fewer plays and ended in punts. This could conceivably include a drive that included three first downs, but those were rare.			

There's another reason why teams don't forfeit a play by punting on third down: College defenses are often more than willing to give up a third-down conversion or two. "Three-and-outs are a big part of [winning]," says Air Force head

---

[157] Insert the overused "Three things can happen when you pass, and two of them are bad," cliché here. The statement, attributed to quite a few former coaches, including Ohio State's Woody Hayes and Texas' Darrell K. Royal, dictated the offensive philosophy of most college football teams. No more.

coach Troy Calhoun. "But more realistically, even six-and-outs are still pretty big." And while the margins shrink a bit, Table 5 shows that he is right.

Of course, nobody sends their offense out on the field with a "Try not to go three-and-out" pep talk. "The goal is never to get a first down or two, then punt," says Fisher DeBerry. "The goal is to score."

Similarly, there are no secret strategies when it comes to winning the field position battle. It basically comes down to having an offense good enough to minimize three-and-outs (or punts in general), having a defense good enough to force a few avoiding turnovers, and having a special teams unit that doesn't forfeit major yardage in the kicking and return games. Easy, right?

****

Above, I referred to field position as "free yardage." What if we actually treated this like real yardage? What if we added the raw field position yardage differential – your average starting field position minus your opponent's, times the average number of possessions in the game (example: Team A has a field position advantage of 10.0 yards per drive, and there were a total of 29 possessions in the game, so its field position yardage margin is plus-145) – to a team's overall yardage margin?

Table 6: 2012 FBS vs. FBS Positive Adjusted Yardage Margin*			
Adjusted Yardage Range	**Wins**	**Losses**	**Win%**
+0 to 24 yards	46	33	58.2%
+25 to 99 yards	117	55	68.0%
+100 to 199 yards	171	27	86.4%
+200 to 349 yards	166	9	94.9%
+350 yards or more	108	0	100.0%
* Adjusted Yardage Margin, in this instance, is the combination of raw yardage differential and field position yardage differential.			

Well, first of all, you'd get an even better explanation of who won a given game. Table 6 looks at what we'll call the "Adjusted Yardage Margin." In the 732 FBS vs. FBS games in the sample, teams that were between just zero and 24 yards better than their opponent won nearly 60 percent of the time, while teams that were 200 or more yards better won almost 97 percent of the time.

To get a better feel for the difference field position can make in this "adjusted" yardage margin, let's take a look at some of the more notable games from the latter portion of the 2012 football season:

Table 7: Adjusted Yardage Margin from Notable 2012 College Football Games		
Date	Score	Yardage Margin* / F.P. Margin / Adj. Yard Margin
1/7/13	Alabama 42, Notre Dame 14	+207 / +30.7 / **+237.7**
1/3/13	Oregon 35, Kansas St. 17	+104 / +25.7 / **+129.7**
1/1/13	Stanford 20, Wisconsin 14	+35 / -54.5 / **-19.5**
12/31/12	Clemson 25, LSU 24	+230 / -202.0 / **+28.0**
12/1/12	Alabama 32, Georgia 28	+167 / +38.5 / **+205.5**
12/1/12	Wisconsin 70, Nebraska 31	+152 / +123.0 / **+275.0**
11/30/12	Stanford 27, UCLA 24	-126 / +170.4 / **+44.4**
11/30/12	N. Illinois 44, Kent St. 37	+222 / -126.0 / **+96.0**
11/17/12	Baylor 52, Kansas St. 24	+238 / -114.2 / **+123.8**
11/17/12	Stanford 17, Oregon 14	-19 / +58.7 / **+39.7**
11/10/12	Texas A&M 29, Alabama 24	+17 / -27.5 / **-10.5**
11/3/12	Alabama 21, LSU 17	-78 / -29.2 / **-107.2**
11/3/12	Notre Dame 29, Pitt 26	+222 / -41.0 / **+181.0**
11/3/12	Oregon 62, USC 51	+67 / +20.8 / **+87.8**
10/27/12	Georgia 17, Florida 9	+3 / +90.0 / **+93.0**
10/27/12	Notre Dame 30, Okla. 13	+58 / -2.0 / **+56.0**
10/20/12	Florida 44, South Carolina 11	-42 / +392.6 / **+350.6**
10/20/12	Kansas St. 55, W. Virginia 14	+201 / +151.0 / **+352.0**
10/20/12	LSU 24, Texas A&M 19	-126 / -11.6 / **-137.6**
10/13/12	Notre Dame 20, Stanford 13	+77 / -107.0 / **-30.0**
* The winning team's margin is shown.		

Adjusting the yardage margin in this way creates both questions and answers. It helps to explain how Clemson barely knocked off LSU despite a yardage margin of plus-230, and it explains how Stanford held off UCLA in the Pac-12 Championship. It adds context to what could seem like a total beatdown of Oklahoma by Notre Dame (actually, the game was tied midway through the fourth quarter until a late Irish barrage). Plus, it helps to explain one of the most statistically baffling games of the year, Florida's 33-point, no-yardage destruction of South Carolina that we discussed in an earlier chapter. It also leaves us searching for more questions about games like Alabama-Georgia, Texas A&M-LSU, Alabama-LSU, and Stanford-Wisconsin. (The answer to most of these new questions: Turnovers and special teams also make a huge difference.)

In the end, starting field position is all about margin of error. If you are allowing your opponent to convert a couple of first downs per drive before you are able to settle in and make a stop, then whether they started at their 20 or 40 might make the difference in whether they get into field goal range. Field position can tilt the field in your favor and allow you to create more scoring opportunities for yourself than your opponent does.

And yes, you still have to convert those opportunities as well.

12. The 'Spread Offense' Meme Dies

Texas A&M fans never hesitate to tell you how talented their team is[158]. It is often true, often not, but that really isn't the point. Aggie Confidence never wavers. And the events of November 10, 2012, in Tuscaloosa, Alabama, gave said confidence enough fuel to burn for quite a while.

In Texas A&M's stunning 29-24 win over Alabama that Saturday, the Aggies proved that they indeed were not lacking in raw talent. But they also proved what they had been lacking in recent seasons: Kevin Sumlin.

We often overestimate the impact of a coach's persona when it comes to new hires. If Tennessee fans had gotten their wish in December 2012, for instance, and the school had hired Jon Gruden, we would have heard endless stories about Gruden's confidence, about his swagger, and about how he carries himself like a winner. That's great, but swagger alone doesn't matter if you aren't very good at your job. Charlie Weis was downright cocky when he was tapped to lead Notre Dame and while media and fans lapped that up over the first couple

---

[158] Adapted from a piece that appeared at SB Nation on November 11, 2012.

of years, it didn't stop the Irish from collapsing in his third season.

Kevin Sumlin, meanwhile, looks, walks and talks like a badass. He oozes confidence and hypnotizes you a bit even when he is simply, confidently delivering the exact same kind of coachspeak you hear from everybody else. But when Sumlin was hired to replace Mike Sherman in December 2011, I was lukewarm to the idea. Sumlin was clearly successful in his first head coaching stint at Houston, but I was concerned that he only won big when Case Keenum was behind center. (Keenum got hurt in 2010, and the Cougars fell to 5-7.) I didn't hate the hire, but I didn't like it as much as others.

As the offseason progressed, however, I started talking myself into Sumlin quite a bit, not because of his record, but because both his attitude and the staff he was putting together. And when it came time to write the 2012 A&M preview in mid-August, I was volunteering to drive the bandwagon, even though I didn't think A&M would get a ton of sparkling play from the quarterback position[159]. In that preview, I wrote the following:

> [I]n a season that saw Texas A&M lose four games by four points or less, they lost an average of 4.3 points per game to sheer luck and bounces. With neutral luck, it is conceivable that 6-6 turns into 10-2. And it is probably worth pointing out that a 10-2 A&M team returns seven offensive starters and all sorts of four-star talent would probably be a top-10 to -15 team heading into 2012. [...]
>
> Now it's Kevin Sumlin's turn. Despite constant expectations to the contrary, A&M hasn't won double-digit games in a season since 1998 and has finished with more sub-.500 seasons (four) than eight-win campaigns (three) in that span. R.C. Slocum was pushed out after a 6-6 campaign in 2002, Dennis Franchione after 7-6 in

---

[159] Whoops.

2007, and Sherman after 6-6 last year, but the Aggies have rarely fared significantly better than those records. But Sumlin has a rare opportunity in College Station: a season for which the expectations might actually be lower than they should be. And now I hop on the bandwagon. Go figure.

(Of course, if Sumlin exceeds expectations in 2012, then look out for the hilarious level of 2013 buzz.)

Swagger and confidence only really matter if you can first put a check in a lot of other boxes. But if we look at the A&M team Sumlin inherited as a blank slate, we probably should have seen the Aggies' great year coming. Sumlin found an experienced, deep set of skill position players (on an offense that requires a lot of them) and one of the best offensive lines in college football. On defense, lack of depth on the line and in the young secondary could potentially be offset by the return of phenomenal playmakers like pass rusher Damontre Moore. And Sumlin's staff was exciting, as well: Air Raid disciple Kliff Kingsbury as offensive coordinator, Jim Tressel disciple Mark Snyder on defense. And because the bones of this program were solid, Sumlin was in position to deliver the one thing A&M didn't have the year before: swagger and late-game confidence.

Yes, Johnny Football matters. Without quarterback Johnny Manziel running the show on offense, A&M almost certainly doesn't win in Tuscaloosa. He is a relentlessly unique player, and the A&M offense conforms to his personality. But Manziel didn't force two fourth-quarter turnovers against Alabama. And Manziel didn't make the physical catches that receiver Ryan Swope made late in the game. And let's face it: Texas A&M had a pretty good quarterback in 2011, too. Ryan Tannehill was the eighth pick in the 2012 NFL Draft, after all. Manziel took the Aggies from good to very good, but Sumlin's impact has been even larger. Despite bad luck, A&M really did blow an incredible number of leads in 2011, faltering late in losses to Oklahoma State, Arkansas, Missouri, Kansas State and Texas (and in a win against Texas Tech, really).

That a team with much the same personnel came through late in wins over Ole Miss and Louisiana Tech was a good sign; that the team came through against Alabama was Sumlin's masterpiece. Swagger, confidence, etc., can matter if the bones of the program are strong. And Texas A&M's beef-fortified bones were not only as strong as I thought in August, they were quite a bit stronger.

****

"There's no one in this league that thought that a quarterback from A&M or Missouri was going do that to this league. Right? No one thought that the pass offenses from the Big 12 entering this league could do that. Me included."
— Gary Danielson, late in the Texas A&M-Alabama game

CBS's Gary Danielson lost track of downs a few times late in A&M's win, but you'll have to forgive him for that. He was going through a bit of an existential crisis at the time. Saying "Right?" after declarative sentences is a relatively common verbal tic, the tiniest hedging of bets. But when Danielson delivered the above quote after A&M scored to take a 29-17 lead in the fourth quarter, the pause seemed both pregnant and indicative of a man losing his bearings a bit.

Danielson has made no secret of the fact that he prefers power football to pass-happy and big football hits to finesse. His hostility toward some recent offensive innovations has been palpable. But that evening he revealed that while he didn't find the spread aesthetically pleasing, he also really, truly didn't think it could move the ball in the SEC. This wasn't some sort of "rawr, pansy ball" reflex — he literally, honestly didn't think it would work. And then it did, with a redshirt freshman, in Tuscaloosa against the best defense in the country.

Happy Ball beat Murder Ball on national television that evening. And while Alabama's own poor execution bore a considerable portion of the blame for the Tide's tumble[160], the numbers were still better than just about anybody (anybody not dripping with Aggie Confidence, anyway) could have imagined: 418 yards, 29 points, 167.3 pass efficiency[161].

When Texas A&M and Missouri came aboard the SEC ship, the No. 1 thing SEC traditionalists (and much of the national media) mentioned was that they would be forced to make offensive adjustments. "The spread won't work in the SEC" took on incredible life despite the fact that spread innovators Gus Malzahn (as Auburn's offensive coordinator) and Urban Meyer (as Florida's head coach) had both won national titles in recent years. The question has never been about "the spread" (a term that, first of all, encompasses about 27 different offenses in and of itself); the question should have always been about talent and execution.

You can make any offense work in any conference if you have the right personnel and are coached well enough. Missouri's offense never really threatened to get off the ground in 2012, but while good defenses (and, potentially, questionable personnel) obviously had a role in that, so did crippling injuries at quarterback and throughout the offensive line.

With a healthy (and fantastic) line, a healthy (and fantastic) quarterback, and strong play from skill positions, Texas A&M averaged 546 yards and 39 points per game in

---

[160] Freshman running back T.J. Yeldon lost an ill-timed fumble for the second straight week, just as he had in the fourth quarter at LSU seven days earlier in a game Alabama nearly lost. Meanwhile, quarterback A.J. McCarron's late-game accuracy was woeful. Twice in the fourth quarter, wide open receivers had to slow down to catch deep balls that, if hitting them in stride, would have resulted in touchdowns; Alabama ended up scoring on neither drive. And this says nothing of A&M cornerback Deshazor Everett's fourth-down interception in the game's final minutes, which was thrown a decent amount behind its intended receiver at the goal line.

[161] For the season, Alabama allowed 250.0 yards per game, 10.9 points, and a pass efficiency of 103.7.

SEC play, and 559 yards and 44 points overall. We can debate whether even Johnny Football can keep up this pace in 2013, but we can no longer even pretend to debate whether "the spread can work in the SEC." It can. It is. Sorry, Gary.

SEC defensive coordinators are very, very well-paid and will adapt, but there's nothing saying that Manziel, Sumlin, and A&M cannot also adapt. This is going to be a fun chess match to watch.

13. Beating, and Becoming, Goliath

During a timeout before what ended up being the game's final play, a 16-yard, fourth-down touchdown run by quarterback Kolton Browning, UL-Monroe head coach Todd Berry said some quick words to his team, and as the players began firing each other up, Berry simply grinned[162]. This was a masterpiece almost three years in the making. ULM, a program that had never finished with a winning record or attended a bowl game since joining the FBS ranks, was about to knock off Arkansas, a Top 10 team. His players were about to dog pile in the end zone. His fans were about to start weeping in the Little Rock stands. And the look on Berry's face suggested he knew it. It was a wonderful moment before an even more wonderful moment.

Let's step back about an hour.

On fourth-and-11 from the Arkansas 40, with time winding down in the third quarter, Browning twirled out of the pocket, somehow escaped a couple of closing Arkansas pass

---

[162] Parts of this chapter adapted from a piece that appeared at SB Nation on September 10, 2012.

rushers, and found Tavarese Maye near the sideline. Maye caught Browning's pass and plunged ahead for the first down, and the Warhawks lived to see another series of downs. Seven plays later, on fourth down again, Browning found Kevin Steed for a one-yard touchdown to bring ULM to within 28-21 with 14:08 remaining.

Browning's escape act was one of many on the night, but it perfectly encapsulated Arkansas' miserable evening in Little Rock, which eventually ended in a devastating 34-31 overtime loss.

We know now that Arkansas was not the team many thought it would be in 2012. Ranked eighth at the time they played ULM, the Razorbacks would start the season 1-4 and finish just 4-8 overall. But this game was still noteworthy for its prototypical upset characteristics. This is the textbook from which you teach your Upsets 101 class.

1. Todd Berry called the perfect underdog game.

From my 2011 ULM season preview:

ULM is one of the biggest 'Davids' in college football. The resources at the two Directional Louisiana state schools (UL-Monroe, UL-Lafayette) are, like the money, minimal, and to win at a program like ULM means taking anything but a direct approach. [...]

In 2010, Berry did his best to do things a bit off-kilter: running when opponents expected the pass, passing when opponents expected the run, keeping things fast-paced (possibly not the best idea for an underdog), employing the underdog-friendly 3-3-5 defense, etc. The results were decent; despite low overall quality, ULM won five games, three by a touchdown or less, and came within a one-point loss to UL-Lafayette of finishing bowl-eligible.

And from the 2012 preview:

> Berry enters year three professing that he has the program right where he wants it. His defenses have been salty, and his offenses creative, but in an improving Sun Belt, however, the bar is a little higher than it used to be.
>
> I am rooting for Berry to succeed for one simple reason: I want creativity and aggression to be rewarded. Nothing is more depressing to watch than a David trying to win games like Goliath would. Taking risks occasionally leads to calamity, but if they pay off enough it might encourage other coaches to take similar risks.

On the second Saturday night in September 2012, Berry painted his masterpiece. ULM went for it on fourth down an incredible seven times and converted an even more incredible six of them. In the second half, the Warhawks converted on fourth-and-10 (19-yard run by Browning), fourth-and-11 (the aforementioned pass to Maye), fourth-and-goal (1-yard touchdown pass), fourth-and-10 (23-yard touchdown pass to Brent Leonard with 47 seconds remaining) and fourth-and-1 (game-winning 16-yard touchdown run by Browning). That's not supposed to happen. If the teams lined up and played again the next week, it might not have happened again. But Berry knew it was the only way ULM was going to win this game – his philosophy is pretty fourth-down friendly regardless – and unlike so many college coaches, he said "Screw it," and rolled the dice.

ULM's game plan was beautifully aggressive: Attack Arkansas quarterback Tyler Wilson as much as possible (and when Wilson gets hurt, attack his backup, too), even if it means you risk some long gains. Stick to your strengths ("We can't run the ball? Fine. We'll have our quarterback throw it 67 times, then rip off some perfect scrambles when the defensive line over-pursues"), maintain preternatural aggressiveness in your game-calling (especially in the second half), and try for fourth-down conversions every time you think you have a chance to score. Arkansas will either stiffen or blink.

2. Arkansas blinked.

In the fourth quarter, during one of the many times the camera caught Arkansas offensive coordinator Paul Petrino yelling at his offensive line, his quarterback, and anybody else within range, all I could think of was the Miracle On Ice. The USSR coach, flipping out because his dominant team was trailing, subbed out his all-world goalie, Vladislav Tretiak, after a goal that wasn't entirely Tretiak's fault. In the face of a determined underdog, he briefly lost his mind, and it hurt his team significantly.

Why this analogy? Because when ULM scored to cut the lead to 28-14, Petrino completely lost the plot.

On Arkansas' first series with Brandon Allen behind center, the Hogs were up, 21-7. Arkansas ran the ball on three of four first downs; Allen completed some big-time passes on second-and-14 and first-and-15, and the Hogs scored to go up by 21 points. That was enough for Petrino to attempt to turn Allen loose despite the circumstances. Arkansas passed on seven of its final nine first downs; those seven passes netted two completions for 17 yards and an interception. Arkansas' last seven possessions ended in five punts, the pick, and an overtime field goal. The line was by no means blocking particularly well for running back Knile Davis and company, but instead of milking a lead, Petrino called plays like his team was trailing. Petrino clammed up, interim head coach John L. Smith looked sad and worried, and the defense just barely missed on quite a few stops. Arkansas first lost confidence, then lost control of the game. Among other things, the incompletions Allen threw kept extra seconds on the clock, and when ULM got the ball at its 10 near the end of regulation, the Warhawks had enough time to drive 90 yards for the tying score.

****

College football is nothing if not contradictory. It is at once a sport with the most well-embedded oligarchy and dominant socialist tendencies. At any given time, one of the sport's blue bloods is a single good hire away from becoming a dominant force again, and on most occasions, only members of the blue-blood club get a shot at the national title (and most major blue-chip recruits). At the same time, however: You get a bowl bid! And you get a bowl bid! And you get a bowl bid! If you win just half of your games, you will probably end up playing in an exotic locale – Mobile! Boise! Shreveport! Detroit! – and getting some free swag over Christmas break.

In a way, bowls are an implicit acknowledgement of the simple fact that most teams are never going to have a serious shot at a national title. You probably won't ever be a real contender, but hey, here's a trip to Honolulu (or San Francisco or Jacksonville, or New York City). In general, though, unless you are one of a small handful of schools, you probably aren't going to see a sustained stay in college football's top tier. And if you get a shot at the national title, you better win it, because you might not get another one.

Using a measure I call Estimated S&P+[163], let's look at the top 10 teams from three different three-decade periods: the 1930s-1950s, the 1960s-1980s, and the admittedly incomplete 1990s-2010s. We'll rank these teams according to the number of times in each span that they ranked in the 90th percentile or better.

---

[163] Explaining Estimated S&P+ is pretty simple: In essence, I took the same "output versus expected output" model that I use for S&P+ and applied it to the only data points available going back to the late 1800s: points scored and points allowed. It is not as accurate as using S&P+, and it certainly not as robust but it is still more effective than simply looking at records or poll rankings.

Table 1: 90th Percentile Est. S&P+ performances		
Top 10 Teams (1930s-1950s)	Top 10 Teams (1960s-1980s)	Top 10 Teams (1990s-2010s)
1. Tennessee (17)	1. Alabama (23)	1. Florida St. (17)
2. Notre Dame (15)	2. Nebraska (21)	2. Oklahoma (15)
3. Duke (14)	3. Oklahoma (19)	2. Florida (15)
4. Alabama (13)	3. USC (19)	4. Ohio State (14)
5. Army (12)	5. Michigan (16)	5. Miami (13)
5. Navy (12)	5. Texas (16)	6. Penn State (12)
7. Michigan (11)	7. Notre Dame (15)	7. Alabama (11)
7. Ga. Tech (11)	7. Penn State (15)	7. Michigan (11)
9. LSU (10)	9. Arkansas (14)	7. Nebraska (11)
9. Oklahoma (10)	10. Auburn (13)	7. Notre Dame (11)
9. Texas (10)		

Four teams – Alabama, Michigan, Notre Dame, and Oklahoma – are in the Top 10 in all three spans of time. LSU (12 times in the 1960s-1980s, 10 times in the 1990s-2010s) and Tennessee (11 times in the 1960s-1980s, 10 times in the 1990s-2010s) have come really close. Six members of the Top 10 from the 1960s-1980s were also in the Top 10 from the 1990s-2010s. The major changes in the power structure came in the reduction of the armed service schools' effectiveness (beginning in the 1950s) and in the emergence of Florida schools over the last 30 years or so, but the power structure has remained remarkably similar over time.

Upsets do happen, however. Frequently.

There are countless ways to win a college football game. It is one of the more charming aspects of this sport. The variance from one team's style to another dwarfs that of the professional game. The difference in talent levels from the power schools to the also-rans is such that the underdog schools face reality pretty quickly. You have to do things a little differently against the power schools, or else you probably aren't going to beat them. Coaches are often up for that challenge.

"Coaches have figured out ways to give themselves a chance when they shouldn't have a chance," says Sonny Dykes "It's what makes college football so cool."

Dykes draws reference to one particular game to make his point. In 2003, when he was the Texas Tech receivers coach under Mike Leach, his 7-5 Red Raiders played in the Houston Bowl against Paul Johnson's Navy Midshipmen. Texas Tech quarterback B.J. Symons completed 41 of 53 passes for 497 yards and four touchdowns. Symons completed passes to Nehemiah Glover, Taurean Henderson, Mickey Peters and Wes Welker at least seven times each, and to Carlos Francis six times. Henderson, a running back, had almost as many receptions (nine) as rushes (11). In all, Tech passed 53 times and rushed 20 times, a 73 percent pass rate, despite the fact that the Red Raiders led for almost the entire game (14-0 at halftime, 24-7 after three quarters) and therefore could have been expected, by general convention, to run a lot in the latter stages of the contest.

Navy, meanwhile, did almost exactly the opposite. Despite facing a deficit for most of the game, Navy's flexbone quarterback Craig Candeto rushed 23 times while completing just two of nine passes. Navy rushed 55 times and passed 13 times, an 81 percent run rate.

With neither school possessing natural historical or geographical advantages, both were forced to make creative hires to win games. At Tech, Leach employed his Air Raid attack (with assistants like Dykes, current West Virginia head coach Dana Holgorsen, and current East Carolina head coach Ruffin McNeill, among others) with great success. In his 10 years as head coach, Leach won 84 games, finished with 10 consecutive winning seasons, and made a solid run at the national title in 2008, ranking second in the polls in mid-November before getting whipped by Oklahoma. He qualified for the same number of bowls in 10 years as Texas Tech had reached in the 26 years before his arrival.

At Navy, Johnson employed his well-drilled Flexbone option attack with solid success. Navy had fallen on hard times, reaching just one bowl in the 20 years before Johnson arrived and going just 1-20 in 2000-01, but after going 2-10 in 2002, Johnson uncorked five straight bowl campaigns. The Midshipmen went 10-2 and finished 24th in 2004; Johnson was hired by Georgia Tech, where he won the (later-vacated) ACC title in 2009[164]; and his successor and former assistant, Ken Niumatalolo, kept both the Flexbone and most of the wins. Navy has gone to nine bowls in 10 years since Johnson arrived and has just once won fewer than eight games in a season in that span.

"On any given Saturday in college football, I think anybody can beat anybody," says Colorado head coach Mike MacIntyre. I think the 85 scholarships[165] has evened things out a little; back when it was 105 scholarships, there was a bigger difference."

Granted, the most talented teams are usually going to win. And in college football, the talent disparity is still vast, even if it isn't as ridiculous as it once was. As former Alabama head coach Gene Stallings so aptly puts it, "I'd rather be the favorite. The favorite is the best team, and the best team usually wins."

Dykes agrees. "If my players are better than your players, then of course I'd shorten the game and rely on my talent to beat yours."

But coaches are willing to get very creative to find the winning edge if they don't have vastly superior talent. "One of college football's biggest strengths has grown out of one of college football's biggest weaknesses," says Smart Football's Chris B. Brown. "There are lots of non-competitive games in a given week, but there are enough games going on at any time

---

[164] From 2010-12, however, Johnson went just 21-19.
[165] Beginning in 1992, the NCAA imposed "an annual limit of 85 on the total number of counters [scholarship recipients] in football at each institution."

that you can always find something competitive and interesting."

According to Brown, the hierarchy of needs for winning a football game is as follows:

1. Talent. The "It ain't about the Xs and Os, it's about the Jimmies and Joes" cliché has certainly been around a while, but it is still true in essence. No matter what tactics a coach uses, over the course of 125 to 200 plays, the team with a talent advantage is going to win more often than not. And while they certainly have flaws and outliers, recruiting rankings are rather predictive because of this. College football recruiting has become its own industry – its own *sport*, really – and that wouldn't be the case if there weren't some basis in reality for the obsession. Some teams are able to succeed at a high level without four- or five-star recruits, but they are notable because they are rare.

2. Development. If you have a specialized system, like the Air Raid or the Flexbone, Brown says you can almost take a shortcut in terms of talent development. Players' roles are very well-defined and specific in such a system. At the same time, however, a coach like Nick Saban has proven that he can both land and develop blue-chip talent as well as anybody, and if you master numbers one and two here, you are the elitest of elite.

3. Scheme. Congratulations, you have landed talent, and you have learned how to develop it! Now you have to figure out how to deploy it.

4. In-game management. In-game decision-making – play-calling, aggressiveness, etc. – is a distant fourth on Brown's list, but that doesn't stop fans from complaining about it the most. It also doesn't stop coaches from attempting to derive an advantage from this.

****

In some ways, life as an underdog is freeing. Coaches at the highest level are typically allergic to risk; the pressure is so immense, and the second-guessing is of such high volume, that it almost feels more sensible to take what is considered the safe play even if stats tell you it isn't the smart play. "It's hard to break out of the norm as a coach," Todd Berry says. "If you're outside of the norm, you get fired pretty quickly if it doesn't work right away."

And to be sure, if you have a large enough talent advantage, playing it safe and risk-free might be the way to go. Jim Tressel developed a reputation as one of the most risk-averse coaches in college football while the head man at Ohio State; he also won 106 games, five BCS bowls, and a national title in 10 seasons in Columbus.

Tressel's conservatism backfired at times in big games – for two years in a row, his team entered the BCS title game ranked No. 1 in the country and lost by double digits, first to Florida in 2006, then to LSU in 2007 – but it was the sensible approach on most occasions. His teams may have struggled against top-tier opponents at times (who doesn't?), but he also almost never fell victim to upsets. After a rocky first season in 2001[166], Tressel's last nine Buckeye squads lost just once to a team that finished with a losing record and just four times to a team that won fewer than nine games in a season. Of their 17 losses in that span, eight came against teams that won at least 11 games.

When you've got all the talent and resources in the world, you can feel free to trust your talent to win games over the course of 60 minutes. When you don't, you get creative, both because it's your only chance of winning, and because there's almost no risk – "They can try something new," Brown says, "and if it doesn't work, Alabama was going to kill them anyway."

---

[166] In 2001, Ohio State went 7-5 and lost to 5-7 Wisconsin, 5-6 Penn State, and 7-4 UCLA, among others.

"I was at Kentucky, Texas Tech, and Arizona," says Sonny Dykes. "Those are hard jobs in those conferences. If we lined up and tried to out-Alabama Alabama, we didn't have a chance." And once you acknowledge that reality – which is tough to do sometimes – you go about doing whatever you think will build an edge.

"Do what others aren't." That's Fisher DeBerry's advice for maximizing your opportunities as a David against college football's Goliaths. If you can create a unique scouting experience, either by running an option offense (like DeBerry did for more than 20 years at Air Force), by executing your own unique version of the spread offense, or, since so many schools have moved toward the spread (and defenses have gotten smaller), by doubling down on an old-school power offense, you can force powerful schools to play at your level.

Over time, the spread has become less of an 'underdog' thing. "Sometimes you stumble onto a new dominant strategy, Brown says, be it the spread, a new variation of a standard offense, or a new defense[167].

Brown points to former Nevada coach Chris Ault as an example of stumbling onto something big. "Ault was unhappy with his offense, so he tried a Pistol set[168] instead of a Shotgun. Within a decade, this simple tweak had caused an earthquake in the college football universe. Nevada set offensive records with dual-threat quarterback Colin Kaepernick running Ault's offense, and it continued to move quite well when Kaepernick took his skills to the San Francisco 49ers. Offensive coaches throughout college football started adding aspects of the Pistol

---

[167] In his *The Essential Smart Football*, Brown talks about Memphis State defensive coordinator Joe Lee Dunn whipping out a 3-3-5 defense to try to beat USC in 1991. It worked well enough that a) Dunn was hired as Ole Miss' defensive coordinator the next season, and b) the 3-3-5 caught on in various areas of the country, including New Mexico (during Rocky Long's time as head coach; now San Diego State's head coach, he employs it there, too) and, now, UL-Monroe.

[168] The Pistol's name comes from basically being a shorter shotgun. Creative, right?

into their offenses, and in 2012, the Pistol made a huge impact at the NFL level with quarterbacks like Kaepernick and Washington's Robert Griffin III[169].

When something works, other coaches notice. And then a chain reaction begins. The spread and its variations have proliferated throughout college football, setting in motion the same set of events that we saw when the Wishbone gained popularity in the 1970s and 1980s. Other offensive coaches adopt it because it works, and then it works to the point where defensive coaches have to adjust for it.

With the Wishbone and the option game dominating, defenses felt the need to get smaller and faster to compensate. That opened the door for a set of bigger, more powerful pro-style options, adept at passing the ball downfield (perhaps via play-action), to thrive. Now, because of the spread, defenses have once again begun to get smaller, in some cases using a nickel back (a fifth defensive back) full time, or close to it, instead of a third linebacker in your standard 4-3 defense.

For a lot of coaches, then, this has led them not toward the spread, but to its direct opposite. In three conferences known for offensive proficiency, schools like Stanford (first under Jim Harbaugh[170], then under David Shaw), Kansas State (under longtime coach/wizard Bill Snyder), and even Western Kentucky (under Willie Taggart, who was hired by South Florida following the 2012 season) found success not through speed and relentless pace, but through power and plodding.

"The spread has been a big equalizer," says Sonny Dykes. "It's become more popular, so what you have to do is stay a little bit ahead of the curve. We've gone to tempo as another great equalizer."

---

[169] From the "Everything old is new again" department, John Thorn points out that the Pistol innovations, along with a lot of the quarterback run plays, draw heavily (though not entirely) from the single wing formations from the first half of the 20th century. "We stand on the shoulders of giants."

[170] Harbaugh became the head coach of the San Francisco 49ers in 2011; naturally, with Kaepernick, he adopted the Pistol and strayed ever so slightly from some of the power concepts that had built Stanford into a national power.

Tempo is an interesting topic. Statistically, it makes sense to shrink a game to a minimal number of plays if you aren't completely sure you will have a per-play advantage. With fewer plays, your team might need fewer breaks to get ahead.

At the same time, however, you can minimize an opponent's physical advantage by wearing the hell out of its defenders. Even a defense that fields 11 five-star blue-chippers isn't going to be as effective when its players are gassed and its substitution patterns are knocked out of rhythm by a no-huddle attack[171].

Of course, you can also play with your tempo the way Greg Maddux played with the speed of his pitches. In UL-Monroe's 2012 upset of Arkansas, Berry's approach changed after halftime. "We went relatively slow early on because we wanted to have a close game at halftime. We ran a lot of plays, but we were at a much slower pace, moving the ball, converting third downs, not worrying about the explosions." On ULM's opening drive, the Warhawks went 67 yards in 12 plays, eating up 5:03 of possession. They averaged 25.3 seconds per play. On their next four drives, all punts, they averaged 33.3 seconds per play. They picked up the pace late in the half, ripping off a 10-play, 73-yard drive in two minutes and 11 seconds, but it finished with no points – they went for it on fourth-and-1 from the Arkansas 2 and failed. ULM trailed by a 21-7 margin at halftime; considering the Warhawks' lack of offensive success, the slow pace did perhaps help to keep the game close, especially considering Arkansas had scored on three of its final five drives of the half (the last drive: three plays, 87 yards, and an easy seven points).

"In the second half, it was a 'two-minute frenzy' type of pace, and we wore the defense out a bit," says Berry. Indeed,

---

[171] Every potential reward has a potential black cloud, of course. A no-huddle is great if you are moving the chains and keeping the defense on the field. But if you aren't getting first downs, a no-huddle offense simply means that you go three-and-out faster, and your own defense gets gassed instead. That's why you'll see a lot of offenses wait until they first convert a first down to go into fourth or fifth gear.

ULM began the half with a 10-play, 64-yard drive that ate up just 2:19 of clock; and again, the drive finished with no points. On third-and-10 from the Arkansas 11, quarterback Kolton Browning was picked off by Arkansas' Ross Rasner. The pace didn't offer immediate help on the scoreboard, but one could certainly make the case that it wore the Arkansas defense down a bit[172].

Of course, it helped that Arkansas quarterback Tyler Wilson had gotten hurt late in the first half. After backup Brandon Allen's initial touchdown drive, the Razorbacks would go scoreless for the rest of regulation, going three-and-out four times in their final six drives (the other two drives: a four-and-out and a turnover). Arkansas' sudden offensive incompetence bought ULM some extra time, and considering the Warhawks finally tied the game with just 47 seconds remaining, they needed every bit of that time.[173]

Around the time Paul Johnson's tenure at Navy was beginning, Berry's at Army was ending. In four seasons as the head coach of the Black Knights (2000-03), he won just five games, six fewer than he had won in his final season at Illinois

---

[172] A couple of weeks later, in a near-upset of Baylor on a Friday night on ESPN, Berry took a completely different approach on the offensive side of the ball. While they thought they might be at an overall disadvantage against Arkansas, the Warhawks knew they could move the ball against Baylor about as well as Baylor moved the ball. So instead of keeping things close early, the general approach was, according to Berry, "Here we go. Let's maintain serve [by scoring every time Baylor does]." It was pedal-to-the-metal football that featured 173 total plays, 1,109 yards, 63 first downs and 89 points. It also featured a tweak from ULM most of us hadn't seen before: a two-quarterback formation. The Warhawks lined up both starter Kolton Browning and backup Cody Wells in the backfield and ran a couple of option-then-pass looks that set Twitter on fire. "We'd been doing the two-QB thing for going on about seven years," Berry says. "We did it at UNLV [when he was offensive coordinator], too. It just happened to be the first time it was on national television."

[173] One other factor in this game that is incredibly common in upsets: At some point, Arkansas' home-field advantage turned sour. The home crowd typically gives you an edge, but if something is happening that they didn't expect – like your team either losing to an inferior program, or at least letting them hang around – there is a palpable air of anxiety in the stadium that can turn the situation into a bit of a home-field disadvantage.

State (his Redbirds went 11-3 and made the 1-AA semifinals in 1999). He went 3-1 against Tulane and 2-41 against everybody else. He won just one of his final 24 games as head man at West Point. Along the way, he learned some lessons that would eventually turn his career around.

"I wasn't as risky at Army as I am [at ULM]," he says. "Here's one thing I definitely learned from Army: Go win the games. Don't worry about what the General's going to say. Don't worry about losing your job, don't worry about pleasing people. Just try to win games. Coach games to win, don't coach to keep things close and be a 'good old college football coach.'"

At ULM, Berry recruits players with chips on their shoulder and a willingness to play the role of both underdog and winner. He also doesn't use the "U" word that often. "We don't play up the underdog thing very much. We have a sign that players see every day; it says 'I didn't come here to play, I came here to win.'

"A lot of players in programs like this, they think that going into a game as the underdog means it's a win if we play it close. You don't play to your potential like that."

After struggling at Army (to put it kindly), Berry moved around a bit; he spent two seasons as Charlie Weatherbie's offensive coordinator and quarterbacks coach at ULM, moved to Miami for one year as Larry Coker's quarterbacks coach in 2006, then spent three seasons as Mike Sanford's offensive coordinator and quarterbacks coach at UNLV. All of these programs faced uphill battles – ULM had never been to a bowl game, UNLV has attended just two bowls since 1984 (and none since 2000), and Miami was undergoing serious staff changes in what would end up being Coker's final year there – and Berry took plenty of notes along the way.

When Weatherbie's time at ULM ended in 2009, the Warhawks hired Berry, not so much to right the ship (that analogy only works if the ship was once right), but to build it. Utilizing a crafty set of tricks, he almost dragged an outmanned ULM squad to bowl eligibility in 2010, going 5-7 with two tight, late losses. In 2011, injuries provided a bit of a setback, but in 2012, ULM leaped forward[174]. The Warhawks upset a highly-ranked (and, as we would later learn, overrated) Arkansas squad in the season opener, nearly did the same to Auburn and Baylor, and jumped out to a 6-2 start. Injuries dragged the Warhawks down again (depth still wasn't where it needed to be), but they still finished 8-5 and made their first ever bowl appearance, a loss to Ohio in the Independence Bowl.

****

Life as an underdog also requires some calculated risks. Going for it on fourth down is frequently cited as a way to put pressure (mentally and tactically) on an opponent that might have other advantages over you. "I treat fourth-down conversions as a turnover," says Bob Stitt, head coach at Colorado School of Mines. "I go for it a lot on fourth down, not because the stats tell me to or anything, but because of confidence. I think we're going to get it.

"We were 58 percent [conversion rate] on fourth downs in 2012, and we went for 36 of them. Our opponents went for 18.[175] We're a lot higher than 58 percent when it's fourth-and-5 or less, too. I'll even go for it on fourth-and-8 when we're on their 40 or so.

"That's a turnover! If you get it, it's like the defense just got you the ball on the opponent's 50-yard line. We've got to be able to have confidence as an offense that, 'Hey, when we get around the 50, Coach is going to go for it.' And the defenders have to have it in their heads that, 'Hey, they're

---

[174] Heading into the 2012 season, Berry gave a great quote to the local *Monroe News-Star*: "The first year it sleeps, the second year it creeps, the third year it leaps."

[175] He admits that those numbers get skewed a bit when your team is losing a lot, and in part because of injuries, Stitt's 2012 team wasn't quite as effective as in years past.

going to go for it, and if they don't get it, we have to get excited and make sure the opponent doesn't get points out of it.'

"Man oh man, it's horrible for the opponent's defense to get you on third down, and they're all cheering, and then they stay out there. 'Oh no, we've gotta stop them again.' And then you get the first down."

Stitt crafts his game plan with this in mind, too. On third-and-long from certain areas of the field, the quarterback knows he doesn't have to go into hero mode. He just takes what the defense gives him because "he knows Coach is probably going to go for it on fourth[176]."

At the FBS level, Berry shares this mentality. "At East Carolina with Steve Logan [as Logan's offensive coordinator from 1992-95], I started doing some of the 'go for it on fourth downs' types of things," he says. "Steve was out there a little bit in terms of breaking convention[177]. I've always gone for it on fourth down a lot, and it takes a while to get to where the players don't treat that like a big deal. The offensive players

---

[176] More from Stitt: With his offense, "Playing bend-don't-break defense doesn't work. You want to keep the opponent's defense on the field; you want fast drives, for better or worse." And has he seen a correlation between explosive offense and leaky defense? In 2012, they couldn't stop anybody for five weeks. They lost their top three running backs and faded on offense, but the defense surged. "I think there's a huge correlation between having a great offense and the defense putting the screws down and having that sense of urgency." He references the Denver Broncos with Tim Tebow in 2011: "They knew they weren't gonna score a ton of points with that offense," and the Broncos' defense began to improve dramatically. His recommendation: "Don't even watch the offense, don't even look at the scoreboard. Just play D." Easier said than done, evidently.

[177] Logan coached under Jimmy Johnson for one year at Oklahoma State, then ended up with future Ohio State head coach John Cooper at Tulsa (Logan's alma mater) in 1983-84. After short stints as a position coach at Colorado and Mississippi State, Logan landed at East Carolina, where he was the offensive co-coordinator in 1990-91 and head coach from 1992-2002. He went to five bowls in seven years from 1994-2001 but resigned after a 4-8 season in 2002. He bounced around NFL Europe for a while, spent two years as Boston College's offensive coordinator, and most recently spent three seasons as the running backs coach for the Tampa Bay Buccaneers.

understand: It's third-and-10, and where we are on the field, fourth-and-3 is probably acceptable.

"If you Google 'fourth down percentages,' you pretty quickly find that it's a good gamble," Berry says.

Brown agrees: "Going for it on fourth down at certain areas of the field isn't an underdog strategy – numbers show it should be the *dominant* strategy, at least unless you have an extreme talent advantage." And as with every other aspect of football, talent does matter. Simply going for it on fourth down isn't a sound strategy if you don't think your guys can get it.[178]

****

Your overall philosophy – the offense you run, the times at which you are willing to go for it on fourth down, et cetera – obviously matters when it comes to pulling an upset. But within the flow of the game itself, you will also need to take advantage of every break and every matchup advantage. You might also need a favor or two from Goliath. And you don't quite know in advance what breaks you might get.

To elaborate on this, let's explore three famous upsets from the upset-laden 2007 season. No season strayed further from the norm than this one, which saw Michigan (three points away from a berth in the national title game in 2006) lose to an FCS team, saw USC (perhaps two to four points away from a berth in the national title game in 2006) lose to then-lowly Stanford at home as a 41-point favorite, and saw a Nick Saban squad fall to Charlie Weatherbie's ULM Warhawks on Senior Day[179].

---

[178] Stitt, once more: "Dropped balls are a horrible, horrible thing with the spread. You're frequently using short passes as a substitute for rushing, and while that is a high-percentage option, it isn't 100 percent."

[179] How crazy was 2007? The following teams all spent at least one week in the AP Top 5: Boston College, California, Florida, Georgia, Kansas, LSU, Michigan, Missouri, Ohio State, Oklahoma, Oregon, South Florida, Texas, USC, Virginia Tech, West Virginia, and Wisconsin. No. 2 USC was stunned by Stanford one

Appalachian State 34, Michigan 32 (September 1, 2007)

The craziest year began with the craziest result. This game didn't have as much of an impact on the national title race as Stanford's win over USC, but it set the table for everything that followed. Appalachian State raced out to an early lead, held on for dear life, then won it in the final 30 seconds, stunning the 109,218 in attendance.

What Mattered: Special Teams. Appalachian State blocked two field goals (from 43 and 37 yards), including an attempted game-winner as time was expiring.

What Didn't Matter: Turnovers. Somehow, ASU survived three turnovers, including one that took place right after Michigan had taken the lead with five minutes remaining in the game. Michigan also recovered two of three fumbles.

What Mattered: Finishing Drives. Appalachian State made seven trips inside Michigan's 40-yard line and scored on six of them – five touchdowns, a field goal, and a missed field goal. Points per trip: 4.9. Michigan created more scoring opportunities and outgained ASU by nearly 100 yards (479 to

---

week, then No. 1 LSU lost to Kentucky and No. 2 California lost to Oregon State the next. New No. 2 South Florida fell to Rutgers, then the next No. 2, Boston College, lost two weeks later. No. 1 Ohio State fell to Illinois on November 10, and two Top 3 teams (No. 2 Oregon, No. 3 Oklahoma) saw their quarterbacks get hurt in upset losses the next week. LSU, back to No. 1, fell to unranked Arkansas, leaving the winner of No. 2 Kansas and No. 3 Missouri (Mizzou won, 36-28) to rise to a stunning No. 1 ranking over Thanksgiving break. Missouri stayed on top for just one week, crumbling in the Big 12 title game against Oklahoma, while No. 2 West Virginia was shocked at home by unranked-and-mediocre Pittsburgh. Only three teams lost fewer than two games that year, and two (11-1 Kansas, 12-0 Hawaii) played schedules that were too weak to get them into the BCS title game. For the first time ever, a two-loss team won the national title when 11-2 LSU took out 11-1 Ohio State in January.

387), but in 11 trips inside ASU's 40, Michigan scored four touchdowns, attempted four field goals (missing two), turned the ball over on downs twice and threw an interception. Points per trip: 2.9.

What Didn't Matter: Leverage Rate. Michigan was constantly able to leverage Appalachian State into passing downs, but dynamic quarterback Armanti Edwards dug the Mountaineers out of holes, time and again. Edwards completed 17 of 23 passes for 227 yards and three touchdowns on the day.

What Mattered: The Start. Appalachian State kicked the eventual game-winning field goal with 26 seconds left, then blocked a Michigan field goal as time expired. That's what we remember. But in the first half, ASU created a cushion for itself that it would later need. A long first quarter touchdown pass from Edwards to Dexter Jackson and three brutally efficient second-quarter drives bought ASU a 28-14 lead near the end of the first half. The Mountaineers' offense would go cold for much of the second half, but the lead bought them enough time to keep things close enough to win it at the end.

Stanford 24, USC 23 (October 6, 2007)

Few upsets have followed the stereotypical upset script more closely than this one. As expected, Stanford's offense struggled mightily against a strong USC defense that ranked second in the country in Def. F/+ in 2007. Stanford's offense ranked 77th in Off. F/+ and was without the services of injured quarterback T.C. Ostrander. The Cardinal punted on their first eight possessions. But a) the Stanford defense held the potent Trojans to just nine points in the first half and 23 for the game, b) the Stanford defense *also* scored a touchdown in the third quarter (a 31-yard interception return by Austin Yancy, one of four interceptions on the day) and held on a goal line stand late in the first half, and c) USC's home field advantage turned sour in the fourth quarter, when the Cardinal started to finally move the ball.

What Mattered: Field Position. Stanford's offense was nonexistent for three quarters, but the Cardinal were consistently able to pin USC in awkward field position. For the game, Stanford punter Jay Ottovegio punted eight times for an average of 42.9 yards (with two downed inside the 20), and USC's average starting field position was a paltry 23.1. The Trojans gained 459 yards and averaged 5.8 per play, but a long field became a 12th Stanford defender, and USC would eventually make a mistake on each drive.

What Didn't Matter: Sustained Offense. On Stanford's first eight drives, the Cardinal gained 59 yards (1.6 per play) and punted eight times. On five occasions, they went three-and-out But punting, defense, and turnovers bought them time, and eventually, the Cardinal, behind backup quarterback Tavita Pritchard, found a rhythm. Their last three drives generated 176 yards (5.5 per play) and 17 points.

What Mattered: Turnovers. USC quarterback John David Booty had an incredibly awful day; he completed 24 of 40 passes for 364 yards but was sacked four times and, more importantly, threw four interceptions. One was returned for a touchdown. Plus, there was only one fumble on the day, committed by USC tight end Fred Davis (who had an otherwise outstanding day: five catches, 152 yards, and a touchdown), and Stanford recovered it.

What Didn't Matter: Third Down Conversions. For the game, USC converted a mediocre seven of 19 third downs (36.8 percent), but Stanford was even worse: five-for-17 (29.4 percent). What ended up mattering more was fourth down: Stanford converted two of two, both on its final, game-winning drive (a 20-yard pass on fourth-and-20, and a 10-yard

255

touchdown on fourth-and-goal), while USC went just one-for-three.

UL-Monroe 21, Alabama 14 (November 17, 2007)

From 2008-12, Nick Saban went an absurd 61-7 at Alabama and won three national titles in four seasons. But the first year in a new locale is often Year Zero, even for good coaches, and it took him a while to find some traction in 2007, his first fall in Tuscaloosa. And when his Crimson Tide lost, 21-14, to ULM – the third of a four-game losing streak to end the regular season – it was difficult to envision all of the success that awaited in the coming seasons.

What Mattered: Turnovers. ULM was plus-4 on the day; the Warhawks recovered both Alabama fumbles and picked off quarterback John Parker Wilson twice in the first quarter. Quintez Secka returned the second interception 42 yards to the Alabama 1, setting up a touchdown that tied the game at 7-7. The Warhawks needed all four of these turnovers to overcome a 127-yard disadvantage in total yardage (409 to 282).

What Didn't Matter: Sustained Offense. ULM gained more than 29 yards in a drive just three times all day. But the one-yard touchdown drive that followed the interception was huge, as was the simple fact that ULM scored touchdowns on all three trips inside the Alabama 30. The Warhawks were able to advance the ball just enough to flip the field – average starting field position: ULM 31.6, Alabama 28.5 – and relied on key moments and mistakes to win the game.

What Mattered: Passing Downs. Alabama's offense was far from spectacular in 2007, but the Tide were particularly undone by their inability to function when they fell behind schedule. Their 65 percent success rate on standard downs was great; their 13 percent success rate on passing downs meant that as soon as they fell into second-and-9 or third-and-7, they were soon punting. Fourth downs didn't help, either: Alabama's last two drives resulted in turnovers on downs; first, Terry Grant was stuffed on fourth-and-2 from the ULM 18, then Alabama quickly went four-and-out in their territory with under a minute left.

****

There is, of course, an elephant in the room here as we talk about upsets and underdog tactics. "Nobody's employing an underdog tactic to win a national championship right now," Football Outsiders' Brian Fremeau reminds us. "They are counting on underdog tactics to win their little world, or their few non-conference games that make a difference to their small rate of success." At ULM, Charlie Weatherbie went 10-14 in the two seasons following the Warhawks' upset of Alabama and was gone. Meanwhile, Alabama went 26-2, attended two BCS bowl games and won a national title in that same span. Then they went 35-5 over the next three years and won another two titles. Upsets create incredible moments on which underdog programs can hang their hats, but they remain underdogs the next week, and most of the weeks that follow. The 2012 ULM team upon which I heaped praise above, after all, went just 8-5.

"It's a different kind of idea of success across college football," Fremeau continues. "For certain programs, it isn't just like they're unable to win a championship, but they're forced to strive for something less — a conference title, eight wins, whatever." College football's socialist tendencies allow for everybody to have their moment, but then the oligarchy resumes power.

Of course, if we go back to Brown's "stumbling across a dominant strategy" idea, it bears mentioning that what began as underdog tactics have gained in national relevance, and that, on rare occasion, teams do indeed break through. In 2010, an

Auburn offense led by one of the South's true spread offense wizards (Gus Malzahn), eked out a title-game win over Chip Kelly's run-first, Oregon spread offense to claim the national title. It took superior talent for both of those teams to reach the title game, talent that only a handful of schools could have compiled, but that single game handed evidence to those who think you can ride what we might call "underdog tactics" to a national title (or, at least, *almost* to a national title).

"Can you win a title with these tactics? Absolutely," says Sonny Dykes. "You have to have a special player, of course, like Auburn did [with quarterback Cam Newton] in 2010. Instead of having six exceptional players, you can possibly have just one or two at key positions. And you have to play a certain level of defense. Defense is like pitching – you're always going to have a chance with good D. Your quarterback won't always play well, but your D can."

****

It was a rather common refrain by that point: On December 2, 2006, Stanford just couldn't hold onto momentum. The Cardinal, playing in The Big Game in Berkeley versus arch-rival California, had figured out a way to put up a fight for a while. With seven minutes left in the third quarter, Stanford's Evan Moore reeled in a one-handed catch and scored a 51-yard touchdown to cut the Golden Bears' lead to 20-17. The score marked just the second time all season that the Cardinal offense had reached the end zone twice in the same game.

The Golden Bears' lead was 23-17 early in the fourth quarter when Cal running back Marshawn Lynch fumbled to give Stanford the ball at the Cal 14. For the third straight drive, however, Stanford's offense went three-and-out, and kicker Aaron Zagory missed a 29-yard field goal wide left. Stanford's offense would gain just 12 yards in its final 17 plays, and a late Cal field goal created an insurmountable 26-17 margin.

Be it because of talent, athleticism, stamina, resolve, some other reason, or *all* of the reasons, Stanford just couldn't hold on in 2006. The Cardinal trailed by just seven points late in the second quarter against Oregon in the season opener, then faded terribly and lost by 38. They built a 27-7 lead midway through the second quarter against San Jose State, then collapsed and lost, 35-34. They trailed Navy by seven points at halftime and lost by 28. They trailed UCLA by seven late in the third quarter and lost by 31. They trailed Notre Dame by four late in the first half and lost by 21. After stunning Washington for their only win of the season, they struck quickly against Oregon State and trailed by only seven late in the first half; they lost by 23.

The loss to Cal was Walt Harris' final game as Stanford's head coach. Just two years earlier, Harris had come to Palo Alto following eight seasons at Pitt. He had gone 52-44 with the Panthers, finished in the Top 25 once, and won the Big East in 2004; but with Harris in charge in Palo Alto, Stanford went just 6-17, and athletic director Bob Bowlsby let him go.

Since Tyrone Willingham had left Stanford for Notre Dame following a 9-3 campaign in 2001, the Cardinal football program had lost its way. Buddy Teevens and Harris had combined to win just 16 games in five seasons.

Enter Jim Harbaugh. The 43-year old University of San Diego head coach had just about the most impressive football lineage imaginable. His father is Jack Harbaugh, a former assistant coach at Michigan and Stanford and head coach at Western Michigan and Western Kentucky (where he won a 1-AA national title in 2002). His brother is John Harbaugh, who was at the time finishing his 23rd season as an assistant and is now a Super Bowl champion as head coach of the Baltimore Ravens. He served as Bo Schembechler's starting quarterback at Michigan for two years, leading the nation in passing efficiency in 1985 and going 21-3-1 in 1985-86. He played for 14 years in the NFL, winning the AFC Player of the Year award in 1995 and coming within an eyelash of reaching the Super Bowl that same year. During his final seven seasons in the NFL, he also served as an unpaid assistant and offensive consultant for his father at Western Kentucky. Once retired as a player from the NFL, he resurrected Rich Gannon's career as quarterbacks coach for the Oakland Raiders, then took the head coaching position at the University of San Diego in 2004. He inherited a Torero team coming off of its best season in a while (8-2 in 2003), and after a sketchy start (USD began the 2004 season 2-4), his squad won 27 of its next 29 games, claiming Pioneer League titles in 2005 and 2006.

Considering he had only been out of football and into full-time coaching for about six seasons, Harbaugh's résumé seemed pretty damn impressive. But when he agreed to become Stanford's head coach, he took on an extremely difficult situation. In a league where USC was once again at or near college football's pinnacle, California was not far from its peak with Jeff Tedford, Oregon State was surging under Mike Riley, Oregon was putting the pieces together, and even Washington wasn't too far removed from national relevance, Stanford had fallen far behind the curve. But there was a glimmer of hope from those decent starts in 2006.

"When we got this job, a friend of mine called me and said, 'If you can teach those kids to win, you'll have a chance,'" says David Shaw, who came to Stanford as Harbaugh's offensive coordinator in 2007. "They were 1-11, but they lost a lot of close games, and they lost close to the best teams. They didn't realize how to finish the game." Indeed, Stanford had faltered in close games, as evidenced above. But still, they weren't losing by three or four points. Only once in their 11 losses did they fall by fewer than nine points. There were injuries involved, but one had to question the talent level of a team that had ranked 104th in the 2006 F/+ rankings, barely ahead of 0-12 Duke and behind 2-10 teams like Memphis and Miami (Ohio).

Harbaugh was going to need to both improve the squad's overall athleticism and maximize the talent he was inheriting. The former would take some time. The latter, not so much. "There were so many big changes," Shaw says, "but the first thing that had to change was attitude. Jim was the best at that. Anybody who's doing anything that doesn't lead to winning, he's going to make them extremely … uncomfortable He wanted people saying to themselves, 'If I want to survive here, I need to be pushing myself and my teammates.' And the staff was very conducive to that."

Harbaugh's first Stanford staff consisted of Shaw (a 34-year old former Stanford receiver who had spent five years as an NFL position coach before serving as an assistant under Harbaugh for a year at San Diego), defensive coordinator Scott Shafer (a 40-year old who had spent six seasons as defensive coordinator at Northern Illinois and Western Michigan and was eventually hired as Syracuse's head coach in January 2013), Willie Taggart (a 30-year old running backs coach who would leave in 2010 to become head coach at his alma mater, Western Kentucky, where he had played for Jack Harbaugh) and a host of young, hungry 30-somethings.

"We made everything about competition," Shaw says. "When a guy realizes there's no more wiggle room, he either begins to compete, or he goes by the wayside."

The turnaround began immediately. In 2007, Stanford improved to 66th in the F/+ rankings, not good enough to compete consistently, but good enough to serve notice. The Cardinal still got beaten around by UCLA (45-17), Oregon (55-31), Oregon State (23-6) and Washington (27-9), but they also pulled off two monumental wins: the upset of USC discussed in the previous chapter, and a 20-13 Big Game win over California, Stanford's first since 2001. Rarely has a 4-8 season been so encouraging.

Stanford improved again, slightly, in 2008, to 5-7 overall and 58th in the F/+ rankings, albeit with losses to USC and California. But the turnaround truly picked up speed in 2009, both on and off the field. The Cardinal signed the No. 20 recruiting class in the country according to Rivals.com that year; the class featured eight four-star signees, five more than Harbaugh's first two classes combined.

"We started to realize as a staff that we needed to recruit kids earlier," Shaw says, "getting Stanford in front of these young men earlier and getting them to realize what it takes to get into Stanford. We need to inspire them early enough to take the right classes to get into this school." The staff also began to realize how they could use Stanford's western locale to their advantage as well. "Let's say we're recruiting a young man from Georgia, and he's getting recruited by everybody in the South. Going to Alabama or Florida would be hard for him because of the locals; but going to Stanford is an out. 'Everybody's not going to hate me if I go to Stanford.'"

Sure enough, out-of-state recruiting picked up drastically in 2009. Harbaugh signed a four-star defensive end from Arizona (Trent Murphy), three players from Texas (including four-star running back Stepfan Taylor[180]), a four-star linebacker from New York (Shayne Skov), a four-star receiver from Georgia (Jamal-Rashad Patterson), and a four-star tackle from Maryland (Terrence Stephens). They also unearthed a two-star defensive end from Wisconsin named Ben Gardner, who would go on to become an all-conference performer.

Of course, they were also doing well locally, reeling in California products and future difference-makers such as tight ends Zach Ertz and Levine Toilolo, running back Tyler Gaffney, defensive back Usua Amanam, fullback Ryan Hewitt, and cornerback Terrence Brown.

The 2009 recruiting class would play an incredible role in the Cardinal's future success, but Stanford didn't have to wait for them to make a difference. The 2009 squad, which featured veterans like senior running back Toby Gerhart (who

---

[180] A year earlier, Stanford had signed a four-star quarterback from Texas as well. Last name: Luck.

finished a very close second to Alabama's Mark Ingram for the Heisman Trophy) and youngsters like redshirt freshman quarterback Andrew Luck, broke through with an 8-5 record and the No. 3 offense in the country according to Off. F/+.

In 2010, they lost Gerhart but remained No. 3 on offense, rose to sixth overall, finished 12-1, and whipped Virginia Tech, 40-12, in the Orange Bowl.

In 2011, they lost Harbaugh to the San Francicso 49ers, replaced him with Shaw, went 11-2, and reached the Fiesta Bowl, where they lost to Oklahoma State.

In 2012, they lost Luck, the No. 1 selection in the NFL Draft, but again won 12 games, reeled in their first conference title in 13 years, and beat Wisconsin in the Rose Bowl.

Once the train got rolling, it just kept charging ahead no matter who stepped off of it. "The guys coming into the program realize what the program is about now: competition," says Shaw. "Everybody coming in is competing for the same spot. We've rewarded high-effort guys with playing time. We play as many guys week-to-week as anybody in the country because we want them to know they'll see the field when they do what we need them to do."

According to Shaw, as one of college football's new (and unexpected) heavyweights, Stanford has begun to become a "circle it on your schedule" game for lower-ranked programs looking to make a name for themselves. "We've seen a lot of people do different things against us. But we don't change our mentality, we don't change what we do. Plus, we haven't cemented ourselves in the football world's psyche as much as we should have by now. There's always the idea that we're going to slide."

On one hand, it is a bit disrespectful to assume a program that improved its win total for four straight years while rising (2007-10), then went 35-5 from 2010-12, will fall off simply because it isn't a historical power. On the other hand, it's pretty basic logic; that's just what tends to happen. You surprise people, make an unexpected run to the top of your conference (or the country) based around a specific coach, player, or cycle of recruits, and over time, you retreat back toward the level of play your program has established over the course of the previous decades. It is really, really difficult to maintain a winning program at an underdog school.

Just ask Jim Grobe.

****

"It started with just being different," Grobe says. "We looked at the personnel, and we didn't want to have any preconceived notions about who could or couldn't play. We wanted everybody to have a fresh start."

Grobe is describing his decision-making process as he took the reins of a beaten down Ohio football program in 1995. Then 42, Grobe had spent more than a decade as linebackers coach for Fisher DeBerry at Air Force. A former starting linebacker at Virginia, Grobe's history was on the defensive side of the ball; but offensively, he saw in Athens an opportunity stemming from the offense DeBerry was running in Colorado Springs. "Coming in, we didn't see a need to be in any certain offense. But we looked around the [Mid-American Conference] and realized that nobody was running the triple option like we did at Air Force. So that gave us a little bit of an edge.

"Defensively, we did the same thing. Most of the teams in the MAC were in a four-man front, so we thought, well, let's play a 3-4 defense and maybe do a little slant-angle with that. Let's make them hit moving targets and be a little bit different on both sides of the ball. Being unique got things going at Ohio."

For most of the previous three decades, Ohio was a coaching graveyard. Accept the job at your own peril. Under Bill Hess, the Bobcats had gone 10-1 in 1968, reaching the Tangerine Bowl (a 49-42 loss to Richmond) and finishing 20th in the AP Poll. But after a decade of mostly middling results

(Ohio won more than six games just once more), his tenure ended with a 1-10 campaign in 1977. Brian Burke managed a few 6-5 seasons in late 1970s and early 1980s, but he never topped six wins and was out after 1984. The two men who followed him, Cleve Bryant and Tom Lichtenberg, won just 17 games – seventeen! – in 10 years. Between 1985 and 1994, Ohio went 4-6-1 in 1988, 4-7 in 1993, and an incredible 9-76-3 in the other eight seasons. They went 0-11 the year before Grobe's arrival.

"Ohio had four separate 12-game losing streaks in the 10 years before we got there," Grobe says. "They were on the nation's longest losing streak when we got there." He once jokingly asked at a local quarterback club meeting "if anybody had any ideas on how to improve on 0-11." The semi-serious answer: "Well, you could just play 10 games…"

So why did Grobe, with no real Midwestern ties (unless you consider Virginia or West Virginia "Midwestern") and no "clean up a mess at your alma mater" obligation, accept the Ohio job in the first place? "The draw was being a head coach. I wanted to see if I could run my own program and be successful doing that. That was my motivation."

Following a 2-8-1 debut season, Grobe had to overachieve just to reach .500. In his final five seasons in Athens, Grobe's Bobcats went 31-25, which seems relatively unimpressive until you realize the destitute state of the program he inherited. It was an impressive enough coaching performance that Wake Forest hired him as its head coach in 2001.

In 2001, Wake Forest was in many ways to the ACC what Ohio had been to the MAC in 1995. The Demon Deacons had experienced sporadic success through the years: John Mackovic had taken them to the Tangerine Bowl in 1979 in a season that saw them ranked as high as 14th at one point. Bill Dooley had engineered an 8-4 season and Independence Bowl win in 1992. And future Indianapolis Colts head coach

Jim Caldwell had, in 1999, pulled off a 7-5 record and an Aloha Classic win over Arizona State.

Still, those three seasons were the lone bright spots for Wake, despite the fact that the school made what were really some relatively decent hires. Mackovic would win 71 games at Illinois and Texas from 1988-97. Mackovic's replacement, Al Groh (who led the Demon Deacons from 1981-86), would lead Virginia to five bowl appearances in six years in the 2000s after a year as head coach of the New York Jets. Bill Dooley (1987-92) won 132 games at North Carolina and Virginia Tech before finishing his career at Wake Forest. And Caldwell (1993-00) would go on to lead the Colts to Super Bowl XLIV (with help from Peyton Manning, of course). But none of them could master the Wake Forest job. Those four coaches had combined for three bowl bids and six winning records in 23 seasons in Winston-Salem; in its history, Wake Forest had won more than seven games in a season just three times and had won fewer than three 30 times.

Caldwell's teams had passed pretty well at times but, for the most part, had no semblance of a running game. That meant for a potentially awkward transition for Grobe, but he and his staff made the most of it.

"At Wake Forest, we didn't think we had the guys to run the Wishbone like we did at Ohio University," Grobe says. "At the end of our tenure at Ohio, we had moved more toward an I-option attack, like those old Nebraska and Colorado teams – lots of option mixed with power off-tackle, toss sweep, play-action, spring draw, spring draw pass. We had a little bit of a background in I-football, and we had a good fullback in Ovie Mughelli[181], so we ran more speed option, more zone option. And we had a good quarterback in James MacPherson. Typically you don't feel good about what you've

[181] Mughelli was an all-conference fullback and four-year starter for Wake Forest and became a two-time All-Pro fullback, first for the Baltimore Ravens, then for the Atlanta Falcons.

got when you get there, but Jim Caldwell left us some pretty good players.

"We just tried to take the personnel we had and tried to be a little bit different. Defensively, we really felt like we didn't have the personnel to be in a 3-4, so we actually went to a 3-3 look and played five defensive backs. That really helped us for a couple of years; it was totally different than what others had in our league. We went back to a four-man front when we got some big guys.

"Our thoughts at both places were to initially try our best to be a little unique." Outmanned at a school that was athletically overmatched by teams like Florida State and Clemson, in a conference that was about to add Big East heavyweights Miami and Virginia Tech, the Demon Deacons were able to more or less hold their own early on under Grobe They went 6-5 in 2001 and 7-6 in 2002 (whipping Oregon, 38-17, in the Seattle Bowl), but they slipped, winning just 13 games from 2003-05.

Over time, Grobe began to conclude that, to win games in Winston-Salem, at a school with high academic standards, he was simply going to have to recruit the best athletes available and use his "do something a little different" strategy to craft a system from year to year. "Our recruiting each year has become simply trying to find the best players we can find. Maybe that's an option quarterback, maybe that's a throwing quarterback. We were running the quarterback a lot, doing a lot option stuff, but then we ended up with Riley Skinner, who doesn't run but throws so well. We had to go to school and learn to throw the ball."

Grobe has never signed a recruiting class that Rivals.com ranked higher than 58th in the country. And in Riley Skinner, he found an unheralded, undersized quarterback that didn't even have a Rivals profile. When starting quarterback Ben Mauk went down in the first game of the 2006 season, Skinner, then an unranked and unknown redshirt freshman, took over and took Wake to unheard-of heights. He completed 70 percent of his passes, threw 17 touchdowns to five interceptions, and led the Demon Deacons to a stunning 10-2 record in the regular season. Wake Forest ranked just 30th in the F/+ rankings but won five one-possession games and outlasted Georgia Tech in a 9-6 bearhug to win the ACC. It was the Demon Deacons' second conference title ever, and the ensuing BCS bowl bid, a trip to the Orange Bowl, was their first.

The passing yards and, to an extent, the wins, continued as Skinner's career progressed. Wake never won another conference title but won nine games in 2007 and eight in 2008. Skinner threw for more than 13,000 yards and 100 touchdowns in his career, and he did so for a coach who, a few years earlier, was running a Wishbone attack.

As talent has cycled through the system, Grobe has begun to notice a problem he probably didn't expect. "With Tanner Price [Skinner's successor, who enters his senior season in 2013 already having amassed 6,666 passing yards and 39 touchdown passes], we've been a throwing team. Now we don't run the ball very well because we've gotten used to throwing. We're really in transition now – we're trying to get back to being more of a running team.

"At a place like Wake Forest, you just go recruit the best players you can, and your schemes might change year to year. That's not what you like to do, but it's something you have to deal with."

Since the 2006 ACC title run, wins have diminished. Wake Forest has still won more consistently than, really, at any point in its history since the 1940s; the Deacs have been to three bowls in six seasons, and they've only had one year worse than 5-7. Another break or two in 2009 and 2012 (each 5-7 seasons), and Wake would be looking at a string of six bowls in seven years. Still, maintaining that higher level has been difficult at a school with no historical advantages and with recruiting difficulties. Wake Forest's story makes Stanford's achievements even more impressive by comparison;

it also reminds us that Stanford has only been winning big for three years.

****

There is a pathway to becoming Goliath. Eventually, almost every coach at an underdog school will falter at different parts of the path; but the checkpoints, the issues every coach faces, remain the same.

1. Inheritance

"When you're a new coach, it's like being a high school coach – you don't really control the type of talent you have," says Brown. "You sometimes have to get creative in the ways you 'get good fast,' and you stumble across some new ideas."

The breaking-in period for a new coach can take so many twists and turns. The first year or two calls on a skillset completely different than what carries a coach when the program is built in his own image.

To make his point, Brown uses the example of Randy Walker at Northwestern. An offensive coach for his entire career, Walker coached running backs at alma mater Miami (Ohio) for two years, then held various jobs at North Carolina (running backs coach, quarterbacks coach, and eventually offensive coordinator) for a decade, ended up at Northwestern for two years and settled in as Miami (Ohio)'s head coach for nine seasons (1990-98). He stabilized a fallen program pretty quickly – after going 2-18-2 in the two years before Walker was hired, the then-Redskins went 26-25-4 in his first five seasons – then took a lovely step forward. Miami went 8-2-1 in 1995, knocking off No. 25 Northwestern and finishing the season by outscoring Ohio and Akron by a combined 95-2. After a 6-5 step backwards in 1996, his final two Miami teams went 18-4; in 1998, Miami lost to an elite Marshall team by 14 and outscored its other 10 opponents (including North Carolina), 300-111.

In 1999, Northwestern hired Walker to replace Gary Barnett, the wizard who had taken the Purple to Pasadena in 1995[182] and won another nine games in 1996 before fading a bit and taking the Colorado job. The Wildcats had averaged only 17.8 points per game in Barnett's final season and would score only 12.8 per game in Walker's first year on the way to a 3-8 record. In the brutal home stretch to finish the 1999 season (final four opponents Wisconsin, Michigan, Michigan State and Illinois went a combined 38-10 in 1999), Northwestern was outscored 135-29.

At this stage in college football, the spread offense was in its infancy. Hal Mumme and his offensive coordinator, Mike Leach, had unleashed gaudy passing stats on the SEC, to the point where new Oklahoma coach Bob Stoops decided to bring Leach aboard as his offensive coordinator in 1999 [183]. Plus, Purdue's Joe Tiller was making serious waves with Drew Brees at quarterback. But these pass-first offenses didn't necessarily appeal to most coaches, including Walker. Walker and his offensive coordinator, Kevin Wilson[184], had a lot of power offense in their background. In a desperate attempt to simply move the ball a little bit, however, Walker and Wilson started tinkering.

---

[182] The loss to Miami was Northwestern's only blemish that year until the Rose Bowl. The Wildcats had upset Notre Dame in South Bend in the season opener and would go on to take out Michigan in Ann Arbor and Penn State and Iowa at home to secure its first Big Ten title since 1936. They would split the conference title at 7-1 the next year, too.

[183] The logic behind Stoops hiring Leach: Kentucky's offense was the one Stoops had the most trouble stopping when he was Steve Spurrier's defensive coordinator at Florida. After just one year, Leach was promoted to head coach at Texas Tech; new Oklahoma coordinator Mark Mangino took the components of Leach's offense, added in a heaping helping of tiny running back Quentin Griffin, and won a national title in 2000.

[184] Bob Stoops would eventually hire Wilson, too. But if you've reached this point in the book without skipping around, you already knew that.

What they came up with was something like the spread-to-run attack that Clemson and offensive coordinator Rich Rodriguez were mastering with dual-threat quarterback Woody Dantzler. In 2001, Dantzler would become the first quarterback in history to pass for 2,000 yards and rush for 1,000 yards in the same season[185]. Northwestern, meanwhile, was establishing something similar; the Wildcats were less explosive than Clemson, but they were devastatingly efficient and powerful on the ground.

In 2000 – again, just one season after nearly complete offensive incompetence – quarterback Zak Kustok passed for 2,389 yards and rushed for 505 [186], while running back Damien Anderson rushed for 2,063 yards (6.6 per carry) and 23 touchdowns. Five Northwestern receivers caught at least 25 passes, while Anderson carried about 25 times per game and Kustok threw in about 10 non-sack carries per game. Northwestern also averaged 82.7 plays per game, an exhausting number even in today's game, but downright revolutionary in 2000. A year earlier, Anderson had gained 1,128 yards on just 3.7 yards per carry, and Kustok and Nick Kreinbrink had combined to throw for just 1,515 yards with a dreadful 42 percent completion rate. But in one offseason, Walker and Wilson figured out how to nearly triple their scoring (from 12.8 points per game to 36.8) and raise their per-play average by 50 percent (from 3.8 to 5.7).

Brown points to one particular game that may have had as much of an influence on widespread acceptance of the spread offense as any other. On November 4, 2000, Northwestern unleashed a furious fourth-quarter comeback to knock off mighty Michigan, 54-51. The Wildcats scored 18 points in the final quarter, eventually finding cracks in

---

[185] At the time, this was an amazing feat, as was Missouri's Brad Smith's own accomplishment of averaging a 2,000/1,000 season over four years. Now, quarterbacks like Texas A&M's Johnny Manziel and Michigan's Denard Robinson have been threatening something closer to 3,000/1,500.

[186] Really, the totals were probably closer to 2,100 passing yards and 700 rushing yards; Northwestern allowed 34 sacks for 239 yards that season.

Michigan's defense with an up-tempo attack that attempted 90 plays in 60 minutes; but that wasn't the most notable part. The balance of the offense was breathtaking. Kustok completed 27 of 40 passes for 322 yards and two touchdowns (including the game-winner with 26 seconds left), while Anderson rushed 31 times for 268 yards; in total, Northwestern rushed for a nearly symmetrical 332 yards.

To date, the spread offense had been mostly used as a way to generate underdog yardage through the air. Northwestern changed the perceptions of how a spread could be used, and it was a couple of coaches grounded in power running who shined this light.

Above, we discussed Brown's hierarchy for winning games – talent, development, scheme, and in-game management. When you inherit talent and you are just starting out at a program, you can't do much about those first two items. Brown: "Steps 1-2 are a longer game, but you can win faster with mastery of steps 3-4." Walker did that in Evanston; in his second season, Northwestern went 8-4. As his program became 'his,' instead of one he had inherited, the results dried up a bit. Wilson took Oklahoma's offensive coordinator position in 2002, when then-coordinator Mark Mangino left to take over at Kansas. Northwestern won just seven games combined in 2001-02 before rallying to win six, six, and seven games in his final three seasons (2003-05). Walker passed away after a heart attack on July 7, 2006.

For some great coaches, the breaking-in period doesn't go exceedingly well. Big-name, experienced coaches might be less interested in tweaking their way of thinking to adapt to the talent at hand, settling instead for short-term pain while they go about recruiting their own type of talent into the program. In 1977 at Florida State, Bobby Bowden took Darrell Mudra's three-win team and turned it into a five-win team. In 1986, Lou Holtz inherited Gerry Faust's ghastly 5-6 Notre Dame team. Holtz went 5-6 in 1987; in 1999, Holtz took Brad Scott's 1-10 South Carolina team and turned it into an 0-11 team.

Also in 1999, Bob Stoops came to Oklahoma and turned John Blake's disastrous 5-6 team into a 7-5 Independence Bowl team[187]. In 2001, after John Cooper had been fired following an 8-4 season, Jim Tressel came to Ohio State and went 7-5. In 2007, Nick Saban inherited a 6-7 Independence Bowl team at Alabama and turned it into a 7-6 Independence Bowl team.

That's why we often refer to a coach's first year as Year Zero, of course. It's a bit of a mulligan. After going 5-6 in his first season, Bowden won 39 games in his next four years in Tallahassee. Then he *really* caught fire in Year 12, kicking off a string of 20 consecutive Top 10 finishes (with two national titles). In South Bend, Holtz improved by three games in Year 2, then won a national title in Year 3; at South Carolina in 2000 he followed up his 0-11 season by going 17-7 and winning two Outback Bowls in Years 2 and 3. In his second year in Norman, Stoops won the national title; he has won at least 10 games in a season 11 times in the last 13 years. As mentioned above, Tressel won a national title in his second year and won a ridiculous 99 games in his final nine seasons. And Saban, of course, went 61-7 and won three national titles in his next five years in Tuscaloosa.

"As a coach, you've got to be open-minded to this business," Ohio head coach Frank Solich says. "There's a lot of creativity out there. You've got to be flexible, open to new ideas."

The early stages of a coach's tenure at a school can be throwaway campaigns, but occasionally a coach will find some lightning in a bottle. "That's what I love about coaching," says New Mexico head coach (and former Notre Dame head man) Bob Davie. "Take the hand that you're dealt, but be able to spin that into a positive." If you can do it, that doesn't

---

[187] Driving through Oklahoma City after Oklahoma's Independence Bowl loss to Ole Miss, I, for some reason, found myself listening to sports talk radio. One listener called in to rant about all of Stoops' mistakes and how Oklahoma fans were once again "settling for mediocrity." That phrase has somehow independently made its way to every Internet fan base in the country and is deployed daily.

guarantee long-term success, but it certainly buys some goodwill for you to spend as the program becomes your own.

2. System versus available talent

"You have to have your niche – you have to have something you do that gives you an identity schematically," says Davie. And to a large extent, that depends on the talent available to you. Great recruiters can reel in more talent, obviously, but considering there aren't that many truly elite recruiters out there (at least, guys who are a couple of standard deviations better than the norm), and considering few "underdog" programs are going to be able to recruit at a national level, it certainly helps when you cater the system to the style of recruit you know you can find in abundance.

Since 2002, the state of New Mexico has produced just 64 players who committed to an FBS school and were given at least a two-star rating by Rivals.com. Eight of these 10 were running backs, and 14 were offensive linemen, but only eight were receivers or tight ends. In this way, it might make sense to build more of a running attack in Albuquerque. That certainly appeals to Davie, anyway. "We're kind of a triple-option team here, and we're running it out of the pistol.

"I've embraced the underdog mentality here," he says. "New Mexico's kind of quirky, kind of different. It's got a small population but is filled with tough, hard-working people." Davie's own brand of football that he defined in previous stops like Notre Dame, Texas A&M, and Pittsburgh caters well to a physical, grinding, run-heavy attack. In this way, he might find what he's looking for from a recruiting standpoint.

"New Mexico was No. 2 in time of possession [in 2012]," Davie notes. "Everybody's speeding the game up, but we have to slow it down." Due to defections, "we had the lowest number of scholarship players in the country, and we played 13 straight weeks. Our identity was to outwork, outhit, and outdiscipline you. Slow the game down, run the ball, force turnovers."

"My plan at Notre Dame wasn't a whole lot different, of course. But you're still forming your identity to the place you are at. That's how it's going to be sustainable. My plan has to be specific to the University of New Mexico."

Coaches adapt similarly elsewhere, as well. Wisconsin produces big, corn-fed offensive linemen like they grow on trees. The Badgers import some running backs, load up on linemen, and pound away at you with great success; they've done so through two different coaching regimes now (Barry Alvarez[188] from 1990-2005, then Bret Bielema from 2006-12).

From 2002-13, the state of Missouri produced 21 quarterbacks rated at three stars or higher by Rivals.com, including five-star Missouri signee Blaine Gabbert in 2008 and high four-star Kansas State signee Josh Freeman in 2006. Both went on to become first-round NFL Draft picks. Meanwhile, the state has produced 17 three-star (or better) tight ends, including 2008 Mackey Award winner Chase Coffman, and 20 three-star (or better) receivers, including first-round draft pick Jeremy Maclin and the class of 2012's No. 1 overall player, Dorial Green-Beckham. It would make sense, then, that Gary Pinkel and Missouri would find some success in keeping those players nearby and running an effective spread offense. (The state doesn't produce nearly as many big-time defenders, by the way.)

Meanwhile, the state of Kansas doesn't produce that many elite high school recruits (and schools like Oklahoma are always major threats to swoop in and nab the ones it does produce), so Bill Snyder found himself a competitive advantage by raiding the local junior colleges for talent. That they are nearly in his backyard has made it easier to scout them and easier to recruit them heavily.

And, of course, the fact that seemingly almost every school in Texas runs its own variation of the spread makes

---

[188] Alvarez, by the way, went 1-10 in "Year Zero" at Madison.

perfect sense considering the proliferation of the spread throughout Texas high schools.

Straying from your base of talent (if there is one) can work out okay, in theory, but you better have a strong recruiting pull of some sort, or your margin for error is minimal. The state of Oregon doesn't produce a large number of elite prospects, but Mike Bellotti (1995-2008) and Chip Kelly (2009-12) were able to craft devastating teams based around the speed they were able to attract to Eugene, in part because of the facilities and unique marketing tools they have deployed with money Nike chief Phil Knight has donated through the years[189]. Rutgers, on the other hand, began to see its effective offense dry up as it attempted to move toward its own variation of a spread attack. In the northeast, you can get the big-time linebackers and power guys. Elite skill position players, however, might be a bit harder to come by if you have a system that needs a lot of them.

3. Culture

It is counterintuitive at first thought: A new coach is able to scrape together some wins with someone else's roster, and as he begins to bring in more highly-touted recruiting classes, the wins dry up a bit. As his own recruits begin to fill in the roster, a coach is sometimes left with a bit of an identity crisis as he transitions between the program he threw together on the fly and the one he intended to create. "A lot of coaches struggle to make the transition from 'making the most of what we have and trying to figure out ways to win,' to 'we have the talent we wanted now, and we're going to change our approach,'" says Brown.

"When you start to win, you start to become able to recruit better players," notes David Shaw. "Good players want to go where they can win games. The key for us is to never,

---

[189] To an extent, Oklahoma State is doing the same thing now with athletics benefactor, and aging jillionaire, T. Boone Pickens.

ever lose that David mentality. Even after winning BCS games, we still try to have the attitude like we're coming off of a 1-11 season. That's the trick. There's no such thing as carryover. We're not going to win games because we won last year."

That is, of course, where culture fits in. And it becomes especially important when you have the opportunity to recruit a higher-caliber athlete. "The biggest thing that gets glossed over in recruiting, something that truly upsets me, is that these kids are looking for the right fit, academically and athletically," Shaw says. "As coaches, we're often guilty of just trying to recruit the highest-rated, best player. But if the kid doesn't fit your team socially, doesn't fit your school, you're doing a disservice to the young man."

You could be doing a disservice to yourself as well. "Getting kids in your program that fit your program help you to have a healthier team," Shaw says. "When the game is on the line, I am a half a field away. It's the kids on the field that have to trust each other, work together, do problem solving on their own. And they can only do that if the locker room is tight and if everybody trusts each other. We can change lines and diagrams on our playbook, but if you have guys who don't trust each other, it's not going to matter."

On average, recruiting rankings are rather predictive of wins. You don't necessarily see "culture problems" at a school like Alabama, at least not with a 99th-percentile coach like Nick Saban involved. (Recruiting rankings certainly didn't help Auburn's Gene Chizik avoid both potential culture issues and, eventually, losses.) But if you are a third-tier team looking to make a jump to the second tier, or if you are a second-tier team looking to take that final step up to "Goliath" status, then finding players of a certain level of quality is only part of the battle.

"The one characteristic we will never waver on is toughness," Shaw continues. "On film, the quarterbacks we recruit need to show it. The cornerbacks need to run up and tackle somebody. We're not going to take the guys with the great combine ratings and no toughness. When we watch guys, we need to see it."

At Colorado School of Mines, another school with lofty academic standards and a potential academic disadvantage, head coach Bob Stitt aims to find a different kind of toughness. "We set up a structured interview and a mental test to determine whether a kid could survive both playing for us and going to such a rigorous school. [Former Nebraska head coach and three-time national champion] Tom Osborne did something similar; I worship Tom Osborne, so if it's good enough for him, it's good enough for me."

Stitt says the structured interview's effectiveness was verified for him when he and his staff decided to take a chance on a player who was more athletically gifted than most of his recruits, but who scored quite low on their test. He quit the team not too long after school began in his freshman year.

The word "culture," of course, can mean so many different things when it comes to a football program: the type of player you recruit, the type of image and attitude you project to your players in practice, style of play on the field, et cetera. And of course, culture becomes an easier thing to build when given players or recruits know you can build a winner.

"Kids aren't dummies," says UTSA head coach Larry Coker. "If they see things that work, it makes them more receptive." If you're at a program that hasn't won much, or if you are just starting out and haven't built much of a winner's reputation yet, "it makes it difficult."

For Ball State head coach Pete Lembo, a Georgetown business school grad and winner at three disparate programs (Lehigh, Elon, and Ball State), culture comes down to something about which you take entire classes in business school. "I have been a head coach for 12 years, and for me it always gets back to organizational behavior. If the coaches are unified and have great chemistry, and if you keep your composure in close-and-late situations, when it's stressful, when there is a lot at stake and the pressure's on, then it will trickle down to the football team. You try to control everything you can control in that regard."

The biggest test of a team's culture, however you want to define that word, is its ability to maintain certain overriding, high-quality characteristics despite changing personnel. Players cycle in and out on a yearly basis, but if you are successful enough for long enough, your reward is the need to replace assistant coaches who got promoted to bigger jobs elsewhere.

A great current example of this is Boise State. Head coach Chris Petersen played a significant role in the Broncos' rise to prominence. He was Dan Hawkins' offensive coordinator from 2001-05, and when Hawkins took the Colorado job, Petersen took over as head coach and established an absurd level of overall success. Under Hawkins, Boise State won 53 games in five years, finishing in the AP Top 20 three times. In seven seasons under Petersen, Boise State has won 84 games and finished in the AP Top 11 four straight years, from 2008-11. In 2012, after losing more starters than any team in the country, the Broncos "fell" all the way to 11-2 and No. 18.

That Petersen has been able to establish this level of success at all, with a small stadium, a small fan base, no elite history, and minimal television revenue compared to other heavyweights, has been nothing short of astounding. It is even more impressive, however, when you realize how many hires he has had to make through the years.

On the offensive side of the ball, Petersen promoted Bryan Harsin, then around 29 years old, to offensive coordinator in 2006. Harsin remained in that position until 2010, when he left for the same role at Texas. (He has since moved on to become Arkansas State's head coach.) Petersen replaced Harsin with Brent Pease, and the offense barely missed a beat. After ranking 17th, 14th, and ninth in Offensive F/+ from 2008-10, the Broncos ranked 14th in 2011.

The precision of the Boise State offense was perhaps on best display in the 2011 season opener, a 35-21 thumping of

Georgia in Atlanta. Georgia was actually able to hold the running game in check – running backs Doug Martin and D.J. Harper combined to gain just 101 yards in 32 carries – but it didn't matter because of the accuracy of the passing game. Kellen Moore completed 28 of 34 passes for three touchdowns, and after a poor early showing (four of Boise State's first six drives ended with punts, and one resulted in an interception), Pease, Petersen, Moore, and the offense found the right buttons to press. Boise State scored touchdowns on four of five drives in the middle of the game, and that was that.

"They were like a flock of birds," says Grantland's Holly Anderson. "I've never seen a team play more cerebrally than that."

Pease was impressive enough in 2011 that, after just one year at the helm, he was offered the same job at Florida.

As good as the Boise State offense has been through the years, however, the defense has potentially been even better. The Broncos ranked fourth in Def. F/+ in 2008, 14th in 2009, first in 2010, 11th in 2011, and 17th in 2012. Petersen hired Justin Wilcox, then the 29-year old California linebackers coach, as his coordinator in 2006; he promoted line coach Pete Kwiatkowski to the position in 2010 when Wilcox left for the same job at Tennessee.

Despite the turnover on the sideline, and despite an apparent reliance on players overlooked by other teams and recruiting services, the train keeps rolling for Petersen in Boise. Perhaps he will eventually make the wrong hire, or a recruiting class or two will fall flat. And maybe it already has. The 2012 Boise State offense had to replace nearly every primary contributor, plus Pease (he was replaced by receivers coach Robert Prince), and fell to 40th in Off. F/+. We don't know that the Broncos will put an elite product on the field again on that side of the ball until they actually do. But history, and culture, are on Petersen's side.

How has Petersen done it? "You'd have to be in the room with him to know," says *Sports Illustrated*'s Stewart

Mandel. "There is obviously a way to win without those five-star kids. Part of that comes down to evaluation. I always find it funny when ESPN shows the fans booing at the NFL draft when a team makes a pick that doesn't fit with all the mock drafts. These teams don't just look at Mel Kiper's list and go, 'Okay, that one's next.' They do have people paid a lot of money to do their own evaluations. There are a whole lot of kids that, for whatever reason, don't garner the stars." And Petersen finds them. He even signed some players from Holland a few years ago. He and his staff find players with one truly elite skill – accuracy at quarterback, route-running at receiver, strength on the defensive line – and coach around the weaknesses.

"They're not just valuing athleticism," says Ed Feng of The Power Rank. They saw pocket presence and accuracy in Kellen Moore and offered him a scholarship despite a distinct lack of anything resembling arm strength or athleticism; he won 50 games and threw for nearly 15,000 yards in four seasons. They always seem to have a 5'11", 290-pound defensive tackle who is mean as hell and as disruptive as any blue-chip, 6'4", 310-pound tackle in the country. Through evaluation, development, and outstanding coaching, Petersen and Boise State have cracked the code for winning in unorthodox fashion.

Of course, Boise State and TCU, under Gary Patterson, are just about the only ones that have consistently done that from a mid-major conference. Whatever "culture" might mean it is difficult to both obtain and keep. As former Alabama coach Gene Stallings notes, "You win football games with football players making plays." If you are attempting to win without the bluest of blue-chip athletes, you are going to be working with almost no margin for error. That hasn't caught up to Petersen or Patterson yet, but it always could.

4. Adaptation

Whether you have created a truly unique system of offense or you are relying on recruiting and tried-and-true methods of moving the ball (or preventing it), eventually opposing coaches will learn the book on your tendencies and weaknesses. And for almost every coach, the balance of power eventually shifts away from you.

"Almost no coach gets to ride off into the sunset," notes Chris B. Brown. "Everybody gets fired, even Tom Landry."

Your ability to fend off the end typically comes down to your ability to stay ahead of the curve. That means either tweaking your system or understanding how to counter the counters. It always eventually comes back to a game of chess.

"We created an 'offensive bible'" at Air Force, says former coach Fisher DeBerry. DeBerry's option attack was quite effective for quite a while, and it came in part from the combination of precision and understanding. "We saw every defense in the world and would document how to react to anything a defense did. If we executed and took care of what we needed to do, there's nobody that could stop us."

From the beginning to the end of his tenure in Colorado Springs (1984-2006), DeBerry says he didn't tweak too terribly much about his attack. "The foundation and the theory of it all stayed the same. We tinkered with motion and things like that. Urban Meyer [when he was Utah's head coach from 2003-04] told me, 'The only difference from what y'all do and what we do is, we snap it between our legs and y'all take it from under center.'"

DeBerry's last few teams were less successful overall, though that was as much because of defense as anything else[190]. The attack was sensible enough at an underdog school like Air

---

[190] Air Force went just 13-21 in DeBerry's final three seasons (2004-06). The Falcons averaged a respectable 27.5 points per game in that span, but they allowed 29.2.

Force that DeBerry's successor, Troy Calhoun, maintained a good portion of DeBerry's system. That makes sense, of course: Calhoun was a quarterback for DeBerry from 1985-88.

For Air Force, it comes down to "realizing there's still a way to run the ball even if you don't weigh as much as somebody else," Calhoun says. Calhoun was an assistant under both DeBerry (1989-94) and Jim Grobe (1995-02), leaning heavily on the triple option. But he also spent four seasons as an NFL assistant under Gary Kubiak; he spent three years with the Denver Broncos (2003-05), then spent a year as Kubiak's offensive coordinator for the Houston Texans.

This pro influence gave him some ideas for tweaking Air Force's option, but not eliminating it. "We do a lot more zone blocking and zone running," he says. "Our guys are going to go through basic training, and that will require you to run one and a half miles in 11 minutes at 7,000 feet. So we're always going to be tiny. What you do tactically has to fit your personnel. We're going to be a zone running team, and we're going to be able to generate some throws through play-action and bootlegs.

"Anybody's preference would be to overwhelm somebody with sheer mass and speed, but we have to find different ways. You have to be resourceful."

And you have to be meticulous in keeping track of how other teams are countering your resourcefulness because they're definitely tracking you.

5. Infrastructure

"When you take over a program, you've got to put the players first. One of the first things we did was, for instance, upgrade the training room. Our training room situation was not good at all. It was horrible in terms of areas for our players to meet with their position coaches, and if we wanted to meet with the entire team, we had to do so in the locker room. So we restructured our second floor and put together a meeting room. That was something the players could identify with right away. One of the very *last* things we did was upgrade our coaches' offices. It leaves the players with a great feeling."

Frank Solich is describing the steps he had to take upon taking the Ohio job in 2005. In the four seasons since Grobe had left Athens, the Bobcats' program had fallen back into what we'll simply call disrepair.

Grobe had derived a bit of an advantage through talent development and tactics, but the general infrastructure of the Ohio program was still far behind that of its peers. The Bobcats had won just 11 games in four years – beginning in 2001, Brian Knorr's first year in charge, Ohio went 1-10, 4-8, 2-10, and 4-7 – and was sinking back toward its historically awful level of play. As is customary, the community noticed. Going 0-5 at home in 2001 and starting the 2002 home campaign with a 31-0 loss to Northeastern, an FCS school, probably didn't help.

"Basically, we inherited a program that was not winning and had not won with any sort of consistency since the 1960s. We had to start to get the community to look at our program again and see what we're all about, to get them to start supporting our program. It was a matter of just paying attention to people and, really, trying to gather support one person at a time.[191]"

The goal of the infrastructure battle is really just to keep pace. When recruits visit your school, they need to see facilities, fan support, et cetera, on par with that of other schools. A kid isn't going to choose a school because of the size of its weight

---

[191] More from Solich: "It's always good to start from the positive. You have to figure out what your program's about, figure out what has to be done differently, and establish a game plan for what it's going to take to get the program built. You have to recruit on the positives. We're an hour and 15 minutes away from Columbus, where we have to fly players in for visits. You'd like to have a heavily populated area to draw players from, and we don't have that. But we do have a university that gives a great education and as good a campus as you're going to find. You can walk to all your classes. The atmosphere is great. Once you're able to get players to campus, they see that. You build off of that instead of the negatives."

room or the number of meeting rooms, but he'll pretty clearly notice if your school is far behind the curve.

There's a chicken-and-egg relationship here, of course. You tend to win when you have more support, both from fans and your own athletic department, and you tend to get more support when you win. But the key seems to be winning just enough to show everybody what's possible. Solich did that; after a 4-7 first season, his Bobcats surged in 2006, winning nine games and reaching a bowl for the first time in 38 years. The facility upgrades and fan outreach had already begun before the wins rolled in, but everything picked up speed.

If you master the game in all five of these areas – if you figure out some tricks with the players you inherit; if you can build depth for your system with local talent; if you can establish your culture and find the players who can maintain it; if you can stay one step ahead of your opponents when they adapt to your ways; and if you can keep up in the arms race of money, facilities, and fans – then you can win some games. You'll still need some luck in the way of injuries, turnovers, and other factors to experience a major breakthrough. You're still going to do weekly battle versus other coaches following the same path as you (with similar experience and capabilities). You're still going to find yourself frequently outmanned by the sport's haves. You're still going to find yourself on an uphill slope for eternity. You're still probably either going to get fired or pushed to resign/retire eventually.

The pursuit of glory, be it one amazing win or a run of amazing seasons, is often futile and forever ongoing. Just like the love of college football.

Acknowledgements

It wasn't my original intent, but a good portion of this book ended up taking on an almost autobiographical feel. Let's continue that here.

First, I owe some obvious and profuse notes of gratitude to everybody who helped to contribute to this book, be it via foreword (Spencer Hall, Jason Kirk), copy editing (Rob Weir), reading just for fun (Ross Taylor[192], Chris A. Brown, my father), contributing Top 10 lists (Ty Hildenbrandt, Dan Rubenstein, and "Senator Blutarsky"), proofing to make sure Chapter 2 wasn't a disaster (John Infante), or interviewing (Holly Anderson, Todd Berry, Bill Barnwell, Chris B. Brown, Greg Byrne, Troy Calhoun, Larry Coker, Bob Davie, Fisher DeBerry, Sonny Dykes, Bruce Feldman, Ed Feng, Bryan Fischer, Brian Fremeau, Steven Godfrey, Jim Grobe, Matt Hinton, John Infante, Pete Lembo, Mike MacIntyre, Stewart Mandel, Paul Myerberg, Rob Neyer, Mike Nixon, Michael Oriard, Rob Paschall, Trent Ratterree, Ralph Russo, Aaron

---

[192] Ross co-founded Rock M Nation with me and has been secretly cleaning up my work for almost six years now.

Schatz, C.J. Schexnayder, David Shaw, Frank Solich, Gene Stallings, Andy Staples, Bob Stitt, Bob Stoll, Mitch Tanney, John Thorn).

The acknowledgements shouldn't stop there, however.

My parents, Betty and Mike, have long encouraged my random, sporadic ambitions and, when I was growing up, accepted that I could entertain myself with a clipboard and dice in the back seat of the car for any road trip of any length, no matter how weird they thought it was. And Kerry and Darlene Rasberry, my second parents since birth, went along with it, too.

My blogging career began in the basement of Jim and Suzan Tuley, my wife's parents. I was a blogger stereotype from the start.

Vickie Hull and Pat Sturm were my first editors. And Kellie Hamm was one hell of an algebra teacher.

Eric Ratterree has been my sports sounding board since age two. Dyrek Willis joined in in high school. And Seth Rosner took over in college. Shaq Hays, too. And Walsh. And Sosa. And Drew. And on and on.

Aaron Schatz brought me aboard at Football Outsiders, giving me a level of legitimacy I wouldn't have otherwise had. Really, his responding to an e-mail of mine in the summer of 2008 got the ball rolling for everything that followed. And three years later, Kevin Lockland sent me a full-time SB Nation job offer the day after my daughter was born.

Beginning in 2009, Marty Couvillan of CFB Stats began sending me weekly data updates during the college football season. It allowed me to both process the weekly mountain of data that college football generates and actually write about it, too. His help has been invaluable; I honestly wouldn't be able to do what I do without him.

Indirectly, Bill James taught me to ask questions; Bill Simmons taught me that if you think in parentheses and footnotes, write in parentheses and footnotes; and Roger

Ebert taught me that if you love your craft, and you're always striving to get better and smarter, people can tell.

The favorite teams I so ineptly chose in the 1980s and early 1990s – the Missouri Tigers, the Pittsburgh Pirates, the Portland Trailblazers, the Miami Dolphins, the New York Islanders, Nottingham Forest – taught me (over and over and over again) that enjoying sports boils down to more than simply winning. There is joy to be found in the people, the traditions, and the little moments. At least, that's what I've always believed. If I didn't, I'd have given up on sports 20 years ago.

And of course, Jamie agreed to marry me and has provided support, encouragement, understanding, and snark. And Erin gave me the extra boost of motivation (and mandatory organization skills) I didn't realize I needed. Love you both. Love you *all*, actually.

I wanted to write a book about college football because I enjoy it and wanted to learn more about it. Now that it's over, I enjoy it more and want to learn even more. I call that a success.

Citations

Below is a per-chapter list of links and citations. But first, let's make some blanket citations. The following sites are invaluable for any fan of college football stats and history:

CFB Stats: http://www.cfbstats.com/

NCAA stats: http://web1.ncaa.org/mfb/mainpage.jsp

James Howell's college football history page: http://jhowell.net/cf/scores/ScoresIndex.htm

Sports Reference's College Football page: http://www.sports-reference.com/cfb/

I cannot tell you how frequently I visit these four sites. They are a must-bookmark for any college football fan.

CHAPTER 1

Pg. 1. Original SBN piece (2011): http://www.sbnation.com/ncaa-football/2011/9/19/2434018/morning-tailgate-im-not-thinking-about-numbers

Pg. 17. Football Outsiders Top 100 list (2010):
http://www.footballoutsiders.com/varsity-numbers/2010/vn-podcast-top-100-redux

Pg. 26. Senator Blutarsky's blog:
http://blutarsky.wordpress.com/

Pg. 26. Solid Verbal home page: http://www.solidverbal.com/

CHAPTER 2

Pg. 43. Chung, Doug J. (2013). The Dynamic Advertising Effect of Collegiate Athletics. Harvard Business School, Cambridge.

Pg. 46. Wallace, Francis. (1951). Dementia Pigskin. Rinehart.

Pg. 48. Staples' Sports Illustrated column (2012):
http://sportsillustrated.cnn.com/college-football/news/20121221/college-football-apocalypse/

Pg. 49. Broeg, Bob. (1974). Ol' Mizzou: A Story of Missouri Football. Strode Publications.

Pg. 54. Oriard, Michael. (2009). Bowled Over: Big-Time College Football from the Sixties to the BCS Era. University of North Carolina Press.

Pg. 56. The Bylaw Blog:
http://www.athleticscholarships.net/bylaw-blog.htm

Pg. 60. Full text for In re NCAA Student-Athlete Name & Likeness Licensing Litigation:
http://scholar.google.co.uk/scholar_case?case=4946922481208536870

Pg. 61. Mike Alden Q&A (2012):
http://www.columbiatribune.com/sports/mu/alden-discusses-year-in-transition/article_b2aaea5b-b88f-5092-8ede-1ad41525268a.html

Pg. 79. Outside the Lines (2013).
http://espn.go.com/espn/otl/story/_/id/8867972/ucla-study-finds-signs-cte-living-former-nfl-players-first-time

Pg. 83. Audio of Greg Schiano interview (2011).
http://media.790thezone.com/Podcasts/1773/Greg_Schiano_6-9-11.mp3

Pg. 84. Miller, John J. (2011). The Big Scrum: How Teddy Roosevelt Saved Football. Harper Perennial.

Pg. 86. Should College Football Be Banned?
http://www.slate.com/articles/sports/intelligence_squared/2012/04/should_college_football_be_banned_the_next_slate_intelligence_squared_debate_is_on_may_8_in_new_york_city_.html

CHAPTER 3

Pg. 88. Original SBN Piece (2011):
http://www.sbnation.com/ncaa-football/2011/9/30/2459745/college-football-rankings-ap-top-25

CHAPTER 4

Pg. 94. Daniel Okrent's Sports Illustrated piece on Bill James (1981):
http://sportsillustrated.cnn.com/vault/article/magazine/MAG1124493/

Pg. 94. SABR founders page:
http://www.sabr.org/about/founders

Pg. 94. Carroll, Bob, Pete Palmer, John Thorn. (1988). The Hidden Game of Football. Warner Books.

Pg. 95. Lewis, Michael. (2003). Moneyball: The Art of Winning an Unfair Game. W.W. Norton.

Pg. 96. Pete Thamel's Sports Illustrated piece on Drew Cannon (2013): http://sportsillustrated.cnn.com/-college-basketball-mens-tournament/news/20130320/drew-cannon-butler/

Pg. 99. Mills, Eldon and Harlan Mills. (1970). Player Win Averages: A Complete Guide to Winning Baseball Players. A.S. Barnes.

Pg. 100. Explaining Total QBR (2011):
http://espn.go.com/nfl/story/_/id/6833215/explaining-statistics-total-quarterback-rating

Pg. 101. 2013 Harris Interactive sports popularity poll (2013): http://www.harrisinteractive.com/NewsRoom/HarrisPolls/tabid/447/mid/1508/articleId/1136/ctl/ReadCustom%20Default/Default.aspx

Pg. 101. Mauboussin, Michael J. (2012). The Success Equation: Untangling Skill and Luck in Business, Sports, and Investing. Harvard Business Review Press.

Pg. 109. Albert, Jim and Jay Bennett. (2003). Curve Ball: Baseball, Statistics, and the Role of Chance in the Game. Copernicus; Revised edition.

Pg. 111. Dr. Bob's homepage: http://www.drbobsports.com/

CHAPTER 5

Pg. 115. Original SBN Piece (2012):
http://www.sbnation.com/ncaa-
football/2012/8/3/3214770/kansas-state-wildcats-football-
preview-2012

Pg. 115. Varsity Numbers interview with Ken Pomeroy (2010):
http://www.footballoutsiders.com/varsity-numbers/2010/vn-
talking-trade-kenpom

Pg. 118. Kansas State 2011 team preview (2011):
http://www.sbnation.com/ncaa-
football/2011/5/16/2173191/2011-kansas-state-football

CHAPTER 6

Pg. 122. Discussion of Gene Stallings' 1992 Defensive Quality
Control Chart at Football Outsiders (2011):
http://www.footballoutsiders.com/college-xp/2011/alabama-
1992-defensive-game-charting

Pg. 126. The Daily Oklahoman's Todd Monken interview
(2012): http://newsok.com/oklahoma-state-football-todd-
monken-says-stats-are-for-losers/article/3795607

Pg. 128. Steven Godfrey's interview with Tommy Tuberville
(2013): http://www.sbnation.com/college-
football/2013/3/27/4146576/tommy-tuberville-interview-
cincinnati-football-2013-texas-tech

Pg. 135. Rob Paschall's Twitter profile:
https://twitter.com/togfootball

CHAPTER 7

Pg. 141. Examples for both the 1961 Orange Bowl box score and the 1930 Rose Bowl box score were found using a date-specific search of the Google News archive: https://news.google.com/

CHAPTER 8

Pg. 161. Andrew Sharp's SBN piece (2013): http://www.sbnation.com/longform/2013/3/7/4071420/sloan-sports-analytics-conference-recap-ssac-2013

Pg. 162. The Varsity Numbers archive at Football Outsiders: http://www.footballoutsiders.com/varsity-numbers

Pg. 171. Belichick, Steve. (2011). Football Scouting Methods. Martino Fine Books; reprint.

Pg. 187. Official NFL page for All-22 film: http://www.nfl.com/coachesfilm

CHAPTER 9

Pg. 189. Original Football Study Hall piece (2013): http://www.footballstudyhall.com/2013/2/14/3984720/college-football-offense-charting-no-back-formation

CHAPTER 10

Pg. 197. Original Football Study Hall piece (2013): http://www.footballstudyhall.com/2013/2/28/4036850/adjusted-completion-percentages-collin-klein-matt-barkley

CHAPTER 12

Pg. 229. Original SBN piece (2012):
http://www.sbnation.com/college-football/2012/11/12/3634692/texas-am-alabama-football-2012-kevin-sumlin-johnny-manziel

Pg. 230. Texas A&M 2012 team preview (2012):
http://www.sbnation.com/2012/8/16/3246590/2012-texas-am-aggies-football-preview

CHAPTER 13

Pg. 235. Original SBN piece (2012):
http://www.sbnation.com/2012/9/10/3307386/arkansas-football-john-l-smith-louisiana-monroe

Pg. 236. UL-Monroe 2011 team preview (2011):
http://www.footballstudyhall.com/2011/4/4/2075236/2011-ul-monroe-football

Pg. 237. UL-Monroe 2012 team preview (2012):
http://www.sbnation.com/ncaa-football/2012/4/4/2924681/2012-louisiana-monroe-football-preview

Pg. 245. Brown, Chris B. (2012). The Essential Smart Football. Amazon Digital Services.

Pg. 246. Chris B. Brown's SB Nation piece on Chris Ault and the Pistol offense (2012):
http://www.sbnation.com/longform/2012/12/27/3792740/pistol-offense-nfl-redskins-rg3

Pg, 254, 257. Pieces of the Appalachian State-Michigan and ULM-Alabama recaps are adapted from a series of "Anatomy of an Upset" pieces at Football Study Hall:
http://www.footballstudyhall.com/anatomy-of-an-upset

About the Author

Bill Connelly is a college sports editor, tennis contributor, and analytics director for SB Nation, a columnist for Football Outsiders, a contributor to the annual *Football Outsiders Almanac,* and the editor of Rock M Nation and Football Study Hall. His work has also been featured at ESPN Insider and the Wall Street Journal. You can follow him on Twitter at @SBN_BillC.

Made in the USA
Middletown, DE
20 November 2019

79072387R00170